Scientific Pollyannaism

"With extraordinary passion and spirit, Yakushko traces the long and tragic history of the role science plays in the demand to be happy. She shows how this demand emanates from a white 'scientific' elite that wreaks havoc upon all those on whom it turns its destructive gaze. Coining the powerful term, scientific pollyanism, she here deconstructs any claim to being 'evidence-based' that these racist and (hetero)sexist uses of science make. In so doing, she redeems scientism's many victims."

—Lynne Layton, *Ph.D., Assistant Clinical Professor of Psychology, Harvard Medical School, USA, and author of* Who's That Girl? Who's That Boy?

"Oksana Yakushko has written a well-researched, historically sweeping, and in fact courageous book that is greatly needed during this dark time in the worldwide rise of the far-right. Her book reveals the deep connection between the forces of racism, misogyny, and classism, on the one hand, and the corrupt uses of science in psychology, on the other. Yakushko critiques the ongoing history of silencing those who suffer by ignoring the sociopolitical contexts that cause the suffering. Creatively, Yaskusko argues that false narratives of happiness, pejorative diagnoses, and the weaponizing of a scientistic cognitivism in service of neoliberal governmentality go hand in hand. Please read this book."

—Philip Cushman, *Ph.D., author of* Constructing The Self, Constructing America: A Cultural History of Psychotherapy

"In her fascinating new book, Oksana Yakushko provides a carefully researched study of the politics of 'positivity.' The emphasis in contemporary culture on positive emotional states serves a status quo that separates happiness from wellbeing and marginalizes examination of suffering from the injustices of social contexts. Indeed, argues Yakushko, an insidious argument is promoted by the happiness industry to suggest that those who are rather out of it suffer some biological or racial fault. Scholarly, incisive, tenacious, provocative, this book will stimulate discussions in many fields and is a compelling example of the power of the pen."

—Christopher Bollas, *Ph.D., psychoanalyst and the author of, most recently,* Meaning and Melancholy

Oksana Yakushko

Scientific Pollyannaism

From Inquisition to Positive Psychology

palgrave
macmillan

Oksana Yakushko
Clinical Psychology
Pacifica Graduate Institute
Carpinteria, CA, USA

ISBN 978-3-030-15981-8 ISBN 978-3-030-15982-5 (eBook)
https://doi.org/10.1007/978-3-030-15982-5

Library of Congress Control Number: 2019935560

This Palgrave Macmillan imprint is published by the registered company Springer Nature Switzerland AG.
The registered company address is: Gewerbestrasse 11, 6330 Cham, Switzerland

This book is dedicated to Marcus, Kai, and Sonia.

Contents

CHAPTER 1

An Introduction to the (Supposedly) Good Life

Promises of a good and happy life, in this world or the next, have always been central to human experience. Answers to the question, "how do I achieve a happy life, how do I live the good life," have been proffered by religious leaders, philosophers, politicians, writers, and, since the establishment of Western scholarship (Ahmed, 2004, 2010a, 2010b; Berlant, 2011; Davies, 2015; Ehrenreich, 2009; Horowitz, 2018; McMahon, 2006). Positivity, especially positive emotional states, holds varied appeals for human communities and its social leaders, often as tools for political control and social management (Ahmed, 2004, 2010a, 2010b; Binkley, 2014; Cabanas, 2016; McMahon, 2006; Yakushko, 2018a).

This book addresses a specific emphasis on positivity (e.g., happiness, optimism, flourishing, well-being) based on Western scholarly theories, empirical data, and scientific rhetoric, which reflect a concerted focus on defining, predicting and controlling human emotional experiences. This work expands on contemporary contributions to the study of enforced happiness and compulsory optimism in the cultural, political, economic, and social spheres (Ahmed, 2010a, 2010b; Ehrenreich, 2009; Horowitz, 2018; McMahon, 2006; Merskin, 2011; Yakushko & Blodgett, 2018). Specifically, I examine the origins and expressions of obligatory positivity in Western scientific practices. I explore not only ways in which this scholarly emphasis on happiness has been shaped by the broader culture (Ahmed, 2010a, 2010b; Berlant, 2011; Binkley, 2014), but also seek to document how cultural rhetoric about human well-being has become driven by "according-to-research" ideologies. Science and scientism have

O. Yakushko, *Scientific Pollyannaism*,
https://doi.org/10.1007/978-3-030-15982-5_1

become among the most influential forces in determining human values and experiences in Western cultures. The guidelines for what constitute a happy or good life stems from scholarly productions rather than sacred texts. These empirically driven admonitions often (through various methods) deny, negate, or villify the full spectrum of human emotional experience while simultaneously requiring a disavowal of human social context. In short, human beings are shamed and chided toward always feeling cheerful, regardless of their individual, social or relational circumstance. They are shaped into Pollyannas.

This scholarly emphasis on achieving happiness through enforced positive emotional states and sets of behavior, I argue, is made in service of maintaining the socio-political status quo. According to this perspective, happiness and well-being are treated as distinct and measurable individual states. Moreover, human affective reactions are presented as disconnected from human rights while injustice and suffering are minimized or denied. In turn, access to happiness is promoted as supposedly achievable by those who possess particular characteristics based on either superior personal predispositions (e.g., divinely or biologically ordained goodness) or concerted behavioral changes (e.g., self-control, determined efforts to use empirical self-help techniques). These human capacities to achieve optimism, I note, are often claimed by scientists to be lacking for entire groups (e.g., women, racial minorities) because of their supposed biological deficiencies or failures to develop control over personal affective states. Lastly, what constitutes happiness is claimed to be knowable exclusively through scientific discovery rather than critical recognition of differing standpoints.

The history of many European civilizations is marked by the accentuation of happiness alongside the denial justice and punishment of those who express unhappiness (Ahmed, 2010a; Ehrenreich, 2010; Horowitz, 2018; Zinn, 2010). In this book I will discuss efforts to demonize negative emotions and those who hold them, such as the witch hunts, which occurred during the so-called Renaissance and Enlightenment eras and were fueled by the privileged scientific theories of the day. I will show that the emphasis on demonizing negative human states and enforcing positivity was further prescribed through Western scientific evolutionary theories of human behavior (e.g., Darwinism, eugenics) and persists today in contemporary Western scientific psychology movements such as "positive psychology." I refer to this production of empirical theories and practices related to enforced and a-contextual positivity as scientific Pollyannaism.

Many historians note that throughout modern Western history positivity and happiness have been the enforced through fundamentalist religions (Ehrenreich, 2009; Horowitz, 2018; McMahon, 2006). Karl Marx referred to religion as an "opiate," designed to pacify and numb; a drugged state, which becomes a symptom and a symbol of a life lived under oppressive conditions. According to Marx (1843/1970),

> Religious suffering is, at one and the same time, the expression of real suffering and a protest against real suffering. Religion is the sigh of the oppressed creature, the heart of a heartless world, and the soul of soulless conditions. It is the opium of the people. The abolition of religion as the illusory happiness of the people is the demand for their real happiness. To call on them to give up their illusions about their condition is to call on them to give up a condition that requires illusions. The criticism of religion is, therefore, in embryo, the criticism of that vale of tears of which religion is the halo. (Introduction, para. 4–5)

As noted in chapters below, use of religious scholarly rhetoric to promote utopian visions of life, whether in earthly state or the afterlife, fueled concerted efforts to rid humanity of all sources of supposed unhappiness. These rationales were central to Inquisition manuals such as the *Malleus Malificarum*, which was grounded in the sciences of its day (e.g., Hellenistic philosophy, medical knowledge). Today, Christian fundamentalism continues to promote positivity as central to both mortal existence and the afterlife (Ehrenreich, 2009). For example, Joel Osteen (2011), a mega-church pastor and a conservative U.S. evangelical Christian star, proclaims in his many sermons and books on happiness (here his *Every Day a Friday: How to Be Happier 7 Days a Week*):

> It is your choice to be happy. Make up your mind to enjoy this day, to have a blessed, prosperous, victorious year. You may have some setbacks and your circumstances may change, but don't let that change your mind. Keep it set to happiness. (p. 5)

Osteen's positivity-focused sermons and books not only draw on prosperity Gospel interpretations of the Bible but also make many references to empirical positivity research. "According to researchers" is a phrase used repeatedly to legitimize Osteen's emphasis on perpetual happiness as both divinely inspired and as empirically valid.

Despite the continued centrality of fundamentalist religious traditions, most Western individuals today hold a more skeptical view of religion's influence on human life (Pew Research Center, 2018). As noted in Pew Research Center studies, individuals around the globe no longer accept blindly accept religious teachings, especially when they oppose the findings of scientific inquiry. This is true of believers just as atheists: most practicing religious individuals will privilege scientific explanations over traditional religious ones, resolving their conflicts between science and faith by favoring empirical views (Pew Research Center, 2018). Moreover, large sections of contemporary Western societies ascribe to openly non-religious and anti-religious worldviews. Western scientists have used these contemporary anti-religious attitudes to attack religion as problematic and dangerous while proclaiming sciences to be salvific and unbiased (see attacks on religion and praise for science by Harris, 2006; Pinker, 2018).

Far from serving as a counter-point to religion, science and some of its scientists appear to have taken over the religious function by preaching absolute truths, providing rigid guidelines for moral living, and claiming to be above bias or cultural influence. The internet is filled with anti-religious, pro-science paraphernalia blazoned with slogans like "In Science We Trust." Almost every Western cultural space requires adherence to claims that their positions are correct "according to research." Scientists themselves demand an unwavering belief that science and scientists are always accurate, balanced, and fair (Hunt, 1999; Pinker, 2018). In the Western world, especially in the U.S., individuals "march for science," and the national public radio plays weekly shows such as "Science Friday," displaying an assumption that science is monolithic, non-ideological, and functions as an unquestioned source of absolute truth. The brand "anti-scientific" is used to attack those who seek to make social change or who engage in rigorous critical discussions about varied empirical assumptions and practices (Hunt, 1999; Pinker, 2002, 2018; Whitney, 1999). Under the guise of condemning supposedly "anti" and "non" scientific perspectives, Western societies have also been pushed to become anti-intellectual, to become disinclined to examine historical, social, and political values that drive science and scientists (Giroux, 2011).

In addition, scholars began to highlight the rise of Western scientism, which promotes exclusively natural biological explanations of human social differences. Blackburn (2005) defined scientism as a "pejorative term for the belief that the methods of natural science, or the categories and things recognized in natural science, form the only proper elements in any philosophical or other inquiry" (pp. 331–332). Sorell (2013) defined scientism as

> *the belief that science, especially natural science, is the most valuable part of human learning—much the most valuable because it is much the most authoritative, or serious, or beneficial.* Other beliefs related to this one may also be regarded as scientific, e.g. the belief that science is the *only* valuable part of human learning, or that the view that is always good for subjects that do not belong to science to be placed on scientific footing. (p. 4)

Scientism, these scholars highlight, especially focuses on offering moral pronouncements, including determinations of what constitute good and bad human behaviors and emotions. In this book, scientism rather than sciences typically underlies what I define as Scientific Pollyannaism.

In this study, I seek to contribute to the work of the scholars such as Ahmed, Berlant, Binkley and others who have criticized current promotion of happiness by focusing specifically on the ways in which scientists, especially social scientists, have sought to elevate their scientific pronouncements about human optimism and positive living to the level of religion. In later chapters, I will describe the demands for contemporary individuals to become Pollyannas about the sciences, which claim to guarantee their happiness and well-being. I will highlight how works by social scientists who promote ideologies for which they require blind faith and a disavowal of common human reactions, such as care for social justice or compassion for other human beings. Francis Galton (1869, 1883), the founder of eugenics or the "science of racial betterment," which is responsible for some of the worse forms of social violence of the 20th century, including the Holocaust, Jim Crow laws, and the Apartheid (Bashford & Levine, 2010; Lombardo, 2011; Yakushko, 2019), openly declared that eugenics must become a form of social creed worldwide. Galton claimed that such religious faith in Darwinist-backed eugenics was needed to guide humanity towards an evolutionary utopia, and his ideas have not gone away. Contemporary social scientists continue to routinely shame people for their "feel-good dogmas" of social equality, while at the same time requiring an absolute acceptance of such supposed scientific truths as "race realism" (i.e., superiority of certain racial groups over others) and genetic gender differences (e.g., "gender feminism," claiming male preeminence over females) (Cattell, 1987; Gottfredson, 1994a, 1994b; Herrnstein & Murray, 1996; Pinker, 2018; Rushton, 1999; Rushton & Jensen, 2005; Whitney, 1999). Raymond Cattell (1987), a leading U.S. psychologist and statistics scholar, proposed a eugenic and racist form of quasi-religious utopia based on supposed sciences of human differences, which he termed the Beyondism. Western individuals are asked or, worse, shamed into accepting, without question, these sciences and scientific proclamations as the "truth." In fact, individual and collective happiness has been continually claimed to be dependent on an unwavering acceptance of science (Melendy, 1914; Popenoe & Johnson, 1935; Pinker, 2018).

In expanding the intellectual (e.g., McMahon, 2006), feminist-political (e.g., Ahmed, 2010a, 2010b), or socio-political (e.g., Binkley, 2014) analyses of enforced positivity, this work focuses specifically on examining historical and socio-political foundations of empirical or scholarly assertions about human happiness and well-being. I use the term "scientific Pollyannaism" to distinguish efforts to justify ideologies of enforced a-contextual positivity through empirical theories and research studies from those originating exclusively in religious or socio-political values. This work will highlight the inter-relationship between scientific and cultural forms of Pollyannaism while drawing specific attention to empirical rationales and epistemological scholarly practices that are distinct to what I term scientific Pollyannaism. Thus, I define scientific Pollyannaism as an empirically-driven effort to enforce happiness as the primary hereditary trait as well as objective (i.e., self-management strategy) while simultaneously minimizing or denying external factors that influence human emotional states.

I take "scientific Pollyannaism" from both the contemporary use of the term Pollyannaism and the original story of an orphaned child named Pollyanna (Porter, 1913). Definitions of Pollyannaism focus on positivity bias, or the tendency to discount other factors and facts by privileging over-optimistic accounts of the self, life, and others. This bias also requires the denial of alternative explanations that are deemed to be negative (Matlin & Stang, 1978). Social scientists Boucher and Osgood (1969) were among the first to use the story of Pollyanna to develop a theory they named a Pollyanna hypothesis, which they defined as a human tendency toward positivity, primarily found in Western forms of cultural communication.

The word "Pollyannaism" is derived from a popular book about an orphan girl Pollyanna, written by Eleanor H. Porter in 1913. Pollyanna's life, like lives of many orphaned children, was filled with trauma, tragedy, and losses. In the story penned by Porter, Pollyanna's key approach to life was described as playing the "glad games"—a type of mind trick that supposedly helped Pollyanna ascribe positive explanations for awful experiences she faced (e.g., loss of her father, neglect and abuse by caregivers). Her perpetually cheery attitude apparently endeared her to people who would much rather prefer to be around happy-go-lucky child than a traumatized suffering orphan.

This book, like many other fairytale-type stories about orphan children, especially orphaned girl children (e.g., Cinderella, Snow White, Annie), is a feel-good story. Being an orphan during the early twentieth century was horrific, placing children at direct risk of poverty, violence, and social exclusion (Bogen, 1992; Morton, 2000; Shealy, 1995; Smith & Merkel-Holguin, 2017). Western societies of that time considered orphans as having deserved their status because of either divine or evolutionary unfitness, thus giving permission for many eugenic scientists to utilize orphans in their studies (Lombardo, 2011; Tucker, 1996). For example, psychologist Goddard (1912) created a sensation with his study of the genetic origins of feeble-mindedness, which he claimed was a menace to all, conducted as an experiment on an orphan child he named Deborah Kallikak. Elimination of feeble-mindedness, claimed to be common among the orphans, was promoted as leading to personal and universal happiness (Davenport, 1910, 1911; Goddard, 1911, 1912, 1917; Popenoe & Johnson, 1935). Famed intelligence scholar Lewis Terman (1916), a eugenicist, Stanford University psychologist and the author of Stanford-Binet intelligence measure, experimented on orphans to show that their inferior intelligence was not only genetic (i.e., based on their defective "germo-plasms") but also linked to their inferior positivity and sociability. John B. Watson (1914, 1919), a behaviorist and a eugenicist, experimented on many orphans, frequently in sadistic ways, to promote the social engineering of people to become happy and efficient. Their works became central to enforced sciences of happiness, or scientific Pollyannaism, to this day, although their problematic origins and practices are sanitized in psychology textbooks.

Less than a generation before Pollyanna's story was published, Europe and its colonizing emissaries were still busy cleansing the world of unhappy or angry individuals, especially women, who were branded as demon-possessed witches (Ankarloo & Clark, 1999; Burns, 2003; Ehrenreich & English, 2010; Ruickbie, 2004; Russell, 1972; Yakushko, 2018b). Just as the witch-hunts against demonically angry witches were dying out, works by Charles Darwin gave rise to social Darwinism and eugenics. Darwinism further ensured that optimism and positivity were treated as signs of evolutionary fitness or goodness while any emotional behavior to the contrary (e.g., anger, sadness, daydreaming) were viewed as marks of evolutionary unfitness, connected to supposedly parasitic genes. It is during the ending of the bloody with-hunts and the emergence of new evolutionary sciences, both of which demonized human deviations from accepted emotional social norms, that Porter penned Pollyanna.

As noted earlier, in Porter's (1913) book *Pollyanna*, the orphan protagonist possessed such an invariably sunny, optimistic, positive, and glowing personality as well as capacity to play her "glad games" that she made everyone around her positive and kind. Pollyanna supposedly not only transcended her difficult social conditions but also gained benefactors, entirely through her bubbly happy attitudes. A happy disposition, Porter assured her readers, could lead to enormous relational and financial benefits. For instance, at the end of the book when Pollyanna is recovering from an accident, which left her bed-ridden, "even Black Tilly who washes the floor" is astounded by Pollyanna's attitude of being "glad for everything," because she [Pollyanna] supposedly "always… think[s] of the gladdest things" unlike "Black Tilly" or other characters (p. 310).

It is this attitude of ignoring one's own and other people's social circumstances (e.g., "Black Tilly who washes the floor") which seemed to have earned Pollyanna a particular symbolic standing in American and Western culture, elevating Pollyanna to a cultural icon and an archetype (Matlin & Stang, 1978). Thus, the story of Pollyanna, written during the era of violent Jim Crow laws and anti-Semitism, of backlash against early feminist movement, and during the rise of scientific eugenics, manages to ignore all of these conditions by making the reader engage in the "glad games." This politics of emotion uses positivity and happiness as forms of social and political control, shaming those on the margins for a lack of positivity that, supposedly, stems from their own lack of goodness and self-control.

Unquestionably, human beings, regardless of their social standing or personal characteristics, experience a full range of emotions, whether joy or sadness, rage or peacefulness. In this book I wish to embrace and celebrate this full spectrum of human emotional experiences and reactions.

In fact, I argue that connection to this entire spectrum of full human emotional capacities is reflective of individual and collective health as well as the vital capacities needed to develop compassion, justice, and democracy. I want to emphasize that the disavowal of so-called negative emotions, especially by scientists in their peer-reviewed empirical and popular writings, is problematic when it demonizes these emotions and when it disconnects human emotional worlds from human social contexts. I argue that scientific perspectives which minimize or even attack the role of the environment or social context while pathologizing normal reactions to traumatic or oppressive social contexts, have dominated Western culture. Porter's (1913) story may well have been a product of the sciences I describe in this book.

These scientific efforts have become an established form of the empirical Pollyanna "glad games," especially in Western psychology. From the early days of psychology in the UK and the U.S., which aligned itself with eugenic and social Darwinist values, to contemporary "positive" psychologies, scientific Pollyannaism has been dominant, popular, and profitable in Western psychology as a discipline. These discourses, I seek to show, are intended to control, to shape, and to keep the privileged apart from unprivileged via promises of happiness as well as shaming failures to obtain it. After all, this pursuit of happiness is promoted as the singular goal of human life, claimed to be achievable without regard for the individual or collective standing, history, or suffering. In turn, individuals are required to maintain their happiness despite social or personal realities by disavowing their right to live full equal human lives. Lastly, in the neo-liberal (i.e., fundamentalist capitalist) social structure, obtaining happiness continues to be treated as a marker of acquired individual wealth (see discussions of positivity "ratios" or "post-traumatic growth"). Individual well-being is sold as achievable either by being born with the correct biological pre-requisites (i.e., genes) or through purchasing manualized empirical self-help programs (Berlant, 2011; Binkley, 2014; Davies, 2015; De La Fabián & Stecher, 2018; Horowitz, 2018; Yen, 2015).

The use of enforced positive emotions in culture, education and the media have gained critical scholarly and journalistic attention (Ahmed, 2004, 2010a, 2010b; Hedges,2009; hooks, 2006; Merskin, 2011; Sloan, 1996). Ahmed's (2010a) writings on happiness highlight that the enforcement and insistence on happiness as an "expectation" may "annul that sense of possibility," in which genuine range of emotional reactions, including positive ones, can occur (p. 592). In addition,

Ahmed has repeatedly asserted that re-claiming the full range of emotions, especially those that have been relegated to the status of "negative" and problematic (e.g., anger, sorrow, regret), is a political act of resistance. "Revolutionary forms of political consciousness involve heightening our awareness of what there is to be unhappy about," stated Ahmed (2010a, p. 592). In contrast, the insistence on optimism and happiness as ideal states is viewed as reflective of cultural-political forms of social compliance, which require denial of oppressive conditions and inequalities and which necessitate routine engagement in disassociation, disavowal, and splitting. These defenses are employed to maintain the individual insistence that, like Pollyanna, the person is always "glad for everything." I review many of these critical contributions in regard to enforced optimism and the rise of "happiness industry" in order to provide a broad theoretical framework for questioning scientific Pollyannaism.

In this work, I take as my starting point the demonization of individuals who were claimed to be unhappy and discontent–the witch-hunts. The witch-hunts, in my view, served as an immediate foundation for Western scientific Darwinist, social Darwinist, and eugenic assertions that only happy and emotionally self-controlled people constitute highest grade of "civilization" and evolutionary fitness. I will connect Darwinist and eugenic bases of Western psychology with their contemporary iterations, which continue emphasize that positivity is a biological and genetic characteristic that can also be enforced and maintained through cognitive and behavioral strategies. Specifically, the contemporary movements of behavioral genetics, positive psychology, and evolutionary psychology will be examined in relation to context-free positivity, which are proclaimed to be the height of mental health. Lastly, I will end with reflections on the little orphan prototype of Pollyannaism. I use psychoanalytic and critical theories to explore how and why traumatized children develop defenses against reality such as playing the "glad games." These theories elucidate the tremendous psychological toll that positivity games can have on an individual life, especially when normal childhood coping reactions to trauma do not give way to more authentic human emotional and relational capacities. Moreover, I will continually emphasize the detrimental impact of enforced happiness without social justice, the importance of historical awareness, the vital role of "negative" emotions to human equality and democracy. I will seek to name alternatives to scientific Pollyannaism, which embrace the full spectrum of human emotions in relation to diverse human social realities.

In contrast to the cheery proclamations of scientific positivity, I will hold spaces for voices of radical critical theorists like Simone de Beauvoir, Frantz Fanon, Betty Friedan, Sara Ahmed and many others who openly addressed the violence of shaming women, racial minority groups, and colonized peoples for not being happy. I will emphasize the writings by scholars who query the economic and social value of optimism in service of social control over people on the margins. I will also hold spaces for poets and writers who have, for the most part, not shied away from acknowledging the entire spectrum of human emotional states. These poets and writers are often on the forefront of questioning happy dissociations, which deny harsh reality in order to maintain a fragile and false sense of safety. These creative voices, in my view, present a radical alternative to scientific Pollyannaism. In fact, negative emotional states and negative reactions to social situations are among the primary reasons for government book-banning worldwide (Karolides, Bald, & Sova, 1999). Books like the *Grapes of Wrath* (Steinbeck, 1939) and *I Know Why the Caged Bird Sings* (Angelou, 1983) were not censored for their sunny dispositions.

The following poem by Ilya Kaminsky (2013), entitled *We Lived Happily During the War*, reminds readers of this human struggle to maintain a full spectrum of emotional reactions in the face of violence:

> In the street of money in the city of money in the country of money,
> Our great country of money, we (forgive us)
> Lived happily during the war.

Scientific Pollyannaism, like religion in Marx' writing, is both a reflection of profound collective anguish and a method of sanitizing suffering. It is also a dangerous opiate, intended to numb and re-direct attention from sources of unhappiness to the desire for a painless utopia. Although interrogating religious Pollyannaism with its promises of the afterlife has become more commonplace, radical interrogation of the false consciousness promoted by scientific Pollyannaism appears to be more rare.

This book is dedicated to such interrogation, as well as to stripping positivity sciences and scientists of their absolute right to demonize human beings as witches, lunatics, feeble-minded, angry Blacks, nasty women, tantrum-throwing children, melancholy migrants, or pessimistic/inauthentic depressives. This book is dedicated to human diversity, to a full spectrum of human emotional reactions, to resisting oppressive social norms, and to using emotional energies to feel compassion or to rage against violence. In this book I call for halting the scientific "glad games" in order to engage in complex and contextual relationships with ourselves and others.

References

Ahmed, S. (2004). *Cultural politics of emotion*. New York: Routledge.

Ahmed, S. (2010a). Killing joy: Feminism and the history of happiness. *Signs, 35*(3), 571–594. https://doi.org/10.1086/648513.

Ahmed, S. (2010b). *The promise of happiness*. Durham, NC: Duke University Press.

Angelou, M. (1983). *I know why the caged bird sings*. New York, NY: Bantam.

Ankarloo, B., & Clark, S. (1999). *Witchcraft and magic in Europe*. Philadelphia, PA: University of Pennsylvania Press.

Bashford, A., & Levine, P. (Eds.). (2010). *The Oxford handbook of the history of eugenics*. New York: Oxford University Press.

Berlant, L. G. (2011). *Cruel optimism*. Durham, NC: Duke University Press.

Binkley, S. (2014). *Happiness as enterprise: An essay on neoliberal life*. Albany: State University of New York Press.

Blackburn, S. (2005). *The Oxford dictionary of philosophy*. Oxford, UK: Oxford University Press.

Bogen, H. (1992). *The luckiest orphans: A history of the Hebrew orphan asylum of New York*. Urbana-Champaign: University of Illinois Press.

Boucher, J., & Osgood, C. E. (1969). The Pollyanna hypothesis. *Journal of Memory and Language, 8*(1), 1–8.

Burns, W. E. (2003). *Witch hunts in Europe and America: An encyclopedia*. Westport, CT: Greenwood Publishing Group.

Cabanas, E. (2016). Rekindling individualism, consuming emotions: Constructing "psytizens" in the age of happiness. *Culture & Psychology, 22*(3), 467–480.

Cattell, R. B. (1987). *Beyondism: Religion from science*. New York: Praeger.

Davenport, C. B. (1910). *Eugenics: The science of human improvement by better breeding*. New York: Henry Holt.

Davenport, C. B. (1911). *Heredity in relation to eugenics*. New York: H. Holt.

Davies, W. (2015). *The happiness industry: How the government and big business sold us well-being*. London, UK: Verso Books.

De La Fabián, R., & Stecher, A. (2018). Positive psychology and the enhancement of happiness: A reply to Binkley (2018). *Theory & Psychology, 28*(3), 411–417.

Ehrenreich, B. (2009). *Bright-sided: How the relentless promotion of positive thinking is undermining America*. New York, NY: Metropolitan Books.

Ehrenreich, B., & English, D. (2010). *Witches, midwives, and nurses: A history of women healers.* New York, NY: Feminist Press.

Galton, F. (1869). *Hereditary genius: An inquiry into its laws and consequences.* New York: Macmillan.

Galton, F. (1883). *Inquiries into the human faculty & its development.* London: J.M. Dent.

Giroux, H. A. (2011). The disappearing intellectual in the age of economic Darwinism. *Policy Futures in Education, 9*(2), 163–171.

Goddard, H. H. (1911). The elimination of feeble-mindedness. *The Annals of the American Academy of Political and Social Science, 37*(2), 261–272.

Goddard, H. H. (1912). *The Kallikak family: A study in the heredity of feeble-mindedness.* New York: Macmillan.

Goddard, H. H. (1917). Mental tests and the immigrant. *Journal of Delinquency, 2,* 243–277.

Gottfredson, L. S. (1994a). Egalitarian fiction and collective fraud. *Society, 31*(3), 53–59.

Gottfredson, L. S. (1994b). The science and politics of race-norming. *American Psychologist, 49*(11), 955–963.

Harris, S. (2006). What is your dangerous idea? In podcast series *Science Must Destroy Religion.* Retrieved on January 14, 2019 at https://samharris.org/science-must-destroy-religion.

Hedges, C. (2009). *Empire of illusion: The end of literacy and the triumph of spectacle.* Toronto: Knopf Canada.

Herrnstein, R. J., & Murray, C. (1996). *The bell curve.* New York: Simon & Schuster.

hooks, b. (2006). *Outlaw culture: Resisting representations.* New York, NY: Routledge.

Horowitz, I. (2018). The happiness of the people. In I. Horowitz (Ed.), *Culture and civilization* (pp. 11–25). New York, NY: Routledge.

Hunt, M. (1999). *The new know-nothings: The political foes of the scientific study of human nature.* New Brunswick, NJ: Transaction.

Kaminsky, I. (2013). Of strangeness that wakes us. *Poetry, 201*(4), 469–478.

Karolides, N. J., Bald, M., & Sova, D. B. (1999). *100 banned books: Censorship histories of world literature.* New York, NY: Checkmark Books.

Lombardo, P. A. (Ed.). (2011). *A century of eugenics in America: From the Indiana experiment to the human genome era.* Bloomington: Indiana University Press.

Marx, K. (1843/1970). *Introduction to a contribution to the critique of Hegel's philosophy of right.* Collected Works. Vol. 3. New York, NY: Cambridge University Press. In J. O'Malley (Ed.), Translated by A. Jolin and J. O'Malley. Retrieved on January 14, 2019 at https://www.marxists.org/archive/marx/works/1843/critique-hpr/intro.htm.

Matlin, M. W., & Stang, D. J. (1978). *The Pollyanna principle: Selectivity in language, memory, and thought*. New York, NY: Schenkman.
McMahon, D. M. (2006). *Happiness: A history*. New York: Grove Press.
Melendy, M. R. (1914). *The science of eugenics and sex life*. New York: W. R. Vansant.
Merskin, D. L. (2011). *Media, minorities, and meaning: A critical introduction*. Philadelphia, PA: Peter Lang.
Morton, M. J. (2000). Surviving the great depression: Orphanages and orphans in Cleveland. *Journal of Urban History, 26*(4), 438–455.
Osteen, J. (2011). *Every day a Friday: How to be happier 7 days a week*. London, UK: Hachette.
Pew Research Center. (2018). *Attitudes toward spirituality and religion: Report*. Retrieved on January 14, 2019 at http://www.pewforum.org/2018/05/29/attitudes-toward-spirituality-and-religion.
Pinker, S. (2002). *The blank slate: The modern denial of human nature*. New York: Penguin.
Pinker, S. (2018). *Enlightenment now: The case for reason, science, humanism, and progress*. New York: Penguin.
Popenoe, P., & Johnson, R. H. (1935). *Applied eugenics* (2nd ed.). New York: Macmillan.
Porter, E. (1913). *Pollyanna*. Boston, MA: Colonial Press.
Ruickbie, L. (2004). *Witchcraft out of the shadows: A complete history*. London, UK: Robert Hale.
Rushton, J. P. (1999). Genetic similarity theory and the nature of ethnocentrism. In K. Thienpont & R. Cliquet (Eds.), *In-group/out-group behaviour in modern societies: An evolutionary perspective*. Amsterdam, The Netherlands: Vlaamse Gemeeschap/CBGS.
Rushton, J. P., & Jensen, A. R. (2005). Wanted: More race realism, less moralistic fallacy. *Psychology, Public Policy, and Law, 11*(2), 328–336. https://doi.org/10.1037/1076-8971.11.2.328.
Russell, J. B. (1972). *Witchcraft in the middle ages*. Ithaca, NY: Cornell University Press.
Shealy, C. N. (1995). From Boys Town to Oliver Twist: Separating fact from fiction in welfare reform and out-of-home placement of children and youth. *American Psychologist, 50*(8), 565–570.
Sloan, T. (1996). *Damaged life. The crisis of the modern psyche*. New York: Routledge.
Smith, E. P., & Merkel-Holguin, L. (2017). *A history of child welfare*. New York, NY: Routledge.
Sorell, T. (2013). *Scientism: Philosophy and the infatuation with science*. London, UK: Routledge.
Steinbeck, J. (1939). *The grapes of wrath* (re-printed 2006). New York, NY: Penguin.

Terman, L. M. (1916). *The measurement of intelligence*. New York: Houghton Mifflin.

Tucker, W. H. (1996). *The science and politics of racial research*. Carbondale: University of Illinois Press.

Watson, J. B. (1914). *Behavior: An introduction to comparative psychology*. New York, NY: H. Holt.

Watson, J. B. (1919). *Psychology: From the standpoint of a behaviorist*. Philadelphia, PA: Lippincott.

Whitney, G. (1999). Introduction. In D. E. Duke (Ed.), *My awakening: A path to racial understanding* (pp. 2–11). Convington, LA: Free Speech Press.

Yakushko, O. (2018a). Don't worry, be happy: Erasing racism, sexism, and poverty in positive psychology. *Psychotherapy and Politics International*, *16*(1), e1433.

Yakushko, O. (2018b). Witches, charlatans, and old wives: Critical perspectives on history of women's indigenous knowledge. *Women & Therapy*, *41*(1–2), 18–29.

Yakushko, O. (2019). Eugenics and its evolution in history of western psychology: A critical archival review. *Psychotherapy and Politics International*, online.

Yakushko, O., & Blodgett, E. (2018). Negative reflections about positive psychology: On constraining the field to a focus on happiness and personal achievement. *Journal of Humanistic Psychology*. https://doi.org/10.1177/0022167818794551.

Yen, J. (2015). Happiness as enterprise: An essay on neoliberal life. *Theory and Psychology*, *25*(4), 541–542.

Zinn, H. (2010). *The twentieth century: A people's history*. New York: Harper & Row.

CHAPTER 2

Demonized Emotions and Tortured Bodies in the Age of Scientific Progress

Contemporary scientific Pollyannaism can be traced to an age that claims the unprecedented development of scientific progress, humanism, and modernity—the Renaissance (Cronin, 2011; Rundle, 1995). This period of European history, roughly lasting from the fifteenth to the seventeenth century, is credited with significant social, political, and cultural developments that underlie the European move away from the so-called "Dark Ages" toward the Enlightenment or the modern era (Bartlett, 2011; Rundle, 1995). The Age of Enlightenment or the Age of Reason, which overlapped with and followed the Renaissance (from the early eighteenth through the nineteenth century), is further praised as the period of unparalleled intellectual, scientific, philosophical, and political progress in Europe and everywhere the Europeans colonized (Conrad, 2012; Fitzpatrick, Jones, Knellwolf, & McCalman, 2004; Gay, 1996).

In the midst of these celebratory histories, which are almost exclusively concerned with wealthy white European males, the experiences and values of marginalized groups remain invisible (Zinn, 2010). According to Hosbawn (1997), an alternative and more accurate view of the Enlightenment should consider it as a "conspiracy of dead white men in periwigs to provide the intellectual foundation for Western imperialism" (p. 336). During these same eras of "rebirth" and "Enlightenment", the religious and political authorities of Europe were engaged in one of its longest and most brutal cleansings of various people considered to be dangerous to their cultures and societies (Ankarloo & Clark, 1999; Burns, 2003; Ehrenreich & English, 2010; Zinn, 2010).

O. Yakushko, *Scientific Pollyannaism*,
https://doi.org/10.1007/978-3-030-15982-5_2

The Inquisition and the witch-hunts are often incorrectly described as being anti-scientific (e.g., pointing to Galileo as a prototype of a persecuted scientist). In contrast, the sciences and scientists of the day tended not to question witch-hunting, which resulted in the eradication of non-authorized forms of knowledge while privileging the exclusively upper-class all-male scientific establishment (Ankarloo & Clark, 1999; Ehrenreich & English, 2010; Yakushko, 2018).

The most infamous and influential witch-hunting inquisition manual, the *Malleus Maleficarum* or the *Hammer of Witches*, was produced by a Catholic priest Heinrich Kramer and initially published in Germany in 1487 (one of its later editions added another Catholic priest Sprengler as a co-author). The *Malleus* is a lengthy book, filled not only with systematic arguments about the existence of witches, their dangers to both individuals and the entirety of European civilization, and the reasons for and the best methods for their extermination, but also with extensive and systematic scientific justifications for its positions. Both Catholic and Protestant societies embraced these explanations about the dangers of witches to society, and the witch-hunts extended to countries influenced by Christianity, including not only Europe but also its growing number of Christianized colonies (Achterberg, 2013; Behar, 2001; Breuer, 2009; Horsley, 1979; Scarre & Callow, 2001; Whitney, 1995). Witch hunts were carried out by both religious and civic authorities in both Catholic (i.e., Spain, France) and Protestant (i.e., Germany, Scotland) countries and commonly occurring in communities which have been celebrating by historians as producing progressive enlightened (i.e., anti-"Dark Age") sciences. Protestantism, often represented as oriented toward questioning religious superstitions associated with medieval Catholicism, was just as engaged in practices of demonizing human beings as witches. Specifically, Ankarloo and Clark (1999) note that "it is undeniable that both Protestant and Catholic governments sponsored witch-hunting… [and in many instances] Protestant rulers were more severe than Catholic overlords in prosecuting witches" (p. 10).

Rationalizing the Demonization and Murder of Witches

Malleus remains largely unacknowledged in popular narratives of European history despite being, for a time, the second best-selling book after the Bible, and despite being named by numerous scholars as "the bloodiest book ever written" (Ankarloo & Clark, 1999; Burns, 2003;

Ruickbie, 2004; Russell, 1972). But some scholars have argued that between late 1400s and early 1700s, the *Malleus* was far more influential on European and colonized world cultures than any other book, again apart from the Bible (Ankarloo & Clark, 1999; Burns, 2003; Ruickbie, 2004; Silverblatt, 1983). According to Burns (2003), the *Malleus Maleficarum* was re-published in twenty revised editions during the 33 years following its publication, with another sixteen editions published by mid-seventeenth century (the Bible was re-published in less than 10 editions in the same time frame). Considering that the printing press was newly invented at the time of *Malleus* release, and that printing and distributing books remained extremely costly, the scale at which the *Malleus Maleficarum* was reproduced speaks to its extraordinary popularity, and its unprecedented influence and social power.

Although the modern reader may wish to dismiss the entire work as the ramblings of a superstitious religion, scholars hold this text as one of the most systematic, scholarly works of its time, drawing on Western philosophy and sciences in addition to theologians and scripture. The writers of *Malleus Maleficarum* cite Socrates, Aristotle, Plato, Seneca as frequently as they cite St. Augustine, St. Thomas Aquinas, or other Christian thinkers. In addition to drawing on scientific and philosophical explanations of ethics and reason in relation to governance or control over supposedly demonized individuals (i.e., lacking rationality, self-control, ethical values, volition), the authors of the *Malleus* drew on existing scholarship in regard to human biological differences. Specifically they emphasized gender differences, which were central to *Malleus*' theory that women were more susceptible than men to the influence of demons. According to Brauner (2001),

> They [authors of *Malleus Maleficarum*] argue that the evil of women stems from their physical and mental imperfections, a notion derived from Aristotle's theory that matter, perfection, and spirituality are purely expressed in the male body alone, and that women are misbegotten males produced by defective sperm. Women speak the language of idiots, Aristotle contends; like slaves, they are incapable of governing themselves or developing into the 'zoon politicon.' Thomas Aquinas adapted these views to Christianity, arguing that because woman is less perfect than man, she is but an indirect image of God and an appendix to man. (pp. 35–36)

The impact of the *Malleus* was not confined to ideology: individuals living across Europe and its colonies between late-fifteenth and mid-nineteenth centuries witnessed public (and often daily) tortures and executions of human beings who were branded as witches, based in the *Malleus*' teachings (Barstow, 1988; Ehrenreich & English, 2010; Scarre & Callow, 2001; Thurston, 2007). Both tortures and executions were conducted in central spaces of most European and colonized settlements as a reminder to the public at large to remain vigilant against demonic influences (Ehrenreich & English, 2010; Scarre & Callow, 2001; Thurston, 2007). Rough estimates suggest that between hundred of thousands to several million individuals, mostly women, were publicly tried, tortured, and executed as witches within the first two hundred years of the publication of *Malleus Maleficarum* (Ben-Yehuda, 1980; Brauner, 2001).

Killing the Healers

Among the individuals typically condemned as witches were women known for their medical knowledge and work healing people with physical and mental health conditions. Midwives, whose herbal and medicinal work would have been vital to their communities, were especially targeted (Achterberg, 2013; Brooke, 1997; Scarre & Callow, 2001; Yakushko, 2018). Because the *Malleus Maleficarum* proclaimed that women's capacity to heal or their medicinal knowledge were not sanctioned by the Church, Christian governments or other established Western institutions, it was claimed that their healing was derived from Satan and was harmful to individuals' spiritual and mental well-being. For example, according to the *Malleus Maleficarum*, "their [female healers] gift of healing is not derived from God," adding that it is the "witch midwives, who surpass all other witches in their crimes" (Part III, Question XXXIV). Thus, women holding positions of authority in their communities as healers were suspect of carrying out demonic works and targeted as witches (Ehrenreich & English, 2010; Horsley, 1979; Whitney, 1995). Meanwhile, in this time of supposed scientific progress and reason, Western universities, schools, and professions (e.g., medicine) accepted only upper class males (Achterberg, 2013; Ehrenriech & English, 2010). Women's knowledge was branded not only as witchcraft but as anti-scientific charlatanism and "old wives tales" (Yakushko, 2018). Women-healers who could attend to both the physical and emotional needs of their communities were killed, their methods proclaimed dangerous. The *Malleus* is filled with repeated injunctions to its reader to pursue the killing of witches and identify their demonic works in an effort to save Western societies and the world at large from great evils and destruction of civilization. Negative emotional states, termed "passions," were among the primary targets of these witch-hunts, deemed hazardous to well-being of individuals and communities.

Ridding the World of Women with "Passions"

Among the unambiguous targets of demonization and witch-hunts were unacceptable feeling states or "passions," especially anger and anxiety. The human body, explains the *Malleus*, is directly created by God and, therefore, is essentially noble. The *Malleus* writers insist, however, that although "the human body is nobler than any other body… [because of] *the passions of the mind the human body changes* and becomes hot or cold [sick], as *is the case with angry men or men who are afraid*" (Part I, Question II). Women, the *Malleus* claims, were second in creation in body and mind and, according to Western secular and religious scholars, biologically and socially inferior. Thus, women were viewed as more susceptible to the demonic influences, especially because of their over-emotional nature: "For though the devil tempted Eve to sin, yet Eve seduced Adam. And as the sin of Eve would not have brought death to our soul and body unless the sin had afterwards passed on to Adam, to which he was tempted by Eve, not by the devil, *therefore she is more bitter than death*" (Part I, Question VI).

Further, according to *Malleus*,

> Therefore, let us now chiefly consider women; and…why this kind of perfidy is found more in *so fragile a sex than in men*. This perfidy is more often found in women than in men, as we learn by actual experience… we may add to what has already been said the following: that *since they are feebler both in mind and body, it is not surprising that they should come more under the spell of witchcraft*. For as *regards intellect*, or the understanding of spiritual things, they *seem to be of a different nature from men*; a fact which is vouched for by the *logic of the authorities*, backed by various examples from the Scriptures. Terence says: *Women are intellectually like children*. (Part I, Question VI)

This lack of mature intellect and rationality was directly and repeatedly related to women's inordinate "passions" and negative emotional states:

> And indeed, just as through the *first defect in their intelligence* that are more prone to abjure the faith; so through *their second defect of inordinate affections and passions they search for, brood over, and inflict various vengeances*, either by witchcraft, or by some other means. *Wherefore it is no wonder that so great a number of witches exist in this [female] sex.* (Part I, Question VI)

Women's terrifying power over others, especially men, first and foremost included their capacity to manufacture negative emotions in others (e.g., hatred, anger, lust, shame, fear): "*they [witches] distract the minds of men, driving them to madness, insane hatred, and inordinate lusts… by the terrible influence of their spells alone, as it were by a draught of poison, they can destroy life*" (Part I, Question II). The section listing the demonic acts women are capable of as witches begins with their influences over emotions. Evil operated through witches, the *Malleus* claimed,

> *First, by inclining the minds of men to inordinate passion*; second, by obstructing their generative force [procreation]; third, by removing the members accommodated to that act [castrating men]; fourth, by changing men into beasts by their magic art; fifth, by destroying the generative force in women [preventing conception]; sixth, by procuring abortion; seventh, by offering children to devils, besides other animals and fruits of the earth with which they work much harm [being bad mothers]. (Part I, Question VI)

Men who were predisposed to feeling anger and other passions, could also be at risk of demonic possession, the *Malleus* warned its readers: "*For it is manifest that a man who has a body so disposed is more prone to concupiscence and anger and such passions; and when they are aroused, he is more apt to surrender to them [demons]*" (Part I, Question VII).

Even women's intense emotional reactions to accusations and torture during their trials were turned against them. The *Malleus* encouraged those in charge of the witch trials, tortures, and murder of witches, not to become influenced by women's emotional states such as when "the witch maintains her denial, or claims that she uttered those words not with the implied intention but in a *vehement and womanish passion*" (Part III, Third Head, Question XXV).

Scholars of the world-wide witch-hunts concur that women's anger was routinely noted as the primary shared characteristic among those who were demonized and violently punished. According to Scarre and Callow's (2001) the demonization of women's anger appears to be the most common pattern among the historical witch hunts, stating the "typical witch... was [supposedly] well known for a quarrelsome and aggressive nature" (p. 26). In contrast, happy housewives and optimistic self-controlled men were viewed as imbued with spiritual grace and goodness.

Undoubtedly, the witch-hunts, especially those exemplified in *Malleus Maleficarum*, were reflective of profound misogyny and nearly obsessive focus on patriarchal control over women's minds, bodies and lives (Brauner, 2001; Burns, 2003; Levack, 1995). According to Levack (1995), the literature produced by European scholars and theologians on witches "is in most cases intensely misogynistic, in the sense that it is demeaning, if not blatantly hostile to women" (p. 145). It is important to note that these European pre-Christian (e.g., Socrates, Aristotle) and Christian cultures placed a significant emphasis on vilifying "passions" and emotions such as anger. As will be noted in later chapters, Simone de Beauvoir, Betty Friedan, and Sara Ahmed have articulated the direct connection between gender oppression and the cultural insistence that women be "happy housewives." Assertions that women are the "second sex," including declarations of their biological inferiority, have often focused on women's supposed lack of emotional self-control. This scientific misogyny, evident during the witch-hunts, was taken up through empirical theories produced by Charles Darwin, social Darwinists and eugenicists. Their writings contributed to the evolution of scientific Pollyannaism as an exclusively scientific (i.e., non-religious) justification for the vilification of negative emotional states and those who expressed them.

References

Achterberg, J. (2013). *Woman as healer*. Boulder, CO: Shambhala Publications.

Ankarloo, B., & Clark, S. (1999). *Witchcraft and magic in Europe*. Philadelphia: University of Pennsylvania Press.

Barstow, A. L. (1988). On studying witchcraft as women's history: A historiography of the European witch persecutions. *Journal of Feminist Studies in Religion, 4*(2), 7–19.

Bartlett, K. R. (Ed.). (2011). *The civilization of the Italian Renaissance: A sourcebook*. Toronto, ON: University of Toronto Press.

Behar, R. (2001). Sexual witchcraft, colonialism, and women's powers: Views from the Mexican Inquisition. In B. P. Levak (Ed.), *Gender and witchcraft: New perspectives on witchcraft, magic, and demonology* (pp. 218–246). New York, NY: Routledge.

Ben-Yehuda, N. (1980). The European witch craze of the 14th to 17th centuries: A sociologist's perspective. *American Journal of Sociology, 86*(1), 1–31.

Brauner, S. (2001). *Fearless wives and frightened shrews: The construction of the witch in early modern Germany.* Amherst: University of Massachusetts Press.

Breuer, H. (2009). *Crafting the witch: Gendering magic in medieval and early modern England.* New York, NY: Routledge.

Brooke, E. (1997). *Medicine women: A pictorial history of women healers.* New York, NY: Quest Books.

Burns, W. E. (2003). *Witch hunts in Europe and America: An encyclopedia.* Westport, CT: Greenwood Publishing Group.

Conrad, S. (2012). Enlightenment in global history: A historiographical critique. *The American Historical Review, 117*(4), 999–1027.

Cronin, V. (2011). *The Florentine Renaissance.* New York, NY: Random House.

Ehrenreich, B., & English, D. (2010). *Witches, midwives, and nurses: A history of women healers.* New York, NY: Feminist Press.

Fitzpatrick, M., Jones, P., Knellwolf, C., & McCalman, I. (Eds.). (2004). *Enlightenment world.* New York, NY: Psychology Press.

Gay, P. (1996). *The enlightenment: An interpretation.* New York, NY: W. W. Norton.

Horsley, R. A. (1979). Who were the witches? The social roles of the accused in the European witch trials. *The Journal of Interdisciplinary History, 9*(4), 689–715. https://doi.org/10.2307/203380.

Hosbawm, E. (1997). *On history.* London, UK: Abacus Books.

Levack, B. P. (1995). *The witch-hunt in early modern Europe.* Essex, UK: Pearson.

Ruickbie, L. (2004). *Witchcraft out of the shadows: A complete history.* London, UK: Robert Hale.

Rundle, D. (1995). A new golden age? More, Skelton and the accession verses of 1509. *Renaissance Studies, 9*(1), 58–76.

Russell, J. B. (1972). *Witchcraft in the middle ages.* Ithaca, NY: Cornell University Press.

Scarre, G., & Callow, J. (2001). *Witchcraft and magic in sixteenth- and seventeenth-century Europe* (2nd ed.). Hampshire, UK: Palgrave.

Silverblatt, I. (1983). The evolution of witchcraft and the meaning of healing in colonial Andean society. *Culture, Medicine and Psychiatry, 7*(4), 413–427.

Thurston, R. W. (2007). *The witch hunts: A history of the witch persecutions in Europe and North America.* Upper Saddle River, NJ: Pearson Education.

Whitney, E. (1995). The witch "she"/the historian "he": Gender and the historiography of the European witch-hunts. *Journal of Women's History, 7*(3), 77–101. https://doi.org/10.1353/jowh.2010.0511.

Yakushko, O. (2018). Witches, charlatans, and old wives: Critical perspectives on history of women's indigenous knowledge. *Women & Therapy, 41*(1–2), 18–29.

Zinn, H. (2010). *The twentieth century: A people's history*. New York: Harper & Row.

CHAPTER 3

The Survival of the Happiest Who (Get to) Control the Resources and Procreation

The modern turn to the sciences rather than religion in the promotion of social values is evident in the works of Charles Darwin and the social Darwinists (i.e., scholars who insisted on explaining human social differences as based on supposed universal patterns of biological evolution) (Bergman 2014; Chase 1980; Gould 1996; Rose and Rose 2010; Tucker 1996). Notably, Darwin (1859) not only claimed to have discovered the "Origin of the Species" but also the "Preservation of the Favoured Races in the Struggle for Life" (the complete title of his book). Darwin's work emerged during the time when the last witch-hunts were being carried out in Europe and North America, as well as at the height of European colonial expansion. Darwin's theory of evolution initially focused on the "fittest" among varied plant and animal species, which supposedly survived and reproduced exclusively by asserting dominance and control over resources and procreation (i.e., males over females). Darwin's subsequent works proclaimed that he found scientific justifications for differences in "status" between varied human races (e.g., English vs. Jews, Irish, Russians, African Blacks) and groups (e.g., males vs. females) via his supposedly empirically grounded theories of evolution (Bergman 2014; Chase 1980). Notably, emotional expression and emotional self-control became one of Darwin's key markers of evolutionary difference between the higher and lower developed species.

O. Yakushko, *Scientific Pollyannaism*,
https://doi.org/10.1007/978-3-030-15982-5_3

Alternatives to Scientific Pollyannaism Found on the Galapagos

Alternative evolutionary theories emerged prior to and during the same time as Darwinist explanations. In fact, at the end of nineteenth century many scientists viewed the French biologist Lamarck as the founder of Western evolutionary theories, rather than Darwin (Packard 1901). Lamarck's (1809) theory of evolution focused on centrality of environmental influences for evolutionary development. Larmarck's theory is exemplified in discussions of how genetically similar organisms could develop in radically different ways based on differential environmental treatment that led to use or disuse of certain functions. According to Lamarck (1809),

> Everything, therefore, concurs to prove my assertion, to wit--that it is not form [genetic, biological endowments], whether of the body or of the parts, which gives rise to the habits of animals and their manner of life; but that, on the contrary, in the *habits, the manner of living, and all the other circumstances of environment*, we have those things which in the course of time have built up animal bodies with all their members. (p. 190)

Thus, Lamarck's theory of evolution primarily emphasized the role of the environment as central in shaping organism's adaptation and development (Butler 1911; Packard 1901). Thus, at the turn of twentieth century, when psychological and social sciences developed as disciplines, Lamarck's evolutionary theory was often recognized as holding more explanatory power than Darwinism in understanding human beings. The vital importance of social context to human development was central in psychoanalysis, which privileged Lamarck's views (Gadjev 2015).

In addition, Russian scientist Kropotkin (1914/2012) set out to confirm Darwin's theory of "the struggle in race for life" in far harsher natural environments than the Galapagos islands—the Siberian tundra. Instead, Kropotkin discovered that among varied parts of the natural world, the "mutual aid" (which became the title of his work), cooperation and interdependence were far more common than the violent struggle to dominate underlying the Darwinist perspective. Thus, Kropotkin openly questioned Darwinist and social Darwinist assumption that human societies evolved through violence and struggle with harsh conditions in which winners supposedly possessed and passed on superior biological traits. Notably, Kropotkin also questioned the mythological fantasies of cave men commonly presented as fact in Darwinist arguments, despite not reflecting actual anthropological evidence. According to Kropotkin, the early periods of humanity were marked by "creative genius" related to what he termed "mutual-aid institutions" of shared human community care:

> For primitive Man--they [Darwinists] maintain--war of each against all was the law of life. In how far this assertion, which has been too willingly repeated, without sufficient criticism, since the times of Hobbes, is supported by what we know about the early phases of human development, is discussed in the chapters given to the Savages and the Barbarians [sic]. The number and importance of mutual-aid institutions which were developed by the creative genius of the savage and half-savage masses, during the earliest clan-period of mankind and still more during the next village-community period, and the immense influence which these early institutions have exercised upon the subsequent development of mankind, down to the present times, induced me to extend my researches to the later, historical periods as well. (Introduction)

In contrast to the violent theories of Darwin and Darwinists, noted below, Kropotkin offered a vastly different vision of humanity and human care, embracing a fuller range of human emotional reactions, including happiness, love, and compassion, as part of human interdependence grounded in social justice:

> Love, sympathy and self-sacrifice certainly play an immense part in the progressive development of our moral feelings. But it is not love and not even sympathy upon which Society is based in mankind. *It is the conscience--be it only at the stage of an instinct--of human solidarity.* It is the unconscious recognition of the force that is borrowed by each man from the practice of mutual aid; *of the close dependency of every one's happiness upon the happiness of all; and of the sense of justice, or equity, which brings the individual to consider the rights of every other individual as equal to his own.* (Introduction)

Kropotkin's views were dismissed as ideological and scientifically incorrect, especially in light of his anarchist social philosophies and his alleged connections to the Russian revolution. His evolutionary theory was rejected as inimical to Western capitalist notions of competition and survival of the fittest (see Robinson's [1908] book entitled *Comrade Kropotkin*).

Similarly, Lamarck's views were also rejected because they did not offer naturalizing justifications for racist and colonial Western systems. Other scholars such as Carpenter (1889) judged Lamarckian and Darwinian views of evolution primarily on their capacity to explain the development of differences in human levels of "civilization," because of social concerns that "ominous change in color" was detrimental to Western societies (p. 4). Even though Lamarckism has remained central to scientific and psychological scholarship from nineteenth century to today, its emphasis on environment and social context is typically minimized or dismissed (Gadjev 2015). Eugenic-based scholars such as John B. Watson (1919) maligned Lamarck's theories as non-scientific. Popular academic eugenic textbooks such as Popenoe and Johnson's (1935) *Applied Eugenics* further claimed to have documented that the influence on Lamarckian evolutionary perspectives resulted in a "racial" decline in Lamarck's native France in contrast to countries such as 1930s U.K., the U.S., and Germany, where Darwinist-based eugenics were dominant. Although psychoanalytic and other critical social theories of human development remain influenced by alternative evolutionary theories, many assertions about human differences and development continue to be tied to Darwinism. Specifically, Darwin's key claims in regard to evolutionary superiority were based on his perceptions of varied emotional states, such as happiness, optimism, and self-control.

The Survival of the Happiest

Thus, Western science embraced Darwin's account of difference within the species as the result of struggle against negative and violent conditions, where survival depends on dominance over others in the fight for resources. Central to these theories was the notion that certain species reached the top of the evolutionary ladder by having superior biological endowments, exemplified by a cheerful disposition and emotional self-control. Thus, after the initial descriptions of violent conflict over resources and control of females among, allegedly, all non-human species on the Galapagos islands, Darwin's (1859) *Origin of the Species* assures British readers: "When we reflect on this struggle, we may console ourselves with the full belief, that the war of nature is not incessant, that no fear is felt, that death is generally prompt, and *that the vigorous, the healthy, and the happy survive and multiply*" (p. 96). Thus, evolutionary warfare was supposedly won by the genetically superior species, and by those who were cheerful while fighting for survival. Their biological dominance over others resulted in continued propagation positivity and emotional self-control in their offspring. In short, it seems clear that Darwin's move to emphasize certain form of intelligence (i.e., British style of educational attainment) and emotional self-presentation (i.e., optimism, restraint) as signs of evolutionary superiority among human beings reflected selective values of wealthy British males. Darwin's evolutionary theorizing not only excluded relational capacities, compassion, physical vigor or environmental adaptability as forms of human goodness but also reinforced the long-standing cultural misogyny and racism common in his day.

Following the *Origin of the Species*, Darwin's (1871) subsequent empirical evolutionary works begin to focus far more on differences between human groups, rather than animal species. Therefore, in his second major evolutionary text entitled *The Descent of Man in Relation to Sex* numerous proclamations are made about women in relation to men, and varied human "races" in relation to British and Nordic "civilizations." In this book, Darwin now openly proclaims that "man has ultimately become superior to woman" (p. 329) and that "the western nations of Europe, who now so immeasurably surpass their former savage progenitors, and stand at the summit of civilization" (p. 141). Emotions, specifically positive happy emotions, supposedly played significant role in development of these differences and served as marks of biological superiority. According to Darwin,

> *A contented, happy tribe will flourish better than one that is discontented and unhappy.* We have seen that even at an early period in the history of man, the expressed wishes of the community will have naturally influenced to a large extent the conduct of each member; and *as all wish for happiness, the "greatest happiness principle" will have become a most important secondary guide and object.* (p. 82)

Pronouncing that the study of varied human races and civilizations could reveal evolutionary strategies of survival and, therefore, fitness among all humans, Darwin (1871) discussed such differences specifically in terms of emotions:

> The races differ also in constitution, in acclimatisation and in liability to certain diseases. Their mental characteristics are likewise very distinct; *chiefly as it would appear in their emotional*, but partly in their intellectual faculties. Every one who has had the opportunity of comparison, must have been struck with the contrast between the taciturn, even morose, aborigines of S. America and the light-hearted, talkative negroes. (p. 131)

Darwin (1871) was among the first popular scientists to openly connect supposed differences in brain sizes and biological appearance to high and low intelligence levels but also to expressions of particular emotions: “With civilised nations, the reduced size of the jaws from lessened use—the habitual play of different muscles serving to express different emotions—and the increased size of the brain from greater intellectual activity, have together produced a considerable effect on their general appearance when compared with savages” (p. 201).

Emotional self-control is further proclaimed by Darwin (1871) to be among the greatest human virtues. Such self-control was also supposed to increase with supposed “grade” of civilization (i.e., lower among the “savages” and highest among the “civilized” British) and to ensure the ever-important notion of male control over females in regard to procreation:

> As no man can practise the virtues necessary for the welfare of his tribe without self sacrifice, self-command, and the power of endurance, these qualities have been at all times highly and most justly valued. The American savage voluntarily submits to the most horrid tortures without a groan, to prove and strengthen his fortitude and courage; and we cannot help admiring him, or even an Indian Fakir, who, from a foolish religious motive, swings suspended by a hook buried in his flesh. The other so-called self-regarding virtues, which do not obviously, though they may really, affect the welfare of the tribe, have never been esteemed by savages, though now highly appreciated by civilised nations. *The greatest intemperance is no reproach with savages. Utter licentiousness, and unnatural crimes, prevail to an astounding extent*... As soon, however, as marriage, whether polygamous, or monogamous, becomes common, jealousy will lead to the *inculcation of female virtue*; *and this, being honoured, will tend to spread to the unmarried females*. How slowly it spreads to the male sex, we see at the present day. *Chastity eminently requires self-command; therefore it has been honoured from a very early period in the moral history of civilised man*. (pp. 119–120)

These supposed differences in emotions and emotional self-control were often evoked as key indicators of the degree of civilization a particular society or individual had achieved. In his letters to fellow scholar Wallace, Darwin (1898) argued: “the struggle between the races of man depended entirely on intellectual and moral qualities” (p. 89). Men, especially British men, were scientifically proven to possess the most civilized and advanced forms of emotional control and expression, in contrast to other, “savage” peoples and to women. According to Darwin (1889):

> With adults, especially of the male sex, weeping soon ceases to be caused by, or to express, bodily pain. This may be accounted for by its being thought weak and unmanly by men, both of civilized and barbarous races, to exhibit bodily pain by any outward sign. *With this exception, savages weep copiously from very slight causes...* A New Zealand chief “cried like a child because the sailors spoilt his favourite cloak by powdering it with flour.” I saw in Tierra del Fuego a native who had lately lost a brother, and who alternately cried with hysterical violence, and laughed heartily at anything which amused him...*Englishmen rarely cry, except under the pressure of the acutest grief*; whereas in some parts of the Continent the men shed tears much more readily and freely. *The insane notoriously give way to all their emotions with little or no restraint.* (pp. 607–608)

Colonization and dominance of the British and Nordic groups over others was associated by Darwin (1889) with their supposedly superior moral and emotional strengths:

> The remarkable success of the English as colonists, compared to other European nations, has been ascribed to *their “daring and persistent energy”*; a result which is well illustrated by comparing the progress of the Canadians of English and French extraction; but who can say how the English gained their energy? There is apparently much truth in the belief that the wonderful progress of the United States, as well as the character of the people, are the results of natural selection; for the *more energetic, restless, and courageous men from all parts of Europe* have emigrated during the last ten or twelve generations to that great country, and have there succeeded best. (pp. 185–186)

Drawing on work of Galton, an infamous eugenicist and Darwin's relative, Darwin (1871) assures that civilized men, even when faced with negative feelings and temptations, can rely on their superior hereditary "volition" to minimize and control their emotional states:

> Galton… see his remarkable work on 'Hereditary Genius,' … has remarked, is all the less surprising, as man has emerged from a state of barbarism within a comparatively recent period. After having yielded to some temptation we feel a sense of dissatisfaction, shame, repentance, or remorse, analogous to the feelings caused by other powerful instincts or desires, when left unsatisfied or baulked. We compare the weakened impression of a past temptation with the ever present social instincts, or with habits, gained in early youth and strengthened during our whole lives, until they have become almost as strong as instincts. If with the temptation still before us we do not yield, it is because either the social instinct or some custom is at the moment predominant, or because we have learnt that it will appear to us hereafter the stronger, when compared with the weakened impression of the temptation, and we realise that its violation would cause us suffering. *Looking to future generations, there is no cause to fear that the social instincts will grown weaker, and we may expect that virtuous habits will grow stronger, becoming perhaps fixed by inheritance.* In this case the struggle between our higher and lower impulses will be less severe, and *virtue will be triumphant.* (pp. 124–125)

In contrast, Darwin (1871) routinely warned that overpopulation among "uncivilized" races, not only African Blacks, but by other particular undesirable groups such as the Irish, would contribute to propagation of morally and emotionally corrupt people:

> *Thus the reckless, degraded, and often vicious members of society, tend to increase at a quicker rate than the provident and generally virtuous members.* Or as Mr. Greg puts the case: "*The careless, squalid, unaspiring Irishman multiplies like rabbits: the frugal, foreseeing, self-respecting, ambitious Scot, stern in his morality, spiritual in his faith, sagacious and disciplined in his intelligence*, passes his best years in struggle and in celibacy, marries late, and leaves few behind him. (p. 93)

Moreover, in Darwin's estimation, distinct emotional states can be used to differentiate varied racial groups, whose emotional proclivities can, supposedly, be traced to evolutionary experiences of climate difference. As noted before, the "civilized" nations, according to Darwin, appear more attractive specifically because facial "muscles serving different emotions led to more civilization" (p. 197).

Darwin (1871, 1889), like Galton and other eugenicists, also encouraged readers to disregard their emotional impulses to feel concern for uncivilized groups, because such feelings detracted from evolutionary necessity of progress. In his section entitled *Natural Selection as Affecting Civilised Nations*, Darwin (1871) praised eugenicists like Wallace and Galton, stating that "natural selection" often operated best among the "savages" because they eliminated their own "weak" whereas higher "morality" of "civilized" races was needed for supposed evolutionary progress:

> With savages, *the weak in body or mind are soon eliminated*; and those that survive commonly exhibit a vigorous state of health. We civilised men, on the other hand, do our utmost to check the process of elimination; we build asylums for the imbecile, the maimed, and the sick; we institute poor-laws; and our medical men exert their utmost skill to save the life of every one to the last moment. There is reason to believe that vaccination has preserved thousands, who from a weak constitution would formerly have succumbed to small-pox. *Thus the weak members of civilised societies propagate their kind. No one who has attended to the breeding of domestic animals will doubt that this must be highly injurious to the race of man.* It is surprising *how soon a want of care, or care wrongly directed, leads to the degeneration of a domestic race*; but excepting in the case of man himself, hardly any one is so ignorant as to allow his worst animals to breed. *The aid which we feel impelled to give to the helpless is mainly an incidental result of the instinct of sympathy, which was originally acquired as part of the social instincts, but subsequently rendered, in the manner previously indicated, more tender and more widely diffused.* Nor could we check our sympathy, even at the urging of hard reason, without deterioration in the noblest part of our nature. *The surgeon may harden himself whilst performing an operation, for he knows that he is acting for the good of his patient; but if we were intentionally to neglect the weak and helpless, it could only be for a contingent benefit, with an overwhelming present evil. We must therefore bear the undoubtedly bad effects of the weak surviving and propagating their kind.* (p. 180)

Darwin (1871) routinely discussed the supposedly negative and amoral emotions accompanying mental illness as signs of evolutionary weakness. He encouraged eugenic methods of ridding the world of individuals who were characterized by high levels of melancholy or anger.

> *In regard to the moral qualities, some elimination of the worst dispositions is always in progress even in the most civilized nations.* Malefactors are executed, or imprisoned for long periods, so that they cannot freely transmit their bad qualities. *Melancholic and insane persons are confined, or commit suicide. Violent and quarrelsome men often come to a bloody end.* The restless who will not follow any steady occupation- -and this relic of barbarism is a great check to civilization… emigrate to newly-settled countries; where they prove useful pioneers. Intemperance is so highly destructive, that the expectation of life of the intemperate, at the age of thirty for instance, is only 13.8 years; whilst for the rural labourers of England at the same age it is 40.59 years… Profligate women bear few children, and profligate men rarely marry; both suffer from disease. (p. 137)

Continuing his proclamations about superior and inferior human beings even among the British, Darwin (1871) praises both the development of eugenic efforts to breed only superior groups as well as the use of "instruction during youth" and "religious feelings" to promote greater evolutionary morality:

> But I have already said enough, whilst *treating of the lower races*, on the causes which lead to the advance of morality, namely, the approbation of our fellow-men--the strengthening of our sympathies by habit--example and imitation--reason--experience, and even self-interest--*instruction during youth, and religious feelings.* A *most important obstacle in civilised countries to an increase in the number of men of a superior class has been strongly insisted on by [eugenicists] Mr. Greg and Mr. Galton.* (p. 137)

The inheritance of superior moral tendencies, which, in Darwin's view, included control over emotional reactions, was frequently emphasized and connected to the evolutionary necessity of higher, civilized nations to become more "moral" (Darwin's examples included "chastity, temperance, humanity to animals") while also fighting with their lower, uncivilized tendencies (e.g., "senseless customs, superstitions, and tastes, such as the horror of a Hindoo for unclean food"). According to Darwin (1871), "*As a struggle may sometimes be seen going on between the various instincts of the lower animals, it is not surprising that there should be a struggle in man between his social instincts, with their derived virtues, and his lower, though momentarily stronger impulses or desires*" (p. 129).

Darwin's Happy Housewives

Gender was central to distinguishing between good and bad emotions. Shame, in Darwin's (1889) view, was primarily related to innately female feelings about sexuality and the body:

> The foregoing facts show that, *as a general rule, with English women, blushing does not extend beneath the neck and upper part of the chest.* Nevertheless Sir J. Paget informs me that he has lately heard of a case, on which he can fully rely, in which a little girl, shocked by what she imagined to be an act of indelicacy, blushed all over her abdomen and the upper parts of her legs. Moreau also relates, on the authority of a celebrated painter, that the chest, shoulders, arms, and whole body of a girl, who unwillingly consented to serve as a model, reddened when she was first divested of her clothes. (pp. 1307–1308)

Many of the emotions that are considered "negative" were also connected to women's lower evolutionary development in contrast to men. In his primary works, such as *The Descent of Men in Relation to Sex* Darwin (1871) discussed that women's development remains "like the young of the species," continually comparing women to children. In his discussion of sorrow related to grief Darwin (1889) stated,

> As far as I have been able to observe, *the grief-muscles are brought into action much more frequently by children and women than by men.* They are rarely acted on, at least with grown-up persons, from bodily pain, but almost exclusively from mental distress. *As children and women cry much more freely than men*, and as grown-up persons of both sexes rarely weep *except from mental distress, we can understand why the grief-muscles are more frequently seen in action, as I believe to be the case, with children and women than with men*; and with adults of both sexes from mental distress alone. (pp. 704–705)

Similarly, women's lower intellectual achievement was also routinely connected by Darwin (1889) to women's inferior genetic or hereditary intellectual capacities. In fact, it is males' dominance over females that supposedly furnished them with superior emotional characteristics like perseverance and self-control:

> *The chief distinction in the intellectual powers of the two sexes is shewn by man's attaining to a higher eminence, in whatever he takes up, than can woman--whether requiring deep thought, reason, or imagination, or merely the use of the senses and hands.* If two lists were made of the most eminent men and women in poetry, painting, sculpture, music (inclusive both of composition and performance), history, science, and philosophy, with half-a-dozen names under each subject, the two lists would not bear comparison. We may also infer, from the law of the deviation from averages, so well illustrated by Mr. Galton, in his work on 'Hereditary Genius,' that if men are capable of a decided pre-eminence over women in many subjects, *the average of mental power in man must be above that of woman.* (p. 328)

Darwin (1871) continued his explanation of males' superiority over females by considering the supposedly central role of males in battle and the slaughter of animals:

> Amongst the half-human progenitors of man, and amongst savages, there have been struggles between the males during many generations for the possession of the females. But mere bodily strength and size would do little for victory, unless associated with courage, perseverance, and determined energy. With social animals, the young males have to pass through many a contest before they win a female, and the older males have to retain their females by renewed battles. They have, also, in the case of mankind, to defend their females, as well as their young, from enemies of all kinds, and to hunt for their joint subsistence. But to avoid enemies or to attack them with success, to capture wild animals, and to fashion weapons, *requires the aid of the higher mental faculties, namely, observation, reason, invention, or imagination.* These various faculties will thus have been continually put to the test and selected during manhood. (pp. 328–329)

Darwin insisted that the superior qualities with which males have been endowed by evolution only passed genetically to other males and not the females:

> *Consequently in accordance with the principle often alluded to, we might expect that they would at least tend to be transmitted chiefly to the male offspring at the corresponding period of manhood.* Now, when two men are put into competition, or a man with a woman, both possessed of every mental quality in equal perfection, save that one has higher energy, perseverance, and courage, the latter will generally become more eminent in every pursuit, and will gain the ascendancy. (p. 329)

Relying on the remarks of other scholars who compare (real or invented) differences between women and men, Darwin (1871) further built his argument for the universal and biological inferiority of women to men by comparing their relative contributions to Western culture and civilization:

> Stuart Mill remarks ('The Subjection of Women,' 1869, p. 122), "The things in which man most excels woman are those which require most plodding, and long hammering at single thoughts." What is this but energy and perseverance?) *He may be said to possess genius--for genius has been declared by a great authority to be patience; and patience, in this sense, means unflinching, undaunted perseverance. But this view of genius is perhaps deficient; for without the higher powers of the imagination and reason, no eminent success can be gained in many subjects.* These latter faculties, as well as the former, will have been developed in man, partly through sexual selection,--that is, through the contest of rival males, and partly through natural selection, that is, from success in the general struggle for life; and as in both cases the struggle will have been during maturity, the characters gained will have been transmitted more fully to the male than to the female offspring. *It accords in a striking manner with this view of the modification and re-inforcement of many of our mental faculties by sexual selection...* Thus, *man has ultimately become superior to woman.* (p. 329)

Men's biologically superior bodies were also, according to Darwin (1871), related to their greater feelings of courage, boldness, perseverance, self-control, dedication, and so on:

> There can be little doubt that the greater size and strength of man, in comparison with woman, together with his broader shoulders, more developed muscles, rugged outline of body, *his greater courage and pugnacity, are all due in chief part to inheritance from his half-human male ancestors.* These characters would, however, have been preserved or even augmented during the long ages of man's savagery, by the success of the strongest and boldest men, both in the general struggle for life and in their contests for wives; a success which would have ensured their leaving a more numerous progeny than their less favoured brethren. It is not probable that the greater strength of man was primarily acquired through the inherited effects of his having worked harder than woman for his own subsistence and that of his family; for the women in all barbarous nations are compelled to work at least as hard as the men. With civilised people the arbitrament of battle for the possession of the

> women has long ceased; on the other hand, the men, *as a general rule, have to work harder than the women for their joint subsistence, and thus their greater strength will have been kept up.* (p. 563)

Women's primary *positive* emotional evolutionary characteristic was to display tenderness, affection, and selflessness, while men's competitive nature is acknowledge to have some downsides, such as their selfishness. Nevertheless, Darwin concludes, "man is more powerful in body and mind than woman." Specifically, according to Darwin (1871):

> With respect to differences of this nature between man and woman, it is probable that sexual selection has played a highly important part. *Woman seems to differ from man in mental disposition, chiefly in her greater tenderness and less selfishness*; and this holds good even with savages, as shewn by a well-known passage in Mungo Park's Travels, and by statements made by many other travellers. Woman, owing to her maternal instincts, displays these qualities towards her infants in an eminent degree; therefore it is likely that she would often extend them towards her fellow-creatures. Man is the rival of other men; he delights in competition, and this leads to ambition which passes too easily into selfishness. These latter qualities seem to be his natural and unfortunate birthright. *It is generally admitted that with woman the powers of intuition, of rapid perception, and perhaps of imitation, are more strongly marked than in man; but some, at least, of these faculties are characteristic of the lower races, and therefore of a past and lower state of civilisation. Man is more powerful in body and mind than woman.* (p. 563)

Darwin's writings in regard to human social differences, including emotional differences based on race, gender, and "grade" of evolutionary development have been minimized and sanitized in historical and psychological scholarship (Buss 2009; Pinker 2018; Shields and Bhatia 2009; Wright 1994). As such, this extensive review and citations are intended to show just how significant the move toward establishing "negative" categories of feelings and emotional states was to the development of scientific Pollyannaism. Darwin's theories, as we have seen, ignore and minimize the socio-historical and contextual factors that led to the patriarchal, colonial, racist world Darwin observed, relying instead on apparently neutral empirical observations about biological endowments found universally in all species.

Whereas during the witch-hunts and Christianized eras of social oppression "negative" emotional states were signs of demonic possession, in Darwin and post-Darwinist scientific theories these affective states and reactions were transformed into inherited biological (genetic) tendencies that could be empirically assigned to gender, race, class and other categories of fitness. As noted above, these assumptions were used not only to justify hierarchical beliefs about human differences but also to institute socio-political policies and norms that create "improved human stock."

References

Bergman, J. (2014). *The Darwin effect: It's influence on nazism, eugenics, racism, communism, capitalism & sexism*. Green Forest, AR: New Leaf Publishing Group.

Buss, D. M. (2009). The great struggles of life: Darwin and the emergence of evolutionary psychology. *American Psychologist, 64*(2), 140.

Butler, S. (1911). *Evolution, old and new: Or the theories of Buffon, Dr. Erasmus Darwin and Lamarck, as compared with that of Charles Darwin*. London, UK: Kessinger Publishing.

Carpenter, E. (1889). *Civilisation: Its cause and cure*. London, UK: George Allen and Unwin.

Chase, A. (1980). *The legacy of Malthus: The social costs of the new scientific racism*. Urbana, IL: University of Illinois Press.

Darwin, C. (1859). *On the origin of species: Or, the preservation of favoured races in the struggle for life*. London: Down, Bromley, Kent.

Darwin, C. (1889). *The expression of the emotions in man and animals*. London: Murray.

Darwin, C. (1898). *The life and letters of Charles Darwin, including an autobiographical chapter* (F. Darwin, Ed., Rev. ed.). London, UK: John Murray.

Gadjev, I. (2015). Nature and nurture: Lamarck's legacy. *Biological Journal of the Linnean Society, 114*(1), 242–247. https://doi.org/10.1111/bij.12439.

Gould, S. J. (1996). *The mismeasure of man*. New York, NY: W. W. Norton & Company.

Kropotkin, P. (1914/2012). *Mutual aid: A factor of evolution*. Mineola, NY: Dover.

Lamarck, J.-B. (1809). Zoological philosophy. In J. A. Hammerton (Ed.) (2008), *The world's greatest books* (Vol. 15). Science. Wm. H. Wise & Co (Online).

Packard, A. S. (1901). *Lamarck, the founder of evolution: His life and work.* London, UK: Longmans, Green, and Company.
Pinker, S. (2018). *Enlightenment now: The case for reason, science, humanism, and progress.* New York: Penguin.
Popenoe, P., & Johnson, R. H. (1935). *Applied eugenics* (2nd ed.). New York: Macmillan.
Robinson, V. (1908). *Comrade Kropotkin.* New York, NY: The Altrurians.
Rose, H., & Rose, S. (2010). *Alas poor Darwin: Arguments against evolutionary psychology.* New York: Random House.
Shields, S. A., & Bhatia, S. (2009). Darwin on race, gender, and culture. *American Psychologist, 64*(2), 111–119. https://doi.org/10.1037/a0013502.
Tucker, W. H. (1996). *The science and politics of racial research.* Carbondale, IL: University of Illinois Press.
Watson, J. B. (1919). *Psychology: From the standpoint of a behaviorist.* Philadelphia, PA: Lippincott.
Wright, R. (1994). *The moral animal: The new science of evolutionary psychology.* New York: Pantheon Books.

CHAPTER 4

Eugenic Scientific Utopias Filled with Socially Engineered Happy Productive People

The previous chapter on Charles Darwin shows the unmistakable movement of Darwinism toward eugenic, defined by Galton, Darwin's relative and British scholar, as the evolutionary "science of racial betterment" (based on Greek words "well" and "born," eu-genics) (Galton, 1865, 1883; Popenoe & Johnson, 1935). According to Galton (1907), eugenics was defined as:

> The science of improving stock, which is by no means confined to questions of judicious mating, but which, especially in the case of man, takes cognisance of all influences that tend in however remote a degree to give to the more suitable races or strains of blood a better chance of prevailing speedily over the less suitable than they otherwise would have had. The word 'eugenics' would sufficiently express the idea. (p. 3)

Eugenics is remembered in Western history because of its association with Nazi Germany's policies of racial purity and, most notably, their extermination of Jewish people, segregation of other racially unfit groups (i.e., gay men), and "mercy killings" of people with disabilities (Kuhl, 2002). It is not so often remembered that that the eugenics was a commonplace social and scientific paradigm, embraced by many countries around the globe as a scientific solution to such problems as physical and mental illnesses, poverty, and war, as well as a technique for creating evolutionary utopias marked by happy controlled societies filled with

O. Yakushko, *Scientific Pollyannaism*,
https://doi.org/10.1007/978-3-030-15982-5_4

happy efficient people (Bashford & Levine, 2010; Lombardo, 2011; Popenoe & Johnson, 1935; Tucker, 1996). These policies included Jim Crow racial segregation laws, constrictive sexual norms, involuntary sterilizations, restrictive vocational tracking, relegation of mentally ill people to abusive asylums, xenophobic immigration policies, justification of colonial practices, the Apartheid, rigid gender laws in regard to women's education, homophobic laws and decrees, appalling behaviorist experiments, and the development of racist and sexist sciences (Bashford & Levine, 2010; Black, 2003; Guthrie, 2004; Lombardo, 2011; Selden, 1999; Smith, 1985; Stern, 2015; Tucker, 1996).

Eugenics was hailed as an empirically-based and groundbreaking pathway toward creating "*harmony with the underlying plan of the universe*" and "*totality of happiness of all sentient beings or of all men*" (Popenoe & Johnson, 1935, p. 214). Humans, eugenicists claimed, could speedily achieve new evolutionary peaks by adhering to established scientific paradigms, including having the unfit accept their inferior social positions or even their own demise in service to the greater social good. Moreover, the eugenicists encouraged evolutionary fit individuals to socially engineer themselves and especially their children toward their primary evolutionary calling to be productive, optimistic, and self-controlled (Davenport, 1910; Galton, 1904; Goddard, 1948; Guyer, 1916; McDougall, 1910; Melendy, 1914; Pearson, 1905; Popenoe & Johnson, 1935; Yerkes, 1923).

For the purposes of this study, individuals or groups will be considered eugenicist when they openly identify themselves as such, either through membership in eugenic-focused organizations (e.g., the American Eugenic Society) or open use of eugenic-specific ideology (i.e., using Darwin's evolutionary theories to propose selective breeding of superior human beings). Certainly, past and present rhetoric about the over-population by marginalized groups, the promotion of racist or sexist ideologies about varied groups' level of "development," or genetic explanations in regard to hereditability of human characteristics as intelligence or optimism, are likely influenced by eugenic and social Darwinist scientific narratives. Nevertheless, I refrain from assigning the term eugenics to these views, while staying in agreement with scholars that these views are racist, colonialist, sexist and so forth (Ruti, 2015; Tucker, 1996). In contrast, as shown in this book, I emphasize specific Darwinist-Galtonian connotations of the term eugenics, which are primarily found in its explicit emphases on both negative eugenics (i.e., not permitting continuation of supposedly inferior human beings) and positive eugenics (i.e., promoting propagation of superior humans together by controlling their social functioning).

The Utopian Visions of Eugenic Racial Betterment

In speaking to the British Sociological Society at a meeting in the School of Economics of London University, which was chaired by a famed statistician Karl Pearson, Galton (1904) summarized not only the definition of eugenics but also its main aims:

> To raise the average quality of our nation to that of its better moiety at the present day, and consider the gain. The general tone of domestic, social, and political life would be higher. *The race as a whole would be less foolish, less frivolous, less excitable*, and politically more provident than now... We should be better fitted to fulfill our vast imperial opportunities. (n.p.)

As noted earlier, Darwin (1889) promoted not only eugenicists efforts "to an increase in the number of men of a superior class" but also focused on improvement of the fit groups' characteristics via such methods as "the instruction in youth" (p. 137). Galton's (1904) vision did include elements of negative eugenics, specifically the evolutionary necessity of eliminating uncivilized races by controlling their procreation or permitting their presumed self-destruction (e.g., in Galton's words, "while most barbarous races disappear, some, like the negro, do not" [n.p.]). But he placed a greater emphasis so-termed positive eugenics as "the science which deals with all influences that *improve the inborn qualities* of a race; *also with those that develop them to the utmost advantage*" (n.p.). In seeking to measure this "improvement" of inborn qualities, Galton called on scientists to determine what constituted good and bad characteristics using empirical methods. Such determination of human fitness and unfitness, Galton claimed, should not be provided by unhappy "cranks" because these individuals would select others who are just like them (i.e., Galton's examples of bad members of society who should be excluded from such selection were not only "criminals" but also "*self-sacrificers, self-tormentors, and other exceptional idealists*"). Thus, according to Galton,

> *A considerable list of qualities can easily be compiled that nearly everyone except "cranks" would take into account when picking out the best specimens of his class. It would include health, energy, ability, manliness, and courteous disposition.* (n.p.)

The foremost assertion about eugenics was that it was scientific and based on accurate large-scale data collection and analysis. Galton (1904) proposed that all academic disciplines, but especially statistics, demography, and psychology, work together to develop large scale data collection studies toward such goals as compiling the eugenic "*golden* book" of thriving families" (n.p.). According to Galton, "the act of systematically collecting records of thriving families would have the further advantage of familiarizing the public with the fact that eugenics had at length become a subject of serious scientific study by an energetic society" (n.p.).

This scientific grounding of eugenics, in Galton's view, should become such a central feature of Western societies as to become their social religion:

> It [eugenics] must be introduced into the national conscience, *like a new religion.* It has, indeed, strong claims to become an orthodox religious, tenet of the future, for *eugenics co-operate with the workings of nature by securing that humanity shall be represented by the fittest races. What nature does blindly, slowly, and ruthlessly, man may do providently, quickly, and kindly.* (n.p.)

Galton (1907) further exclaimed:

> *Happy the child, especially in these inquiring days, who has been taught a religion that mainly rests on the moral obligations between man and man in domestic and national life*, and which, so far as it is necessarily dogmatic, *rests chiefly upon the proper interpretation of facts about which there is no dispute*– namely, on those habitual occurrences which are always open to observation, and which form the basis of so-called natural religion. (p. 152)

Upon Galton's death, obituaries in regard to his legacy specifically emphasized this point of his work. In a letter to the *Eugenics Review*, another relative of Charles Darwin, Sir Francis Darwin (1915), praised Galton's eugenic work in an obituary. F. Darwin quoted Galton's views, reiterating that eugenics must become "a new religion" (p. 15). According to F. Darwin, other scientists and social leaders must join his famed relative Charles Darwin in openly supporting Galton's "hereditary improvement" work, because of their efforts "to do something for the moral and physical qualities of the race" (p. 16).

Social Darwinism (i.e., application of Darwinist theories of plant and animal evolution to human social differences) and eugenics were indeed embraced by many British and American scientists with religious fervor (Darwin, 1888; Davenport, 1910; Galton, 1865, 1904; McDougall, 1914, 1921; Pearson, 1905, 1911; Yerkes, 1923). Eugenicists around the globe shared similar concerns over what was thought to be the evolutionary harmful impact of undeveloped or "primitive" national groups, especially from non-Nordic or Germanic ethnicities, as well as of people who were poor, mentally ill (e.g., melancholic and daydreaming individuals), physically ill, non-heterosexual or sexually unchaste (Popenoe & Johnson, 1935). An oft-cited quote on eugenics by British sexuality scholar Havelock Ellis ably summarized eugenics for the public: "The superficially sympathetic man flings a coin to the beggar; the more deeply sympathetic man builds an almshouse for him so that he need no longer beg; but perhaps the *most radically sympathetic of all is the man who arranges that the beggar shall not be born*" (Guyer, 1916, p. 301).

Eugenicists refused claims that they were biased, and continually referred to their extensive statistical and scientific experimental work in support of their ideas (Brigham, 1923; Davenport, 1910; Galton, 1865, 1904; McDougall, 1914, 1921; Pearson, 1905, 1911; Yerkes, 1923). For example, Pearson'(1905), a founder of the field of statistics and a leading UK eugenicists, in highly popular book entitled *National Life from the Standpoint of Science*, claimed his work to be especially "powerful" in its "*effect on the mind of a true scientific education, which enables a man or woman to form judgments freed from individual bias*" (p. 107). The same book includes Pearson's scientific denouncements of "romantic sympathy for the Red Indian," while praising "America" for its "masterful human progress following the inter-racial struggle" (p. 25), supposedly evident in the extermination and control over same "Red Indian." Pearson's many claims, drawing on statistical data and scientific observations, proclaimed that Darwin's evolutionary theory was verified "chiefly by way of war with inferior races," starting that "this is the natural history view of mankind." (p. 44). This book, like most other books by eugenicists, painted an optimistic picture of Western- and Western-controlled worlds, encouraging readers to not succumb to negative feelings of remorse about violence toward evolutionary unfit groups but to cheerfully and optimistically embrace science-based explanations of human differences.

Moreover, their scientific proclamations repeatedly emphasized that changes in environment had minimal influences on individuals' supposed evolutionary unfitness. According to Guyer (1916) in *Being Well Born: An Introduction to Eugenics*:

> *It is sometimes urged that we [eugenicists] are not dealing in such cases with degenerate strains, but merely with unfortunate individuals who have been subjected to pernicious surroundings from the beginning.* And it can not be denied that parents who are mentally defective, dissipated or syphilitic afford most noxious developmental and environmental conditions for their children. But when one notes how intimately the moral degeneracy in such stocks is bound up with some degree of feeble-mindedness, he [Charles Davenport, leading U.S. eugenicist] is strongly skeptical toward the sufficiency of such an interpretation, although environment undoubtedly intensifies the results. Concerning this point Davenport says: "We have certain methods of testing whether it is bad environment or bad breeding which produced these people. Some of the children have been taken at an early age and 'placed out' [orphans]. We have traced their subsequent history. In most cases *they have turned out quite as bad as those who have remained at home.* In a few cases they have turned out well, but it is also true that some of the children who remained at home in bad environment have turned out well." (p. 273)

Happy Eugenic Brains and Resilient Germo-Plasms

The above summary of eugenic views highlights the use of orphans, especially twin orphans, in studies to prove genetic inferiority of certain groups. In addition to these studies on orphans as well as statistical evidence of the inferiority of many racial and national groups (Brigham, 1923; Galton, 1869, 1883, 1907; Pearson, 1905), eugenicists emphasized studies on brains as supposedly providing unquestionable empirical bases for their claims. For example, Schultz (1923), a eugenicist biologist, published a study on differences between "Negro" and "White" brains, claiming that brains of Black children were "proportionately smaller" than those of White children and therefore not as developed (p. 19). Notably, his and many other historical studies with similar claims have been later re-published by racist scientists such as Rushton and

Ankney (2009) in the *International Journal of Neuroscience* claiming that brains of African Americans have been found smaller than that of Whites over the past century in numerous studies (i.e., comparison of supposed brain sizes and their relation to both intelligence and emotions remains a primary concern of eugenicists and racists).

Smaller brains were routinely connected to not only lower intelligence but to supposed difficulties with inhibition of negative affects (e.g., anger, melancholy), impulsivity (e.g., sexuality, criminality), and many other similar difficulties (Davenport, 1910, 1911; Popenoe & Johnson, 1935). These findings were claimed to be based exclusively on systematic empirical research using advanced statistical methods. Evans (1931), who led the American Eugenic Society's Committee on Formal Education, stated that eugenics was a "method of direct scientific observation rather than methods of secondhand or hearsay evidence" (p. 29).

Women's brains were routinely promoted as being vastly different than male brains, because of women's primary evolutionary tasks of child bearing and rearing as well as caring for males in their lives. Mary R. Melendy (1914), the University of Chicago medical science faculty, produced a lengthy treatise entitled *The Science of Eugenics and Sex Life*, in which she deluged the readers with images and scientific discussions of supposed brain studies related to eugenics and gender differences. According to Melendy, women's brains reflect their essential "love-nature:"

> *The lower part of her brain, near the spinal cord, is most actively nourished by the blood supply; hence it is not strange that the very foundations of her being rest upon sentiment rather than upon reason. Normally, woman lives to be beloved, and intuitively does those things which are lovely.* (p. 44)

Similarly, the eugenic scholar Arabella Kenealy's (1920) stated in her book entitled *Feminism and Sex Extinction:*

> Masculine intellection, pure and simple, is initiative, vigorous, enterprising; analytical, logical, critical; its outlook rational and concrete, its disposition just and honest. Capable in the degree of its virility, of strenuous and sustained endeavour, of keen concentration and close application; taking nothing for granted, but questioning and demanding proof of all things, it is an admirable executive agent of Mind. *Per se*, however, it is rational and deductive, judicial and judicious, rather than inspirational and creative. *The blending with it of the Woman-faculty in him quickens his male brain by contributing the emotional element; endues it with intuitive sensibility, fructifies it with female creativeness.* (p. 29)

Brain, Kenealy asserted, reflected two essential sides of human nature and was differentially developed in males and females:

> As in the two sides of the body, appear, surely, *the factors of Dominance and Recessiveness—in other words of Maleness and Femaleness*; of strength and activity upon material planes, and of inhibition upon these… the two orders of Sex-characteristics (derived from parents of opposite sex) are centred, respectively, in the two sides of the body, and in the two brain-hemispheres allied, respectively, with these. (pp. 52–53)

Measuring Goodness and Happiness

Because large scale statistical studies on cultural groups or brains were difficult to conduct, eugenicists especially focused on phenomena that they believed more readily revealed evolutionary differences between individuals and groups, such as intelligence and its emotional and behavioral correlates–morality, productivity, optimism and self-control (Galton, 1869, 1883, 1907; Popenoe & Johnson, 1935). Galton (1865) in his highly popular *Hereditary Talent and Character*, re-published in the U.S. in *Macmillan Magazine*, claimed that his empirical investigations of intelligence and personality among "great men in history" and Cambridge University graduates confirmed the hereditary nature of these characteristics. He further highlighted that non-Nordic groups' lack of intelligence was evident especially through such measurable characteristics as higher levels of "melancholy" among indigenous tribal peoples and inborn impulsivity among Black Africans.

Galton (1869) in his *Hereditary Genius* routinely tied optimism and self-control to intelligence and high achievement among groups he studied, such as in contrasting Cambridge graduates and other "great men of history" to supposedly primitive groups. Galton observed that

> *The number among the negroes of those whom we should call half-witted men, is very large.* Every book, alluding to negro servant in America is full of instances I was myself most impressed by this fact during my travels in Africa. *The mistakes the negroes made in their own matters, were so childish, stupid, and simpleton-like, as frequently to make me ashamed of my own species.* (p. 339)

Galton further claimed that "the Australian type is at least one grade below the African negro" (p. 339). In contrast, the superior evolutionary people, according to Galton, specifically upper class British white men, were "*cool in danger, sensible in council, cheerful under prolonged suffering, human to the wounded and sick, encouragers of the faint-hearted*" (p. 48), all because of their "natural gifts" (i.e., hereditary genetic endowments) (p. 49).

Inheritability of not only superior intellect but also superior personality characteristics was repeatedly studied and publicized by eugenicists. In his book entitled *Being Well-Born: An Introduction to Eugenics* Guyer (1916), a zoology professor at the University of Wisconsin, explained:

> Galton showed by this method [statistics] long ago, and Pearson and his school have extended and more clearly established the work, that *exceptional mental qualities tend to be inherited.* While on the average the children of exceptional parents tend to be less exceptional than their parents, still they are far more likely to be exceptional than are the children of average parents. By this method Professor Pearson has shown that such *mental and temperamental attributes as ability, vivacity, conscientiousness, temper, popularity*, handwriting, etc., *are as essentially determined as are physical features through the hereditary endowment.* (p. 19)

Huxley (1936), another British promoter of eugenics, referred to multiple scientific studies on differences between individuals of upper and lower social classes. He suggested that "docility" and "industrious submissiveness" were descriptive of "the lower majority" whereas "intelligence, leadership, and strength of character" were common "in the upper few" (p. 25).

Mary R. Melendy (1914), a University of Chicago medical faculty, summarized many studies about supposed dangers of negative emotional states, indicating that the lack of eugenic fitness results in individuals who are emotionally not "*harmonious... [and] cannot be allied to the great life-centers of the universe, and the whole nature suffers in consequence*" (p. 82). Melendy further asserted, using evidence from empirical studies, that the eugenic focus on emotional self-control, especially by women and children, is vital because

> *the mental emotions reach the physical centers and affect the circulation and nervous system.* Prof. Henry Wood says : "It has long been conceded by scientific and medical men that *hate deforms, disintegrates and destroys the physical organism; that anger, hatred, ill-will and anxiety bring mental and physical chaos.* While this fact has been conceded and accepted by all, we have been slow to recognize that the opposite of hate will have an opposite effect; *that if hate destroys, love builds up, renovates and restores." A sunny disposition is most beautifying.* (p. 82)

Thus, intelligence and its emotional as well as moral correlates became the cornerstone of scientific studies and policy suggestions for eugenicists worldwide, especially in the U.S. (Brigham, 1923; Popenoe & Johnson, 1935; Terman, 1916; Thorndike, 1909). For example, Terman (1916), a Stanford psychologist considered the founder of psychological and intelligence testing, documented supposedly significant correlations between positive emotional states and higher intelligence. In Terman words, psychology's contribution was vital to American and Western societies precisely because of its potential eugenic applications, since "considering the tremendous cost of vice and crime…it is evident that psychological testing has found here one of its richest applications" (p. 12). Consistent with claims by Darwin, social Darwinists and eugenicists, Terman declared that non-Nordic or supposedly inferior racial groups were identified by their lower intellectual as well as negative emotional states. Human "dullness," Terman asserted, "seems to be racial, or at least inherent in the family" and found with "extraordinary frequency among Indians, Mexicans, and negroes" (p. 91).

The "Stupendous" Costs of Caring for the Unfit

In addition, eugenicists argued that treatment of physical and mental disorders was detrimental to evolution by encouraging the presence of the unfit. They claimed that natural resilience and resistance to these illnesses (e.g., melancholy, alcoholism, syphilis, tuberculosis) were the evidence of natural selection and the survival of the fittest (Popenoe & Johnson, 1935). Both in the U.S. (e.g., Tuskegee syphilis study) and worldwide (e.g., Mendel's tuberculosis experiments in concentration camps), studies were prompted by Darwinist and eugenic interests in identifying genetic differences in resilience (Bergman, 2014; Black, 2003; Kuhl, 2002; Lombardo & Dorr, 2006). Eugenicists frequently declared that treatment of the unfit resulted in enormous economic and social costs. According to Guyer (1916),

> Doctor Charles L. Dana, member of the National Committee for Mental Hygiene, estimated in 1904 that the actual cost of caring for feeble-minded and insane in the United States amounted to sixty million dollars, to which should be added the corresponding loss in industrial activity on the part of the afflicted,—at least twenty million dollars more, and he figures that the amount was increasing at the rate of four per cent.

> per annum. *Many investigators concur in the opinion that our insane and feeble-minded alone cost us far above one hundred million dollars. Adding to this economic burden the cost of our delinquents and criminals the total expense becomes stupendous. And when we consider still further the even greater burden of suffering of the unfortunates themselves and the sorrows of those to whom they are dear, a burden not measurable in money, the feeling that something must be done to relieve the situation becomes overpowering.* (pp. 257–258)

Those who offered medical or social services to the evolutionary unfit groups were proclaimed to be mercenary. These providers of care were said to be seeking financial gain from treatment of those who may contribute to degeneration of society rather than improving the lives of those who were fit to procreate (Popenoe & Johnson, 1935). In addition, scientific studies were evoked to claim that helping the eugenically unfit integrate into the fit hereditary groups could not only serve to decrease racial fitness of the entire population (Brigham, 1923; Popenoe & Johnson, 1935) but would cause individuals from the inferior groups to become "discontent," "neurotic" and "inefficient" (Huxley, 1936, p. 24).

The Scientific Efforts to Rid the World of the "Evolutionary Unfit"

The costs caring for the unfit were used as further rationale for not offering treatment as a policy of "negative" eugenics, leading to the removal of people viewed as "unfit," or detrimental to evolution and to Western societies. In their best-selling books on eugenics, used in both academic institutions and promoted to the public entitled *Applied Eugenics*, Popenoe and Johnson (1935) referenced numerous scientific studies, and made suggestions such as "*many of those who commit suicide are to be credited to the mentally diseased part of the population, and if they could make way with themselves 20 or 30 years earlier, their demise might be a eugenic gain*" (p. 98). Eugenic experiments were conducted in which people suffering from serious illnesses were denied available medical treatment in order to test their resilience (Lombardo, 2011), as, for example, the infamous Tuskegee syphilis study in the American South (Black, 2003; Lombardo, 2011). As Popenoe and Johnson (1935) stated, permitting infected individuals to die benefited evolution because "*the selective action of the disease (syphilis)… tends to eliminate some of the mentally deficient and mentally diseased, and also those lacking in self-control*" (p. 94). Ridding the world of illnesses and unwanted social conditions was to be achieved by ridding the world of individuals and groups who were marked by these undesirable traits. Believing themselves to be highly moral (i.e., social Darwinists and eugenicists emphasized that because they were the evolutionary fittest, they possessed the highest moral characteristics, which justified their actions), eugenicists claimed to offer another gradual approach to improving the human race: segregating the fit and unfit, while sterilizing the unfit in order to stop the propagation of inferior genes.

The segregation and sterilization of the evolutionary unfit was routinely presented as improving their quality of life, making them "happier" (Popenoe & Johnson, 1935). In the U.S. these efforts were promoted by many scientists, such as H. H. Goddard (1911, 1912, 1917, 1948), one of the foremost eugenic scientists and famous American psychologist, who directed a notorious asylum for the "feeble-minded" in Vineland, NJ. Responding to public concerns that many of the "colonies" or asylums for evolutionary unfit people were inhumane (e.g., according to popular eugenic works such as Popenoe and Johnson's (1935) *Applied Eugenics*, Goddard's asylum in Vineland, NJ operated as a hard labor colony), Goddard (1911) insisted that "*institutions for the feeble-minded… are the happiest places in the world*" (p. 269). In his other writings Goddard (1919) argued for the removal of supposedly unfit individuals' voting and political rights in efforts to create a Socratic "aristo-democracy:" an ideal democracy where "benevolent aristocracy" of eugenically superior individuals had the right to "tell them [the unfit] what to do to be happy" (Goddard, 1919, p. 237). The scientific Pollyannaism of eugenics was evident in the routine and frequent promises of happiness for all, supposedly achievable through the application of empirically-determined eugenic principles. According to Goddard (1911), "*the elimination of… feeble-mindedness would result in an enormous improvement in happiness and… achievement in every community*" (p. 262).

Happy "Mothers of the Race"

Central to eugenic goals of utopian future societies was an emphasis on ensuring that males of superior groups made procreative choices toward racial betterment by selecting only fit females, who were proclaimed to be "mothers of the race." Feminism, which emerged as an influential movement in the early twentieth century Europe and the U.S., was only accepted by eugenicists as long as women maintained their primary evolutionary role as mothers and wives, and recognized their biological position as different-but-equal (i.e., their celebrated position as mothers) (Popenoe & Johnson, 1935). However, feminism that demanded full human equality for women was deemed as evolutionary problematic. According to Kenealy's (1920) *Feminism and Sex Extinction*, feminist menace was evident in re-shaping females into an evolutionary unfit "hard and mannish woman," women who regarded children as "by-products... some hobby or career" rather than "realizing the new generation as the Vanguard of Life and Evolution... which beyond every other human achievement counts in the Universe" (p. 101). Moreover, feminists, according to Kenealy, could engage in all manner of evolutionary problematic behaviors such as becoming ultra feminine, interested in contemporary culture rather than their homes, or being affected by an "educational strain" (p. 101). She claimed,

> *their womanhood... lightly rooted in neurotic systems, the women of this sect are unstable and erratic, seeking distraction for their restless, ill-balanced forces, in cards, crazes, drugs*; fads and freaks. Unfitted for wifehood and motherhood—some by faulty heredity, but a far greater number by educational strain and consequent warp—some of these ultra-feminised and frequently interesting creatures absorb themselves feverishly in public movements; religious, social or political. (pp. 101–102)

Eugenicists also claimed that there were some benefits to males' supposed unbridled biological sexual urges, even toward unfit women, asserting that the rape of enslaved Black women by White slave owners had the evolutionary salubrious effect of raising levels of intelligence among African Americans in subsequent generations (Popenoe & Johnson, 1935). According to Popenoe and Johnson (1935),

> From the beginning [slaves brought to the U.S.]... have mixed to some extent with the Whites, mainly through *irregular matings* of white males with black females... In the later generations doubtless some better germplasms was added to the Negro race through the black concubines taken by white men. (p. 299)

On the other hand, the rape of White women by Black men was considered to be crime against Nature, thus supposedly necessitating lynching. According to Hadden's ("M.D., Fellow Royal College of Surgeons") introduction to Melendy's (1914) *The Science of Eugenics and Sex Life*, eugenics endorsed methods by which "the worthless or injurious had to be got rid of, cast out, expelled, or ejected from society… [such as] lynching for rape and other racial crimes in various localities" (p. 3). He notes, however, that "lynching is unavailing to stop rape" (p. 17), calling for eugenic sterilization of racial minority groups and their segregation from the evolutionary fit, promising the prevention of sexual violence by racially unfit men toward racially fit women.

Women's non-heterosexual intimate interests were likewise deemed dangerous to evolutionary progress. Popenoe and Johnson (1935), focused on numerous examples of problematic sexual behavior by adolescents, especially adolescent girls, including masturbation, pre-marital sexuality, or same-sex erotic interests. They promised the readers that eugenic forms of sterilization would "reduce there being 'sex offenders'" and that, according to their research, "promiscuity, adultery, and other anti-social conduct… would not have occurred had it not been for sterilization" (p. 155). Eugenic scientists, such as Melendy (1914), promoted the idea that women's same sex desire was the result of abnormal sexual organs such as enlarged clitoris and labia. The Sonoma State Asylum, part of the eugenic human betterment asylum system in California, was infamous for sterilizing women and girls who were proven to be "evolutionary unfit" based on their irregularly shaped genitalia (Stern, 2015).

Sterilization of supposedly unfit women was promoted as central to eugenics. Guyer (1916) stated, "According to Goddard [leading U.S. psychologist] the feeble-minded woman is about three times as likely to find a mate as a feeble-minded man, hence it would seem to be of much greater importance to sterilize the woman than the man" (p. 326). Goddard (1911) routinely encouraged sterilization of women including via radiation, but majority of these operations included major abdominal surgery. The loss of lives to surgery-related complications, according to eugenic scholars, were necessary for betterment of all humanity (Goddard, 1911; Guyer, 1916). Guyer (1916) described the procedure of "salpingectomy" or removing "a section of the oviduct… the operation is a more serious one as it usually involves opening the abdominal cavity and the accompanying hazard of infection" (p. 325). Eugenicists, who actively promoted sterilization, claimed that it had salubrious effects on both the people who were sterilized as well the society at large (Goddard, 1911; Guyer, 1916; Melendy, 1914; Popenoe & Johnson, 1935).

Women who were deemed fit for procreation were encouraged to view themselves as “different but equal,” a language frequently used by eugenicist to position themselves as supposedly supporting feminism or women’s rights by maintaining that women should receive better support for their strategic role as breeders (Popenoe & Johnson, 1935). According to eugenicists, women’s supposed evolutionary biological uniqueness required them to remain chaste until marriage, be sufficiently seductive to attract and keep the male, and to focus on the development of their motherly and wifely skills in order to maintain their households and keep support of their male (Guyer, 1916; Hague, 1913; Holbrook, 1897; Melendy, 1914; Popenoe & Johnson, 1935; Scharlieb, 1912). Optimism and cheerfulness were viewed as crucial to these women’s evolutionary tasks. Evolutionary sciences, eugenicists claimed, explained women’s key biological role as wives and mothers. According to Kenealy (1920),

> The girl’s transition to womanhood is seen, on the contrary, to be one almost entirely of adaptation, physiological and psychical, to the functions of wifehood and child-bearing. Her growth ceases. She loses, in place of gaining, nerve and muscle-power. While, *in becoming emotional*, her changed mentality unfits far more than it fits her to cope with life at first hand; with life unadapted, that is, and herself unshielded by the male. Her intelligence at eighteen is normally less keen and active—although of higher and more subtle quality and trend—than it had been at twelve. (p. 114)

This transition to motherhood and commitment to it was viewed as the highest and the only calling women should pursue for the sake of evolutionary development of society. According to Nearing (1912) in his book the *Super Race* women were responsible for developing the “Super Race” by birthing and raising the “Super Man,”

> *Women bear the race in their bodies*; at least half of the qualities of the offspring are inherited from them; as mothers, they educate the children during the first six years of their lives, and then, as school teachers and mothers they play the leading part in education until the children reach the age of twelve or fourteen. The youth of the race is in women’s keeping. *They shape the child clay. The twig is bent, the tree is inclined by women’s hands.* (p. 81)

In *Womanhood and Race Regeneration* by Mary Scharlieb (1912), a medical doctor and a eugenicist, further explained,

> It is no exaggeration to say that *on woman depends the welfare of the race*, for not only is she the parent most intimately in contact with the growing child, but her influence is generally paramount both with her husband and with her grown-up family. It is merely a truism that the *race will be whatever the women of the race make it*. (p. 5)

Scharlieb repeatedly insisted that women use science and scientific information to improve their household work as mothers and housewives or else become overwhelmed with their household duties to such an extend to even cause their own "premature senility and death" (p. 30). Moreover, she warned that

> *Many women who suffer from "nerves," from "brain fag," from being too "highly strung," would have escaped these curses had they been trained to do their household work in the way that involves least friction and least fatigue.* Here is an almost untrodden field of research which calls aloud for the best work and the highest intelligence of which women are capable, *a work that will be amply rewarded in the happiness of their homes, and the welfare of their husbands and children*. (p. 30)

Many eugenicists emphasized that intermarriage between a eugenically fit and unfit individuals could be disastrous, and warning especially about its drastic negative effects on individuals' emotional life. For example, a common narrative shared in the *Book of Eugenic Marriage: A Personal Guide to the New Science of Better Living and Better Babies* by medical doctor W. Grant Hague (1913), highlighted supposedly a common disastrous effects of such intermarriage:

> Take for example the life of a *young wife who marries a man with disease in his blood*. She begins her wedded life with certain commendable ideals. She is young, enthusiastic, ambitious, strong, and she inherently possesses the right to aspire to become an efficient home-maker and a good mother. She gives birth to a child, conceived in love, and during her travail she beseeches her Creator to help her and to help her baby, as all women do at such a time. Her baby is born blind and it is a weak and puny mite. The mother recovers slowly, but she is never the same vigorous and ambitious woman. Later her strength fades away, her enthusiasm falters, the home is blighted and seems a desecrated spot. The baby is a constant worry, it is always sick, it needs expensive care and it exhausts the physical remnant

> of its mother's health. It finally dies and is laid away, not forgotten, but a sad, sad memory. The ailing and dispirited mother is informed that she must submit to an operation if she desires to regain her health, if not to save her life. She returns from the hospital–not a woman–*a blighted thing, an unsexed substitute for what once was a happy, sunny, healthy, innocent girl.* This is not an overdrawn tale,–it is a true story, a common, every-day story. (p. 6)

In contrast, Hague (1913) pronounced that according to eugenic sciences, a eugenic marriage between two supposedly evolutionary fit individuals, where a husband is responsible for his wife's potentially weak mental states (e.g., worrying about her baby) by "directing" her "mental attitudes," would result in an idyllic home that avoided all negativity:

> His [husband] principal aim, of course, will be that she will not worry or have cause to worry. He will so *direct her mental attitude that she will dwell only upon the bright side of the picture*; she will thus strive to realize the hope that the baby will be strong and healthy, and she will, prompted by his encouragement and devotion, try to do her duty faithfully. Working together in this way, much can be done that means far more than we know of, and in the end the little one comes into the world a welcome baby, created in love and born into *the joy of a happy, harmonious, contented home.* (pp. 79–80)

This scientific eugenic contribution, like many other applied eugenic works, emphasized vital importance of "happy thoughts" and controlling any unwanted "negative" emotional or cognitive states. In further advise to pregnant mothers who are supposedly carrying the evolutionary fit progeny, women were admonished:

> *If she will keep in mind that the most important element in the success of the whole period, and consequently the degree of her own health, happiness, and comfort, as well as that of her unborn baby, is the character of her own thoughts from day to day, and month to month, she will be complete master of the situation. By constantly dwelling on happy thoughts*, reading encouraging and inspiring books, admiring and studying good pictures, working with cheerful colors in sunny rooms, exercising, dieting, and sleeping in a well-aired room, she will have no cause to regret her share in the task before her, or the kind of baby she will bring into the world. (pp. 80–81)

Thus, in addition to controlling behaviors considered evolutionary regressive (e.g., sexuality outside of heterosexual marriage, life or vocational choices that precluded primary focus on motherhood), women were also encouraged to control their thoughts, especially ridding themselves of supposedly negative feelings and inner states. Noting periods in women's lives, which these eugenic scientists considered a times of vulnerability for women in relation to possibly rise of negativity (e.g., post-partum depression), their advise focused on encouraging women to remain always in control of their lives, especially by heavy scheduling of all the activities, and by being continually pleasant to others. For example, following child's birth, when women were noted to be depressed, overwhelmed, and tired, eugenic medical doctors such as Hague (1913) provided the following "empirical" advise specific to the post-partum period:

> *Be cheerful, encourage him [husband] to tell of his hopes and plans, and show an interest in his health and in his work. Do not forget the dominating influence on your efficiency, and on your happiness which the study habit possesses.* Interest yourself in some art, cultivate your mind, and soon, sooner than you think, you will have forgotten your troubles and you will have regained your [pre-maternity] health. *There is no other way to do it.* (p. 135)

Thus, the eugenic social goals (i.e., so-called positive eugenics) required that evolutionary fit individuals paired for procreation, maintain not only impeccable physical, but also mental and emotional health. Hague's (1913) stated that "parenthood is the supreme function of the race… it must not be indifferently undertaken;… it demands the most careful preparation;… it is a duty which can only be carried out eugenically by the highest attainable health of body and mind and *emotions*" (p. 17). Specifically, a moral education focusing on women's emotions (e.g., their cheerfulness, self-control) was hailed by Hague as vital to eugenic and evolutionary progress, and "*that any educational system [of women] which ignores the emotions is not only inadequate but reprehensible in the highest degree*" (p. 22).

Mary R. Melendy (1914), a University of Chicago scientist, insisted in her lengthy popular contribution entitled *The Science of Eugenics and Sex Life* that this emotional education required what she termed "brain training" (p. 83). Melendy asserted that negative thoughts, which resulted in negative emotions, must be systematically rooted out of women's minds in order to maintain the healthy brains required for eugenic evolutionary health. Melendy's brain training is remarkably similar to contemporary versions of American cognitive-behaviorism, with its focus on thought-replacement, behavioral self-control techniques, breathing or meditation exercises to rid self of negative feelings, and positive visualizations. Her key summary of eugenic scientific advise for women stated that the positive eugenic brain re-training requires that women

> *Never look on the dark side of anything. If it has no bright side, don't look at it at all.* Look at something else. *Never speak or even think ill of another.* Don't "jump at conclusions" by judging unfavorably even if circumstances are suspicious. Never take any desired favor for granted. If you follow this rule you never need fear being cheated or disappointed. *Try to find something good in every person you meet. Read good books, think good thoughts, lead pure lives, observing the laws of health. These habits once formed become literal brain-paths along which it grows easier and easier for the thoughts to travel, bringing gladness, health and symmetry to every nerve and tissue. In countless cases such results have been achieved.* (p. 83)

The emergence of significant number of scholarly parenting books by eugenicists marked another turn of using their empirical work to encourage parents to maintain optimistic children who were never angry (e.g., tantruming) or sad (e.g., whining). Before eugenic-based psychologies of control, specifically by behaviorist John B. Watson, began to produce massively popular books on parenting, many other eugenic medical doctors and scholars emphasized that evolutionary fitness in a child required their emotional positivity and compliance. For example, Holbrook (1897) in his book *Homo-culture—Or, The Improvement of Offspring Through Wiser Generation*, who was the leader of U.S. Social Hygiene movement, editor of the scientific Journal of Social Hygiene, contributor to multiple topics such as the "Brain Hygiene" and chastity-focused sexual hygiene campaigns, summarized a letter from a mother of an "evolutionary fit" daughter in the following way:

> From the time she was born she was like an exquisite rosebud–the flower of pure, sanctified, happy love. *She never cried at night, was never fretful or nervous, but was all smiles and winning baby ways, filling our hearts and home with perpetual gladness.* To this day, and she is now fourteen years

> old, I have never had the slightest difficulty in bringing her up. She turns naturally to the right, and I never knew her to be cross or impatient or hard to manage. She has given me only comfort; and I realize from an experience of just the opposite nature that the reason of all this is because my little girl had her birthright. (pp. 60–61)

Hollbrook further encouraged mothers to employ such strategies as ending the day with their children while tucking them to sleep with the following positive affirmations:

> You will not have bad dreams. You will not see ugly faces or wake up with a fright. *Tomorrow you will wake up good-natured, full of life, and will be good boy (or girl, as the case may be), and do your best to make mother happy and proud of you.* (p. 223)

In contrast, unfit children were believed to be produced by unfit individuals, including from unions between fit and unfit people because parasitic germo-plasms or genes supposedly diluted superior evolutionary endowments of the eugenically fit. Eugenically fit women (i.e., Nordic White middle or upper class women) were especially warned against the dire evils of inter-racial sexual relations. Popenoe and Johnson (1935) listed both psychological as well as medical data supposedly showing the disastrous problems of children born from parents of different races (e.g., their inner organs mis-sized). Being a multiracial person was claimed to be worse than being of one specific race. According to the American eugenicist and zoology professor Guyer (1916),

> Of the American mulatto one not infrequently meets with the assertion that he is on *the average inferior mentally, morally and physically to either the white or the negro race.* Thus Doctor J. B. Taylor states that, "It is demonstrated by well-attested facts that these hybrids of black and white are vastly more susceptible to certain infections; *their moral as well as physical stamina is lower than that of either original race.*" Others would deny that conclusive evidence to this effect exists. However, it is certain that under existing social conditions in our own country *only the most worthless and vicious of the white race will tend in any considerable numbers to mate with the negro and the result can not but mean deterioration on the whole for either race.* There is certainly not one iota of evidence that the crossing of any two widely different human races will yield superior offspring in any respect and there are many indications that such intermixture lowers

> the average of the population. Our evidence derived from plant and animal breeding is also against pronounced crosses. *The inferiority of the mongrel is universally recognized.* (p. 295)

White women were warned that if they engaged in sexual or marital relations with non-White men, even if they re-married and procreated with a White man later in their lives, were liable to pass on racially parasitic effects of their racially unfit sexual relations, precisely because of women's supposed emotional vulnerabilities.

> Odious and startling evidence that *because of woman's vital emotionalism and sensitive psychology*, her nature retains ineffaceable vestiges of all that has happened to her, is the fact that a woman's children by a second husband may resemble her first husband far more than they resemble their father. A significant and repulsive adulteration of type, and one so intrinsic that a woman who had been previously wife to a negro or a Chinaman will present her second husband, typically European, with offspring of negroid or of Mongolian type. That husbands and wives come to resemble one another in physiognomy and characteristics, is further indication of the subtle and potent temperamental fusion and implications of the mysterious sex-union. (Kenealy, 1920, p. 175)

In addition to remaining perpetually happy, dedicated to children and their households, resistant to sexual allure of unfit men, and being behaviorally self-controlled, women were encouraged to not become over-educated and tax their brains with knowledge beyond what was needed for their role as mothers and wives. Women were actively steered to choose evening over regular day school, and to become teachers or librarians so that their career pursuits did not interfere with their primary eugenic mission as mothers (Popenoe & Johnson, 1935). For example, women were warned that engaging in intellectual pursuits would be highly costly, especially emotionally: "the woman of average brain, however, attains the intellectual standards of the man of average brain *only at cost of her health, of her emotions, or of her morale*" (Kenealy, 1920, p. 155).

Moreover, women's self-control, especially in regard to their sexual chastity was routinely emphasized as paramount for evolution. Melendy (1914) asserted that women's "sex-nature must be kept in an absolutely healthy condition. Such a condition can be reached, and retained, only by pure, temperate, abstemious lives" (p. 85). According to Kenealy (1920), "*that beyond all the other virtues, personal purity is essentially the highest, and is racially the most valuable of all the Woman-qualities...* once she has deviated from the monogamous code, she is dangerously likely never after to conform to it" (p. 170). They were urged to refuse succumbing to "racially parasitic" tendencies such as not only governing their sexual lusts, but also using any alcohol, reading "trashy novels," capitulating to melancholy or depression, daydreaming, engaging in "manly" physical fitness pursuits (i.e., sports) or limiting their food intake (Hague, 1913; Kenealy, 1920; Melendy, 1914; Popenoe & Johnson, 1935; Saleeby, 1911; Scharlieb, 1912). Popenoe and Johnson (1935) in highly popular book *Applied Eugenics* cited studies by UCLA psychologists, which found that women who pursued so-termed masculine college subjects and performed well academically were reported to be unhappy because "*extremely high scholarship in women* seems to be a deterrent to marriage or associated with something that is a deterrent" (p. 105). They encouraged women to pursue "the evening high school and university extension courses that have been so popular during the past decade might well give more attention to marriage and the family" (p. 262). Another typical eugenic warning, given to women who wished to participate in vigorous sports, included the following:

> When girls in course of developing the maternal function, with all its attendant psychical implications, are strained by athletics, by over-culture or industrial exhaustion, the vital resources are so diverted from the evolution of this function as to cause incapacitation in them, partial or complete, for wifehood, and for the bearing of sound and fine offspring. Sterilisation, absolute or partial, is induced; with dwarfed structure, *blighted emotions and warped instincts.* Even in women who have developed normally, disease or atrophy of reproductive organs may follow constitutional strain or undue effort. (Kenealy, 1920, p. 120)

Following this eugenic scientific advice was supposed to grant women happiness via marital bliss and ideal motherhood. According to eugenic scientific advice by Melendy (1914), "The quarrels, separations and divorces now of such frequent occurrence would be unheard of if all about to marry would be *guided by judgment and science, which are the true friends, not the foes, of happy love*" because only such eugenic knowledge guaranteed "*the promise of absolute joy and delight in your union, and in the thought of those you may bring into life with the priceless heritage of being "well-born"!*" (p. 215). Thus, evolutionary unfit women were vilified, sterilized, and proclaimed to be the causes of social unhappiness whereas eugenically fit women were admonished to "*never look on the dark side of anything*" (Melendy, 1914, p. 83) and follow rigid rules of personal behavior and thought control.

Building the Wall Against the Unhappy Hordes of Unfit Immigrants

The evolutionary unfit, according to eugenicists, were dangerous especially because of their supposed emotional volatility, negativity, and lack of self-control, which affirmed their uncivilized and parasitic status. Immigrants in both Europe and the U.S., most of whom were fleeing political instability and persecutions in their countries of origin, were perceived as a problem, in particular because of their supposed lack of emotional control (Yakushko, 2018). Their distress was deemed reflective of their biological hereditary inferiority (i.e., parasitic germo-plasms) and further confirmed via data about their lack of intelligence, which involved testing them at ports of entry, as well as via subsequent data about their poverty and illnesses (Goddard, 1917; Guyer, 1916). For example, according to Davenport (1911), Harvard University biologist and the leader of the American eugenics movement, eugenic sciences were important to the U.S.

> on account of the recent influx of immigrants from Southeastern Europe, [who] rapidly become darker in pigmentation, smaller in stature, more mercurial, more attached to music and art, more given to crimes of larceny, kidnapping, assault murder, rape, and sex-immorality… than were the original English settlers. (p. 219)

Thus, from late 1800s to World War II eugenics became an influential and visible socio-political movements which promised to create happy societies and offered empirical justifications for closing the borders to the evolutionary unfit groups (Yakushko, 2018). American politicians, like U.S. senator Johnson, used eugenics-based rationales to create some of the most restrictive immigration policies, such as Johnson-Reed Act of 1924 that denied immigrant entry to almost all non-Anglo-Saxon immigrants, especially Jews, Slavs, and southern Europeans (Tucker, 1996). The influence of eugenics on contemporary immigration policy is evidenced not only by the traces of its ideologies, but the direct involvement of many American eugenics scholars in debates (Brigham, 1923; Davenport, 1911; Goddard, 1917). Margaret Sanger (1919, 1921) openly used eugenic justifications to promote women's control over sexual reproduction by supporting sterilization or limited birth options among eugenically inferior immigrant women while actively promoting increased fertility among eugenically superior, native-born American women. Capitalist entrepreneurs also used eugenics-based business promotions: Kellogg introduced the benefits of "flow," which was claimed to reduce eugenic weaknesses through an Anglo-Saxon diet of cereal grains, not common for most immigrant communities, and marketing expensive toilet attachments designed to improve bowel movements claimed to rid the body of negative or toxic (i.e., evolutionary parasitic) physical and emotional waste (Cogdell, 2010).

Immigration was a focus for every American eugenic scholarly journal: articles and governmental policy review columns alike expressed concerns about border control and the entry of evolutionary unfit groups into Western societies (*American Breeders Magazine: A Journal of Genetics and Eugenics*, 1912; *Eugenical News*, 1916–1922; Yakushko, 2018). According to Brigham's (1923) popular coverage of the American psychology's most influential study, with a population of nearly two million military personnel, scientific study proved the dangerous decline of intelligence due primarily to U.S. immigration policies. Brigham openly disputed the perception that Jews were intelligent and thus welcome to the U.S., stating that "our figures… tend to disprove the popular belief that the Jew is highly intelligent" (p. 190). These scientific facts were used to further propagate xenophobic and anti-Semitic views. In his initial promotion of centrality of eugenic sciences to U.S. socio-political well-being, Harvard University's Charles Davenport (1911) claimed that studies involving

> The Hebrews showed the greatest proportion of crimes against chastity … there is no question that, taken as a whole, the hordes of Jews that are coming to us… with their intense individualism and ideals of gain at the cost of any interest, represent the opposite extreme from the early English and more recent Scandinavian immigration with their ideals of community life in the open country, advancement by the sweat of the brow, and the uprearing of families in the fear of God and the love of country. (p. 216)

Brigham (1923) further asserted that indisputable empirical data found in "our study of the army tests of foreign-born individuals has pointed at every step to the conclusion that the average intelligence of our immigrants is declining" (p. 197). In his estimate, "there is no doubt that the more recent immigrants [i.e., Jews, Slavs, southern Europeans, Irish] are intellectually closer to the negro than to the native-born white sample" (p. 199). Concerns were also routinely expressed about immigration across the Southern U.S. border. According to the *Eugenical News* (1928), an official publication of the American Eugenics Society, repeatedly called for a dedicated response to "the alarming influx of Mexican Peons [who would] inject another serious color problem into American life" (p. 24).

The threat of immigration was routinely evoked in all eugenic writings. For example, every American journal of eugenics included a special section for discussing immigrants and migration as well as governmental policies in regard to immigration (e.g., *Eugenical News*, 1916–1922). Guyer (1916), in his popular book *Being Well Born: An Introduction to Eugenics*, praised efforts to test all immigrants at entry points for any signs of eugenic weakness. The following summary provides a glimpse into the rhetoric surrounding immigration as well as concerns publicly promoted by eugenicists in regards to "hordes" of immigrants:

> During the decade from 1900 to 1910, 8,500,000 foreigners came to the United States, of whom 5,250,000 remained to make a permanent home. This shows how rapidly our whole population might be radically changed. In recent years the source of our immigrants has shifted proportionately from northwestern Europe to southern and eastern Europe (Italy, Austria-Hungary and Russia), and whether for weal or woe this new blood must inevitably leave its impress upon us. *Does it not behoove us then to seek with anxious eyes some knowledge of these invading hordes with whom we are to mingle our life-blood*? Even the most superficial examination may well cause us grave concern. (p. 281)

Guyer, like other eugenicists, employed numerous statistical studies to prove the problematic eugenic qualities of these new immigrants.

> We find that in one year (1908) at Ellis Island alone, 3,741 paupers, 2,900 persons with contagious disease, 184 insane, 121 feeble-minded, 136 criminals, 124 prostitutes and 65 idiots were denied entrance, and yet, according to the estimate of Doctor F. K. Sprague, of the United States Public Health Service, probably only about 5 per cent of the mentally

> deficient and 25 per cent. of those who will become insane have been detected. When confronted by such data we can begin to realize what we are facing. Others estimate that from 6 to 7 per cent. of the immigrants who are now arriving are feeble-minded. We learn further that recently while the foreign-born population of New York state was about 30 per cent., the foreign-born population of the insane hospitals of the state was over 43 per cent., and at one time approximately 65 per cent. for New York City. In one year (1908) 84 per cent. of the patients in Bellevue Hospital, New York City, were of foreign parentage. Paresis, which probably always has syphilis as its antecedent, is proportionately twice as prevalent among foreigners as among natives in New York City. (pp. 281–282)

Xenophobic and racist rhetoric, supposedly grounded in multiple studies and demographic analyses, framed in terms of evolutionary threat posed by the unfit, was the central feature of American eugenics (Black, 2003; Tucker, 1996; Yakushko, 2018).

The Advanced Western Sciences of Eugenic Human Betterment

Since the late 1800s, eugenic scholars have produced a tremendous number of scholarly books, scientific journals, and empirical research articles, directing their works toward both scientific and popular audiences (Bashford & Levine, 2010; Lombardo, 2011; Tucker, 1996). Eugenic scholarship enjoyed a high scholarly standing, endorsed as it was by an array of famous scientists (e.g., Darwin, Galton, Pearson in the UK; Davenport, Yerkes, Goddard, Thorndike, and Terman in the U.S.) as well as top educational institutions, including Cambridge, University of London, Harvard, Columbia, Stanford, UCLA, Johns Hopkins, Yale, and many others (*American Breeders Magazine: A Journal of Genetics and Eugenics*, 1912; *Eugenical News*, 1916–1922).

Seeking to differentiate itself from European and specifically psychoanalytic influences, U.S. psychology sought to fully embrace biological explanations of all human behavior, specifically Darwinist evolutionary theories and their corresponding eugenic promises to socially engineer human beings into becoming happy and efficient (Black, 2003; Yakushko, 2019). Although moral religious traditions played a factor in shaping the values promoted by early American psychologists such as

William James, Stanley G. Hall, and many others, these influences were always placed within the context of experimental empirical research and its claim to knowledge of universal, neutral, a-contextual and biological human functions (*Eugenical News*, 1916–1922; Guthrie, 2004; Tucker, 1996). In its struggle to differentiate itself from philosophy and align itself more closely with medicine, as well as in its search for sources of funding, especially government funding, the emerging field of American psychology found an impeccable ally in eugenic movement (Walsh, Teo, & Baydala, 2014).

Open affiliation with eugenics was common among key early U.S. psychology scientists. The first president of the American Psychological Association (APA), Stanley G. Hall (1903, 1917a, 1917b), was listed in numerous eugenic publications as its primary authority (*Eugenical News*, 1916–1922). Hall's works included cheery religious contributions, which also provided a rationale for eugenic studies, as for example his 1905 *White Man's Burden in Relation to Inferior Races* and his 1917b *Jesus the Christ in Light of Psychology*. Negative emotional characteristics and behaviors, according to Hall (1881) are the marks of inferior groups, such as "rapacious Jews" he viewed as intent on destroying Western civilization via such theories as Marxism (p. 202).

Another key U.S. psychologist, Robert Yerkes (1923), Harvard scholar and director of numerous American academic societies, not only produced a significant number of scholarly and popular eugenics publications, but also passionately promoted eugenics as the only scientific method capable of improving all aspects of American life. In his article entitled *Eugenic Bearing of Measurements of Intelligence in the United* States, Yerkes (1923) stated, "eugenics, the art of breeding better men, imperatively demands reliable measurement of human traits of body and mind… Scientific method has been commanded effectively to make available facts concerning bodily form and physiological processes" (p. 225). Discussing the central role of psychology as a discipline, Yerkes hailed the replacement of "reflection" and "introspection" (i.e., foci of psychoanalysis) in regard to human experience with statistical data collection, experimental methods, and comparative animal studies (p. 225). Psychology, Yerkes claimed, was ideally positioned to support eugenic efforts to rid humanity of the unfit while engineering those who were fit to contribute to the eugenic goals of social harmony and happiness. According to Yerkes,

> Eugenics needs accurate and reasonably complete description of human behaviour as partial basis *for methods of control*. It may look to psychology hopefully for accurate descriptions of traits of mind and their expressions in action, for measurements of the *manifold features of intellect, feeling, will, temperament, character-in fine for the scientific description of the human personality*. (p. 226)

Intelligence assessments became the cornerstone of American eugenic psychology sciences, in part because eugenicists such as Galton (1869) believed a well-functioning intellect to be the cornerstone for all superior human characteristics, such as emotional and behavioral self-control. The advanced scientific studies on intelligence conducted by Robert Yerkes (Harvard; founder of many fields of psychology including intelligence testing and animal [comparative] psychology), John B. Watson (Johns Hopkins; founder of behaviorism), Carl Brigham (Princeton; developer of SAT), Edward Thorndike (Columbia; founder of educational psychology), Lewis Terman (Stanford; founder of intelligence testing and twin studies genetic research) and many other leading psychologists, invariable produced results that placed African Americans, non-Nordic "foreign-born," and all other racially unfit groups in inferior categories not only because of their supposedly lower intelligence but also because of their negative emotional states, lack of morality, and absence of self-control (Brigham, 1923; Terman, 1916; Yakushko, 2019; Yerkes, 1923).

Many of these psychologists used the threat of dire social conditions, such as war, to promote the necessity of Darwinist and eugenic theorizing in psychology. Robert Yerkes (1920) edited a volume entitled *The New World of Science: Its Development During the War*, in which he invited various top American psychologists to justify eugenic Darwinist psychological views not only with visions of peaceful utopias, but also by promising superior of American troops in upcoming wars. Yerkes stressed that U.S. psychology was poised to become the best scientific method of engineering specific segments of American society such as its military:

> *The theory of psychological service was that human factors should be appreciated, measured, and intelligently used, that so far as feasible chance, personal whim or bias, and convention should be replaced by action in the light of reasonably accurate and thorough information. In a word, that the army should utilize what may be called "human engineering," just as it attempts to utilize other forms of engineering which have to do primarily with non-living things*. (p. 358)

Meanwhile, eugenic-based research was published in leading journals of psychology. For example, the *Journal of Applied Psychology*, founded in 1917, has continued to promote its commitment to a "psychology… applied to practical problems could ***enhance human happiness, well-being, and effectiveness***" (Kozlowski, Chen, & Salas, 2017, p. 237). Its contents from journal's first issue until World War II carry numerous examples of eugenic psychologies search to "enhance human happiness, well-being and effectiveness." A dominant theme among its publications are studies claiming to demonstrate that greater quantities of "White blood" among non-White individuals resulted in higher intelligence, morality, self-control, etc., as well as lower levels of intelligence among African Americans due to genetic hereditary factors (e.g., Gregg, 1925; McGurk, 1953). For example, Sunne's (1917) article claimed to confirm numerous significant differences between tested "White" and "negro children," including the finding that African Americans possessed inferior "facility in control of words," reduced "fertile imagination," inferior "resistance to suggestion," inferior "kinaesthetic discrimination and motor control," and inferior "logical capacity" (pp. 82–83).

The Journal of Comparative Psychology was dedicated to the Darwinist study of differences in animals and the application of these observations to humans. Among the articles on rats, mice, snakes, primates and so on, multiple scholarly works comparing human "species" differences, especially racial and national differences. In one of the journal's publications, Hunter (one-time president of the APA) and Sommermier (1922), claimed to have confirmed "positive correlation between increasing degree of white blood in the American Indian and… intelligence" (p. 277). Many other studies on the degree of "White blood" were likewise used to prove the inferiority of non-White individuals. According to Young's (1929) publication in this journal there was a "noticeable decrease of intelligence as we go from white children to light negroes and then to dark negroes" (p. 344). Responding to public critique of eugenic psychology's tendency to focus on intelligence testing in a country where educational opportunities were remarkably unequal (see Walter Lippman, 1922, expose against eugenic intelligence testing), psychologists turned their attention to other areas in which the White Anglo-Saxon race could be proved inherently genetically superior. One tactic involved measuring color preferences, which were claimed to be unaffected by environmental factors such as access to education. These studies repeatedly found that White individuals and people with supposedly higher White blood concentration had a marked preference for the color blue, and that greater intelligence and educational levels among minorities even shifted their own color preference toward blue (i.e., superior group's color) as well (e.g., Gesche, 1927; Hurlock, 1927). On the other hand, non-blue color preferences were routinely discussed as pointing to shared lower evolutionary progress among racial minorities. For example, Gesche (1927) commented on the results of his study, stating "it is interesting to note than in both the mixed blood Indian and Mexican sequence of color Yellow is least esteemed" (p. 308). Girls and women of differing races, these studies claimed, after being differentiated by their racial preferences, apparently shared an affinity for the color pink as a secondary preference (Hurlock, 1927).

Other publications in this "comparative" psychology journal focused on emotions and empathy. For example, Margaret Washburn (1923), one of the few women-psychologists and second female president of the APA, published her "comparative" study on lack of empathy or compassion toward other people's difficulties, apparently only found among her Jewish participants, claiming that such a "striking national difference" distinguished Jews from other national groups (p. 429). In another offering by this journal Skaggs (1930) claimed to have proven women being markedly more "emotional than the men subjects" (p. 413).

Many academics, including psychologists who studied human emotional differences, not only incorporated focus on eugenics in their scientific studies, writings, and academic coursework but also served as influential political and social leaders toward expanding eugenic based policies (Black, 2003; Guthrie, 2004; Stern, 2015; Selden, 1999; Tucker, 1996; Yakushko, 2019).

Among those who openly promoted the social engineering of human beings based on experimental Darwinism-grounded research was John B. Watson (1914, 1919), founder of one of the most recognized American psychology movements—behaviorism. Watson (1914, 1919), who was listed as a founding member of the American Eugenics Research Association together with Yerkes, Hall, and Charles Davenport eugenic publications (*Eugenical News*, 1916–1922) mentions eugenic-based goals as an inspiration for behaviorism (i.e., prediction and control of behavior, human engineering, genetic biological origins of human differences). The *Eugenical News* (1916) also noted that the newly formed American Eugenic Organization boasted the following top psychologists as its members:

> new active members of Eugenics Research Association... C. C. Brigham, Psychological Laboratory, Princeton, N. J., G. Stanley Hall, Clark University, C. E. Seashore, State University of Iowa, Lewis, M. Terman, Stanford University, Calif., John B. Watson, Johns Hopkins Hospital. (p. 53)

A significant number of APA presidents and top psychologists, including Hall, Yerkes, Watson, Bingham, Thorndike, Seagram, Angell, Thorndike, Hollingworth, Doge and others, wrote openly eugenicist scholarly and popular contributions and were listed as leaders of American eugenics societies and organizations (*Eugenical News*, 1916–1922). In the U.S., eugenicist scientific narratives focused on what they called "human betterment," promising to improve by testing and controlling human beings. Angell, for example, ran a celebrated eugenic "human betterment" laboratory at Yale University, hailed as the largest academic eugenic lab in the world (*Eugenical News*, 1916–1922). In addition, the restrictions on immigration and practices of segregation and sterilization were primarily justified through the scholarly efforts of these psychologists (Bashford & Levine, 2010; Lombardo, 2011; Tucker, 1996; Yakushko, 2019).

These scholars also assured the public that, according to their research, seeking to change the environment in which individuals operated was unnecessary and inadequate to eliminating undesirable social practices or conditions (i.e., poverty, lack of educational success, divorces). According to Guyer (1916),

> *While many an enthusiastic humanitarian is laboring under the assumption that if we can improve external conditions human deficiencies will disappear, the student of heredity realizes that this is in large part a delusion unless we can secure an accompanying improvement in intrinsic qualities of the human species itself through the suitable mating of individuals.* Just as the intelligent farmer to-day demands selected seed as well as good soil and proper cultivation, so one with the facts of heredity at hand would, as he views social problems, urge the fundamental importance of having selected stock with which to start. No shifts or shapings of environment will ever enable men to "gather grapes of thorns or figs of thistles." (p. 294)

Guyer provides the following proof from research conducted by leading American psychologist and education scholar Edward Thorndike:

> Professor Thorndike undertook experiments with groups of school children of high and of low initial ability respectively to determine whether equal opportunity or equal special training would produce an equalizing effect in easily alterable traits such as rapidity in addition and the like. *Without exception he found that at the end of such experiments, although both groups had improved, the superior individuals were farther ahead than ever, that equality of opportunity and training had widened rather than narrowed the gap between the two classes.* Others who have made special studies on the causes of individual differences have come to the same conclusion; *namely, that individuals differ widely by original nature and that similarity in conditions of nurture and training will not avail in deleting these differences.* (p. 295)

Guyer, like other eugenicists from its inception to today (e.g., Bouchard, 1996; Terman, 1916), celebrated the use of twins orphaned and separated at birth to prove the genetic determinants of human differences in intelligence and personality. Guyer (1916) claimed "even in twins, as both Galton and Thorndike have shown, there is no tendency for similar education, home life and the like to render those originally different any more similar with advancing years" (p. 295).

The reduction of humans to animals, stripping individuals of such supposed-uniquely-human capacities as "introspection" and "consciousness" became another practice central to American psychology. In his behavioral manifesto, Watson (1914) claimed that there is no difference between "man" and "brute" (i.e., human and animal.) Robert Yerkes (1907) produced numerous books that proposed that understanding differences between and within animal species (e.g., comparing mice capable of learning mazes through electric shock stimulations or survive drowning versus those who were not) could reveal key facts helpful to explaining successful and unsuccessful human adaptation. Since animals, unlike humans, could be caged, starved, mutilated, and discarded in experiments, their use was claimed by American psychologists to offer unlimited benefits toward successful social engineering of ideal human beings as part of their positive eugenics vision. Entire journals were dedicated to studies of experiments on caged animals, such as *The Journal of Comparative Psychology*. Watson (1914) once boasted of mutilating and killing at times over 600 rats for a single experiment.

In addition to these experiments, psychologists pursued larger scale studies, which offered them access to significant sources of funding, visibility with the American public and politicians, and professional differentiation from other disciplines. Among such studies were the Army mental tests planned, executed, analyzed and published by prominent American psychologists (Gould, 1996; Guthrie, 2004; Tucker, 1996; Yakushko, 2019). Robert Yerkes, who led this work, recruited technicians for this study via such publications as the *Eugenical News* (1916–1922), and lauded that journal in many of his publications (Yerkes, 1920, 1923).

Thus, the Army Mental Tests were claimed to offer the height of scientific, experimental, and unbiased research in psychology (Brigham, 1923; Yerkes, 1923). In the forward to a highly popularized summary of these tests, Yerkes (1923) stated that "It behooves us to consider their reliability and their meaning, for *no one of us as a citizen can afford to ignore the menace of race deterioration or the evident relations of immigration to national progress and welfare*" (p. viii). Brigham's summary of the Army Alpha and Beta (i.e., literate and illiterate participant versions) results, like other eugenicists writings, are filled with complex descriptions of measurements and statistics, multiple tables as well as references to biology and brain. Brigham took pains to explain that their rigorously scientific methods mitigated any influences of the environment, social context, or location since all of the nearly two million tested men were engaged in the same occupation (i.e., these men's background or social context was claimed to not matter). Conclusions of the study were promoted as bias-free and essential to all social spheres. Nordic or Anglo-Saxon individuals were found to possess superior intellectual qualities in contrast to all other racial and ethnic groups. In Brigham's summary, "our results showing the *marked intellectual inferiority of the negro are corroborated by practically all of the investigators who have used psychological test on white and negro groups*" (p. 190). Evoking the work of many other psychologists and education scholars on the necessity of racial segregation in schools, Brigham stated that "the average negro child can not advanced through an educational curriculum adapted to the Anglo-Saxon child in step with that child" (p. 194).

These scientific findings also highlighted supposedly problematic morality, lack of self-control and negative emotional characteristics of non-Nordic individuals, especially African Americans. In his other contributions related to the Army mental tests Yerkes (1920) explained that American Jim Crow laws and policies were based on:

> *Fact, which was brought into clear relief by the wholesale examining of colored and white men in the draft is the intellectual inferiority of the negro.* Quite apart from educational status, which is utterly unsatisfactory, the negro soldier is of relative low grade intelligence… this also is in the nature of a lesson, for it suggests that *education alone will not place the negro race on a part with its Caucasian competitors.* (pp. 376–377)

Yerkes further described numerous studies showing that African Americans were prone to undesirable behavior: they were overly-gregarious and cheerfully naive akin to developmentally disabled individuals. The inauthentic character of this apparent happiness was, it was claimed, evidenced by a propensity for anger, laziness, melancholy, and lack of self control. According to Yerkes,

> All officers without exception agree that the *negro lacks initiative, displays little or no leadership, and can not accept responsibility*… all officers seem further to agree that the *negro is a cheerful, willing soldier, naturally subservient.* These qualities make for *immediate obedience, although not necessarily for good discipline, since petty thieving and venereal disease are commoner than with the white troops.* (p. 742)

These Army testing findings were consistent with other eugenic studies in regard to African Americans. Harvard biologist Davenport (1913), who led many American eugenic scholarly efforts, further explained in the *State Laws Limiting Marriage Selection in Light of Eugenics* that African Americans have "*a strong sex instinct, without corresponding self-control; a lack of appreciation for property distinction… a certain lack of genuineness—a tendency to pass off clever veneer for the real thing, due to inability or unwillingness to master fundamentals,*" (p. 34) though Davenport also elevated supposedly desirable qualities among African Americans such as their "*good-nature, keen sense of humor [and] dog-like fidelity… when treated kindly*" (p. 32).

In addition, Grant's (1921) *The Passing of the Great Race*, using the result of the mental testing studies among the military personnel, warned of dire consequences if eugenic strategies were not followed:

> neither the black, nor the brown, nor the yellow, not the red will conquer the white in battle. *But if the valuable elements in the Nordic race mix with inferior strains or die out through race suicide, then the citadel of civilization will fall for mere lack of defenders.* (p. xxxi)

While profound anti-Black racism permeated the writings of American eugenic scholars, non-Nordic or Anglo-Saxon minority groups, as well as individuals placed in broad categories of the "feeble-minded" (e.g., people with disabilities or living in poverty), were held to lack proper hereditary traits. Among their supposed hereditary failings were improper emotional states and lack of emotional self-control. Wiggam (1923) in his popular contribution to eugenic scholarship, the *New Decalogue*, claimed that all eugenically unfit people had "*high temper, uncontrollable fits of anger, feebleness of will, inability to hold a social ideal permanently in mind, lack of ambition to provide as good homes as their neighbors... and mental 'drive'*" (p. 58). As noted above, the scientific community was also given to anti-Semitic and xenophobic views, holding that Jews and non-Nordic immigrants lacked the genetic background necessary to becoming good, happy citizens. These "indisputable" assertions, made by leading scholars, identified Pollyannaism as a biological trait found only among the evolutionarily fit (Brigham, 1923; Davenport, 1910, 1911; Guyer, 1916). Later scholarship has found that pre- and post-World War II immigrants fleeing violence abroad (i.e., Jews escaping the Holocaust) were made to adhere to a code of silence about their trauma and distress (Danieli, 1984; Yakushko, 2018). American scholars, just as the American public, demanded Pollyanna-like behavior from all immigrants or else they would indeed be branded as evolutionary unfit, as sick, and as lacking proper emotional self-control.

Eugenic studies and scientific results were especially promoted to the public and policy makers, setting the stage for central role of psychologists in determining what constituted human fitness, including human emotional fitness. The result were used to encourage immigration authorities "*only to admit those who are superior to the median American in mental endowment as far as this is shown by approved mental tests*" (Evans, 1931, p. 16). Eugenic writings from the early twentieth century celebrate the use of psychology tests to identify and remove undesirables from immigration lines at ports of entry, based on their observed "feeble-minded" emotional states, resulting in denials of entry and deportations if they failed them (Selden, 1999; Yakushko, 2018, 2019). H. H. Goddard (1917, 1919), famously tasked with administering these eugenic tests, claimed that over 80% of Jewish, Slavic and Southern European immigrants tested as feeble-minded, and that his psychological evaluations increased deportations of such immigrants by over 500%. It seems that not playing Pollyanna marked immigrants for intelligence testing and deportation, even after traumatizing experiences of war and violence, and the long voyage from Europe to the U.S. They were pulled out of waiting lines and taken to separate testing rooms, where they were administered supposedly highly psychometrically valid and culturally relevant tests developed by leading psychologists like H. H. Goddard, R. Yerkes, and L. Terman (i.e., assessments that allowed testing of illiterate or non-English speaking individuals). Failing to achieve adequate scores was used as further proof that immigrants were feeble-minded parasites, whose lack of evolutionary fitness would harm U.S. society. As this and the previous examples demonstrate, the application of scientific Pollyannaism to marginalized groups has had a long and brutal history; one which continues to live on in attitudes and representations of minorities (Merskin, 2011; Yakushko, 2018, 2019).

The Army mental tests and other similar eugenic studies were popularized as scientific solutions to social problems. According to Brigham's (1923) summary, "the deterioration of American intelligence is not inevitable... if public action can be aroused to prevent it. There is no reason why legal steps should not be taken which would insure a continually progressive upward evolution" (p. 210). Among these steps were segregation of the unfit, their sterilization, severe restriction of immigration from non-Nordic countries via ports of entry, closure of Southern borders, vocational and educational tracking of minority individuals, and the enforcement of miscegenation laws to ensure the "prevention of the continued propagation of defective strains in the present population" (Brigham, 1923, p. 210).

Tales of Finding Genetic Origins of Beauty and the Beast

Among the most prominent scholars contributing to scientific Pollyannaism was leading U.S. eugenicist, H. H. Goddard. In addition to coordinating the Ellis Island eugenic intelligence testing, Goddard was known for establishing scientific tests that show the biological or genetic origins of evolutionary unfitness among human beings. Goddard was best known for directing the school for "Feeble-Minded Boys and Girls at Vineland, NJ," where he carried out most of his eugenic testing experiments (Bashford & Levine, 2010; Lombardo, 2011; Selden, 1999; Smith, 1985; Tucker, 1996). He was a student of Stanley G. Hall and close colleague and friend of Yerkes, Thorndike, and many other American psychologists, well-known for their eugenic commitments.

Goddard's (1912) study of the "Kallikak" family (a pseudonym denoting Greek terms for "beauty" and "ugliness") claimed to track hereditary lines of feeble-mindedness and genetic superiority across multiple generations and communities. The Kallikak study was hailed as one of the first eugenic studies of behavioral genetics and continued to serve as a foundation for claims that personality traits (e.g., positive attitude, self-control), as well as intelligence, were grounded in genetic inheritance.

Based on interviews, observations, and, ultimately, direct testing using Binet intelligence measure, Goddard claimed that such hereditary characteristics as intelligence, health, moral choices, career success, optimism, and sexual morality among over 400 Kallikak family members could be traced back through the generations to a choice made by Martin, a "revolutionary hero." Martin's initial poor choice was an affair with "nameless tavern girl," which produced out of wedlock multiple eugenically problematic offspring, which in turn resulted in generations of family members who lacked intelligence, were poor, obtained divorces or had children out of wedlock, and were physically disabled, ill, angry, or melancholy. In contrast, Goddard claimed to empirically show that when Martin decided on evolutionary superior path of "marrying an upstanding Quaker woman," this choice resulted in generations of eugenically superior individuals, including prominent wealthy businessmen, academicians, and politicians who displayed positive personality traits and high intelligence.

Goddard's key evidence in his case for eugenics was a descendent of the "nameless tavern girl" called, in the study, Deborah Kalliak: an orphaned child who was shuffled between numerous state institutions until, at the age of eight, she was sent to Goddard's Vineland home. Based on extensive empirical testing of Deborah, Goddard asserted that she not only inherited borderline levels of intelligence (i.e., Deborah struggled to read although she apparently possessed strong mathematical skills and memory) but also a low moral character (i.e., she was deemed too outspoken, selfish, seductive, occasionally melancholy, and prone to daydreaming).

Goddard's conclusions, based on his supposedly indisputable scientific evidence in Deborah's and her family case, decried the social dangers of "feeble-mindedness" as a form of higher grade evolutionary unfitness in contrast to other levels such as idiocy (i.e., mental disability). According to Goddard (1912, 1917, 1919), unlike other clear signs of eugenic weakness (e.g., obvious intellectual or physical disability), feeble-mindedness could only be detected by trained psychologists or associates through systematic testing, using statistically validated measures. The feeble-minded, Goddard (1912, 1917) claimed, were especially threatening to society because, like Deborah Kallikak, they could appear as ordinary and good-looking to eugenically fit people, thus resulting in the propagation of unfit, hereditarily weak individuals. As Goddard (1912) explained it, Deborah was "seemingly normal to the untrained eye, and obviously attractive, such a woman would have little trouble finding suitors and bearing children" (p. 97). Individuals like Deborah were to be identified, classified, segregated, and sterilized—all for the protection and happiness of current and future society (1911, 1912, 1917, 1919).

The Kallikak study and the experiments at Vineland became the cornerstone of eugenic policies world-wide and remained among the most cited scientific studies supporting influence of heredity throughout 1960s. So foundational was it to the development of Behavioral Genetics as a scientific field. According to Selden (1999), that between 1914 and 1948, 62% of high school biology books covered Kallikak study as the most popular study on heredity. The Kallikak study and Goddard's methods were turned to again and again by eugenicist scholars as well as legal experts. Hunter (1914) in his *Civic Biology Presented in Problems* bemoans the fact that

> Hundreds of families such as [the Kallilaks]… exist today, spreading disease, immorality, and crime in all parts of this country… they not only do harm to others by corrupting, stealing, and spreading disease, but they are actually protected and cared for by the state out of public money. Largely for them the poorhouse and the asylum exists. They take from society but they give nothing in return. *They are true parasites.* (p. 263)

Fisher (1924) in his article entitled *The Elimination of Mental Defect* published in the *Eugenics Review*, stated that Goddard's methods were best suited for the identification and elimination of the "feebleminded, alcoholic, criminalistics, epileptic, insane, migranious, neurotic, paralytic, tuberculous, and tramps" (p. 114). The Kallikak study was used in the Supreme Court decision to uphold involuntary sterilization of Carrie Buck, a young woman who was blamed for her own rape and institutionalized as a feeble-minded prostitute (Lombardo, 2011). It was used to justify segregation in schools, as well as the institutionalization of many individuals found eugenically unfit according to IQ and personality testing (Smith, 1985; Tucker, 1996). It was also used for wide-spread sterilization programs in both the U.S. and, famously, in Nazi Germany, where massive sterilization programs were enacted against those considered racially impure (Black, 2003; Lombardo, 2011; Smith, 1985; Tucker, 1996). Goddard's book was translated twice into German, first in 1914 and again in 1933. In the introduction to the 1933 re-print, translator Karl Wilker names H. H. Goddard as the most significant contributor to the Nazi "law for the prevention of sick or ill offspring" because his study showed "just how significant the problem of genetic inheritance is" which "no example shows so clearly as the Kallikak study" (Kuhl, 2002, p. 41).

Goddard produced numerous other scientific studies, many of them popularized in books addressed to a public audience. In his speech to the American Academy of Political and Social Science, entitled the *Elimination of Feeble-Mindedness*, Goddard (1911) discussed the different categories and gradations of stupidity established by eugenic study, paying particular attention to associated emotional states, in order to advocate for the elimination of the feebleminded. Claiming that care, including mental health and educational treatments, were expensive, Goddard pointed out that these individuals made others unhappy: "He [the idiot] is a source of expense and trouble. No matter how freely the trouble may be met by those nearest of kin, it is nevertheless true, that a child so afflicted is *a constant source of unpleasantness and unhappiness to all those who have to do with him*" (pp. 261–262). Worse then "idiots" were the so-called "imbeciles," who were described as violent and lacking in self control. As such, Goddard claimed, "The elimination of this grade of feeble-mindedness would *result in an enormous improvement in happiness and possibilities of achievement in every community*" (p. 262). Ironically, it was the "morons" or high-functioning "feeble-minded" that were especially dangerous, because they were easily over-looked by those not trained in psychological testing. These individuals, Goddard claimed, lacked moral standards, self-control, or economic acumen: they were empirically proven to be criminal, given to poverty, sexually promiscuous, and emotionally volatile. According to Goddard,

> In consequence of these two characteristics [lack of success in "competition" with others and lack of "prudence" leading to need for social services] of the moron, he becomes an enormous drag upon society, and *the elimination of this grade of feeble-mindedness would be the greatest boon of all.* (p. 263)

Deriding individuals in this category as especially prone to poverty and prostitution, as shown in "laboratory studies," Goddard concluded that, "These are the people who cannot be taught decent living, and through their ignorance of things, which they have not the capacity to learn, they spread disease, through their person and their untidy surroundings. *They are thus a menace to public health as well as to morals*" (p. 263). To achieve the goal of their elimination, Goddard proposed several courses of action. The first was segregation of the unfit from the rest of society and from members of the opposite sex in "colonies" where they lived "in conditions of absolute sexual seclusion" rendering them "incapable of reproduction" (p. 268). Responding to concerns that segregation into such "colonies" and "institutions" would not only be costly but also inhumane, Goddard assured that sufficient number of experts (i.e., psychologists, behavioral technicians) could be made available for their detention, and that "*institutions for the feeble-minded that are the happiest places in the world*" (p. 269). In discussing the sterilization of the feeble-minded, Goddard argued that over-population by those who appear healthy but are actually feeble-minded called for more drastic measures, such as "castrating the males and ovariotomy for the females" (p. 270). He also praised new techniques such as "sterilization by X-rays" (p. 271).

Other "scientific" suggestions made by Goddard throughout his career included removing the feeble-minded from their parents by the State (Goddard, 1911), relegating them to hard labor and menial jobs (Goddard, 1919), removing their voting and political rights to create Aristotelian "aristo-democracy" (Goddard, 1919), severe restricting immigration from non-Nordic countries (Goddard, 1919), training psychologists whose primary task was to identify and segregate the feeble-minded (Goddard, 1911, 1917, 1919), and encouraging eugenically fit parents to raise happy, moral, and self-controlled children (Goddard, 1948). For example, in their highly popular book. *Applied Eugenics*, Popenoe and Johnson (1935) praised "the Training School, Vineland, N. J." in their chapter, *Feeble Minded Men Are Capable of*

Much Rough Labor by displaying a photograph showing men dressed in prison-line uniforms clearing forested area, a photo reminiscent of hard labor camp images. The photograph included an explanation that "Most of the cost of segregating the mentally defective can be met by properly organizing their labor, so as to make them as nearly self-supporting as possible. It has been found that they perform excellently such work as clearing forest land, or reforesting cleared land, and great gangs of them might profitably be put at such work, in most states" (p. 192). Hollingworth (1924), a noted education scholar and a eugenicist, also praised Goddard's work on identifying individuals with "innate permanent, hereditary superiority" (p. 299).

On Testing Intelligence and Finding (Un)Happiness

Another top American psychologist, known for his key role in the development of intelligence testing (e.g., the Stanford-Binet intelligence measure), Stanford University psychologist Lewis Terman, was also a leading American eugenicist. Terman's (1916) key work on intelligence constantly focused on supposed "dullness," which in his view "seems to be racial, or at least inherent in the family" and found with "extraordinary frequency among Indians, Mexicans, and negroes" (p. 91). Terman provided numerous cases of individuals from lower to the highest levels of intelligence, especially focusing on how these varied levels of intelligence corresponded to positive emotions and self-control. For example, Terman discussed a "girl, age 12; mental age 10; IQ approximately 65" although "from very superior family" claiming that these characteristics and levels of intelligence are "the type from which prostitutes often come" (p. 83). Other children with IQ in the range of 70 and 75 are described as "*unruly, boisterous, disobedient, stubborn, and lacking sense of propriety*," or as "*quiet, sullen, indifferent, lazy, and stubborn*" (p. 86).

In contrast, a child with IQ measurement of 130 is described by Terman as having "*social and moral traits of the very best. Is obedient, conscientious, and unusually reliable for her age. Quiet and confident bearing, but no touch of vanity*" (p. 97). Other children with high intelligence are described as "*a wonderfully charming, delightful girl in every respect*, a favorite with young and old, as nearly perfection as the most charming little girl could be," or as someone who "*leads his class. Attractive, healthy, normal-appearing lad. Full of good humor. Is loving and obedient*" (p. 99).

A famous education scholar and eugenicist, Leta Hollingworth (1924) similarly connected levels of intelligence with levels of individual and group happiness in her *Children Above 180 IQ Stanford-Binet*, focusing especially on the top "gifted" students:

> There is thus an "optimum" intelligence, from the viewpoint of personal happiness and adjustment to society, which is well below the maximum. The exploration of this concept should yield truths of value for education, and for social science as well. The few children who test at the very top of the juvenile population have a unique value for society. On them depends in large measure the advancement of learning. *If they fail of personal happiness and human contact, their work for society as a whole may be impaired or lost.* (p. ccix)

Utopian Promises of Eugenic Scientific Pollyannaism

Eugenic scientific Pollyannaism further contributed to epistemological values and empirical strategies, which promoted a-contextual positivity and moral goodness in Western academic traditions. Their methods and findings were represented as unbiased and unquestionable. As this study has shown, they made use of experimental large-scale data or supposedly biologically-based research that relied on statistical explanations of normality (e.g., bell curve and bell shapes of normality) and on tests developed and collected by psychologists with specific ideological values taken as universal or objective (e.g., intelligence or cheeriness as superior human traits). Their scientific efforts minimized or denied social context, including rejecting and vilifying alternative theories of evolution (e.g., by Lamarck) as well as context-focused psychological theories (e.g., psychoanalysis). Their scholarship was promoted as universally true, impartial or neutral, and responsive to social problems (e.g., promising ending to wars, poverty, and illness).

Moreover, eugenics and eugenicists, offered to better individuals and society with promises of individual and collective happiness. Ignoring the political, economic, and social challenges common in early twentieth century Western societies and denying the relevance of racial, gender, and economic inequalities was central to the eugenic sciences. To achieve utopian states of individual and social happiness, Western individuals were asked to subscribe to scientific Pollyannaism views. Non-compliance or resistance to these views was accused of being unscientific. Eugenics was represented as the pathways toward future without wars, illnesses, or poverty. Negative eugenics would ensure that the evolutionary unfit were eliminated, while positive eugenics would guarantee that those born with superior genetics would maintain happy, productive, self-controlled utopian lives (Davenport, 1910, 1913; Galton, 1869, 1883; Pearson, 1905, 1911; Popenoe & Johnson, 1935). In the words of one of the most popular eugenic books, used for both public information and for academic classes, eugenics was the only way to ensure "*harmony with the underlying plan of the universe*" and "*totality of happiness of all sentient beings or of all men*" (Popenoe & Johnson, 1935, p. 214). Guyer (1916) wonders,

> What shall the home of the future be with regard to its most important assets, the children? Shall we as a people continue to be confronted at every turn by the dull countenance of the imbecile, the inevitable product of a bad parental mating; or the feeble body and the clouded intellect of the child sprung from a parentage of polluted blood; or the furtive cunning of the born criminal, the will-less mind of the bred degenerate, or the shiftless spawn of the pauper? *Or shall it be a type with laughing face, with bounding muscles, with unclouded brain, overflowing with health and happiness—in short, the well-born child?* (pp. 338–339)

The lasting impact of this version of scientific Pollyannaism can be found in versions of behaviorism, especially the behaviorism developed by John B. Watson, which sought to socially engineer infants and young children to become happy and efficient people.

References

American Breeders Magazine: A Journal of Genetics and Eugenics. (1912). Washington, DC: American Breeders Association.

Bashford, A., & Levine, P. (Eds.). (2010). *The Oxford handbook of the history of eugenics.* New York: Oxford University Press.

Bergman, J. (2014). *The Darwin effect: It's influence on nazism, eugenics, racism, communism, capitalism & sexism.* Green Forest, AR: New Leaf Publishing Group.

Black, E. (2003). *War against the weak: Eugenics and America's campaign to create a master race.* New York: Four Walls Eight Windows.

Bouchard, T. J. (1996). Galton lecture: Behaviour genetic studies of intelligence, yesterday and today: The long journey from plausibility to proof. *Journal of Biosocial Science, 28*(4), 527–555.

Brigham, C. C. (1923). *A study of American intelligence*. Princeton, NJ: Princeton University Press.

Cogdell, C. (2010). *Eugenic design: Streamlining America in the 1930s*. Philadelphia, PA: University of Pennsylvania Press.

Danieli, Y. (1984). Psychotherapists' participation in the conspiracy of silence about the Holocaust. *Psychoanalytic Psychology, 1*(1), 23–42.

Darwin, C. (1888). *The descent of man and selection in relation to sex*. London: Murray.

Darwin, C. (1889). *The expression of the emotions in man and animals*. London: Murray.

Davenport, C. B. (1910). *Eugenics: The science of human improvement by better breeding*. New York: Henry Holt.

Davenport, C. B. (1911). *Heredity in relation to eugenics*. New York: H. Holt.

Davenport, C. B. (1913). *State laws limiting marriage selection examined in the light of eugenics*. Cold Springs, NY: Eugenics Record Office.

Eugenical News. (1916–1922). Monthly publication of the Eugenics Record Office, Cold Springs, NY. Retrieved on February 22, 2018 from https://babel.hathitrust.org/cgi/pt?id=coo.31924063788834.

Evans, W. S. (1931). *Organized eugenics*. New Haven, CT: American Eugenics Society.

Fisher, R. A. (1924). The elimination of mental defect. *Eugenics Review, 16*, 114–116.

Galton, F. (1865). Hereditary talent and character. *Macmillan's Magazine, 12*(157), 318–327.

Galton, F. (1869). *Hereditary genius: An inquiry into its laws and consequences*. New York, NY: Macmillan.

Galton, F. (1883). *Inquiries into the human faculty & its development*. London, UK: J. M. Dent.

Galton, F. (1904). Eugenics: Its definition, scope, and aims. *American Journal of Sociology, 10*(1), 1–25.

Galton, F. (1907). *Probability: The foundation of eugenics*. London, UK: Clarendon Press.

Gesche, I. E. M. A. (1927). The color preferences of one thousand one hundred and fifty-two Mexican children. *Journal of Comparative Psychology, 7*(4), 297–311.

Goddard, H. H. (1911). The elimination of feeble-mindedness. *The Annals of the American Academy of Political and Social Science, 37*(2), 261–272.

Goddard, H. H. (1912). *The Kallikak family: A study in the heredity of feeble-mindedness*. New York: Macmillan.

Goddard, H. H. (1917). Mental tests and the immigrant. *Journal of Delinquency, 2*, 243–277.

Goddard, H. H. (1919). *Psychology of the normal and subnormal*. New York: Dodd, Mead.

Goddard, H. H. (1948). *Our children in the atomic age*. Mellott, IN: Hopkins Syndicate.
Gould, S. J. (1996). *The mismeasure of man*. New York, NY: W. W. Norton & Company.
Gregg, J. E. (1925). The comparison of races. *The Scientific Monthly, 20*(3), 248–254.
Guthrie, R. V. (2004). *Even the rat was white: A historical view of psychology*. Upper Saddle River, NJ: Pearson Education.
Guyer, M. F. (1916). *Being well-born: An introduction to eugenics*. New York, NY: Bobbs-Merrill Company.
Hague, W. G. (1913). *The eugenic mother and baby: A complete home guide*. London, UK: Hague.
Hall, G. S. (1881). *Aspects of German culture*. Boston: J.R. Osgood.
Hall, G. S. (1903). The white man's burden versus indigenous development of the lower races. *The Journal of Education, 58*(4, 1438), 83.
Hall, G. S. (1917a). *Jesus, the Christ, in the light of psychology*. New York: Doubleday, Page.
Hall, G. S. (1917b). Practical relations between psychology and the war. *Journal of Applied Psychology, 1*(1), 9–16. https://doi.org/10.1037/h0070238.
Holbrook, M. L. (1897). *Homo-culture—Or, The improvement of offspring through wiser generation*. London, UK: M. L. Holbrook.
Hollingworth, L. S. (1924). Provisions for intellectually superior children. In M. V. O'Shea (Ed.), *The child: His nature and his needs* (pp. 277–299). New York, NY: The Children's Foundation.
Hunter, G. W. (1914). *A civic biology: Presented in problems*. New York: American Book.
Hunter, W. S., & Sommermier, E. (1922). The relation of degree of Indian blood to score on the Otis Intelligence Test. *Journal of Comparative Psychology, 2*(3), 257–277.
Hurlock, E. B. (1927). Color preferences of white and negro children. *Journal of Comparative Psychology, 7*(6), 389–404.
Huxley, J. S. (1936). Eugenics and society. *Eugenics Review, 28*(1), 11–31.
Kenealy, A. (1920). *Feminism and sex extinction*. London, UK: T. Fisher Unwin.
Kozlowski, S. W., Chen, G., & Salas, E. (2017). One hundred years of the *Journal of Applied Psychology*: Background, evolution, and scientific trends. *Journal of Applied Psychology, 102*(3), 237–253.
Kuhl, S. (2002). *The Nazi connection: Eugenics, American racism, and German national socialism*. New York: Oxford University Press.
Lippman, W. (1922). The mental age of Americans. *New Republic, 32*(412–417), 9–11, 213–215, 246–248, 275–277, 297–298, 328–330.
Lombardo, P. A. (Ed.). (2011). *A century of eugenics in America: From the Indiana experiment to the human genome era*. Bloomington, IN: Indiana University Press.

Lombardo, P. A., & Dorr, G. M. (2006). Eugenics, medical education, and the public health service: Another perspective on the Tuskegee syphilis experiment. *Bulletin of the History of Medicine, 80*(2), 291–316.
McDougall, W. (1914). Psychology in the service of eugenics. *The Eugenics Review, 5*(4), 295.
McDougall, W. (1921). *National welfare and national decay*. London: Methuen & Co.
McGurk, F. C. (1953). On white and negro test performance and socio-economic factors. *The Journal of Abnormal and Social Psychology, 48*(3), 448–450.
Melendy, M. R. (1914). *The science of eugenics and sex life*. New York: W. R. Vansant.
Merskin, D. L. (2011). *Media, minorities, and meaning: A critical introduction*. Philadelphia, PA: Peter Lang.
Nearing, S. (1912). *The super race: An American problem*. New York: B. W. Huebsch.
Pearson, K. (1905). *National life from the standpoint of science*. London: Adam and Black.
Pearson, K. (1911). *The scope and importance to the state of the science of national eugenics*. London, UK: Dulau and Company.
Popenoe, P., & Johnson, R. H. (1935). *Applied eugenics* (2nd ed.). New York: Macmillan.
Rushton, J. P., & Ankney, C. D. (2009). Whole brain size and general mental ability: A review. *International Journal of Neuroscience, 119*(5), 692–732.
Ruti, M. (2015). *The age of scientific sexism: How evolutionary psychology promotes gender profiling and fans the battle of the sexes*. Toronto, ON: Bloomsbury.
Saleeby, C. W. (1911). *Woman and womanhood: A search for principles*. New York: Kennerley.
Sanger, M. (1919, February). Birth control and racial betterment. *Eugenical News*.
Sanger, M. (1921). The eugenic value of birth control propaganda. *Birth Control Review, 5*(10), 1–10.
Scharlieb, M. M. A. D. B. (1912). *Womanhood and race-regeneration*. New York, NY: Moffat, Yard.
Schultz, A. H. (1923). Comparison of white and negro fetuses. In C. B. Davenport, H. F. Osborn, C. Wissler, & H. H. Laughlin (Eds.), *Scientific papers of the second international congress of eugenics* (Vol. 2). Baltimore, MD: Williams & Wilkins.
Selden, S. (1999). *Inheriting shame: The story of eugenics and racism in America*. New York: Teachers College Press.
Skaggs, E. B. (1930). Studies in attention and emotion. *Journal of Comparative Psychology, 10*(4), 375–419. https://doi.org/10.1037/h0071298.

Smith, J. D. (1985). *Minds made feeble: The myth and legacy of the Kallikaks.* Rockville, MD: Aspen.
Stern, A. M. (2015). *Eugenic nation: Faults and frontiers of better breeding in modern America.* Berkeley: University of California Press.
Sunne, D. (1917). A comparative study of white and negro children. *Journal of Applied Psychology, 1*(1), 71–83.
Terman, L. M. (1916). *The measurement of intelligence.* New York: Houghton Mifflin.
Thorndike, E. L. (1909). Darwin's contribution to psychology. *University of California Chronicle, 12*(1), 65–80.
Tucker, W. H. (1996). *The science and politics of racial research.* Carbondale, IL: University of Illinois Press.
Walsh, R. T., Teo, T., & Baydala, A. (2014). *A critical history and philosophy of psychology: Diversity of context, thought, and practice.* New York, NY: Cambridge University Press.
Washburn, M. F. (1923). A questionary study of certain national differences in emotional traits. *Journal of Comparative Psychology, 3*(6), 413–430.
Watson, J. B. (1914). *Behavior: An introduction to comparative psychology.* New York, NY: H. Holt.
Watson, J. B. (1919). *Psychology: From the standpoint of a behaviorist.* Philadelphia, PA: Lippincott.
Wiggam, A. E. (1923). *The new decalogue of science.* Indianapolis, IN: Bobbs-Merrill.
Yakushko, O. (2018). *Modern-day xenophobia: Critical historical and theoretical perspectives on the roots of anti-immigrant prejudice.* New York, NY: Springer.
Yakushko, O. (2019). Eugenics and its evolution in history of western psychology: A critical archival review. *Psychotherapy and Politics International* [online].
Yerkes, R. M. (1907). *The dancing mouse: A study in animal behavior.* New York, NY: Macmillan.
Yerkes, R. M. (Ed.). (1920). *The new world of science: Its development during the war.* New York, NY: Century Company.
Yerkes, R. M. (1923). Eugenic bearing of measurements of intelligence. *The Eugenics Review, 14*(4), 225–229.
Young, P. C. (1929). Intelligence and suggestibility in whites and negroes. *Journal of Comparative Psychology, 9*(5), 339–359. https://doi.org/10.1037/h0075409.

CHAPTER 5

From the Science of Human Betterment to the Science of Behavioral Control

One of the most insidious influences of scientific Pollyannaism can be found in efforts to control individual and social lives. Common to these efforts is the insistence that eugenic scientific assumptions and practices must be true because they are empirically validated and based on research by scientists. Their persistent emphasis was on measuring supposed human fitness as well as on engineering or shaping people to be happy, self-controlled, and efficient in order to create cheerful and successful (i.e., globally dominant) societies. Emotional states considered anything other than positive were not only disparaged, but proclaimed to be dangerous for evolution. Thus, Western psychologists, influenced by eugenics, developed theories of behavior and therapy that focused on emotional control and on discrediting or suppressing non-positive emotional states. Behaviorism, the most "American" form of Western psychology, reflected these values.

The Eugenic Roots of American Behaviorism

As noted above, John B. Watson, the founder of behaviorism, whose work remains foundational to its practices and assumptions, was a leader in multiple eugenic organizations and openly used eugenic values in his writings. The *Eugenical News* (1916–1922) celebrated the development of a new American eugenic scholarly organization by highlighting its prestigious roster of members:

O. Yakushko, *Scientific Pollyannaism*,
https://doi.org/10.1007/978-3-030-15982-5_5

> new active members of Eugenics Research Association… C. C. Brigham, Psychological Laboratory, Princeton, N. J., G. Stanley Hall, Clark University, C. E. Seashore, State University of Iowa, Lewis, M. Terman, Stanford University, Calif., John B. Watson, Johns Hopkins Hospital. (p. 53)

John B. Watson, together with Charles Davenport and Robert Yerkes, chaired this organization's key committee on testing the heredity of mental traits (*Eugenical News*, 1916–1922). Watson's open commitment to eugenics is visible in his work with the Mental (Sexual) Hygiene committee, headed by a leading American eugenicist, one time president of the American Eugenic Society and Yale university professor Irving Fisher. Together with another American psychologist and one-time president of the American Psychological Association K. Lashley, Watson carried out numerous studies designed to promote eugenic sexual re-education films with titles such as *Fit to Win* (Watson & Lashley, 1920).

Eugenicists from Galton (1869) onwards stressed the vital importance of developing the hereditary characteristics of fit individuals (i.e., positive eugenic agenda). For example, Gueyer (1916), in his book *Being Well Born*, gave the following rationale for making the shaping of early behavior as a key goal of eugenics:

> For if the education which we give our children of to-day, or the desirable moral conduct which we inculcate does not affect the offspring of succeeding generations through inheritance, then the actual progress of the race is much slower than is commonly supposed, and the advance of modern over ancient times lies more in an improvement in extraneous conditions through invention and the accumulation and rendering accessible of knowledge, than in an actual innate individual superiority. And when we face the issue squarely we have to admit that there is no more indication of the inheritance of parentally acquired characters as regards customs, knowledge, habits and moral traditions than there is of physical features. In fact, if such acquirements were inherited then we should soon have a race which would naturally, spontaneously as it were, do what its ancestors did with effort. Yet we do not find the children in our schools reading, doing sums and developing proper social relations without ceaseless prompting and urging on the part of the teacher. Indeed I can testify that this necessity carries over even into a university. *In short, the habits and standards of each generation have to be instilled into the succeeding generation.* (pp. 155–156)

Shaping children's supposed inherited characteristics, especially in regard to their emotional or moral lives, became the primary focus of American psychological theory of behaviorism. This chapter draws parallels between Watson's eugenic-influenced assumptions and commitments to Darwinism with his acontextual view of human functioning, his scientific experiments (especially on infants and young children), and his use of his standing as a scientist to shame and shape the American public. I later trace Watson's work to contemporary iteration of scientific Pollyannaism in psychology, found in cognitive-behavioral "positive psychology."

Watson's (1914, 1919, 1928) writings routinely promoted the superiority of particular inborn behavioral capacities (e.g., lack of emotional reactions such as crying in children). He offered behavioral manipulations of human characteristics toward an ideal eugenic functioning, marked by optimism, efficiency, and control over sexual impulses. In his writings, Watson frequently refers to eugenic-based theories and authors. He also frequently justified behaviorism within Darwinist hereditarian views (i.e., Watson needed to claim space for behavioral interventions in the otherwise biologically determinist scholarly environment) and routinely substantiates his own theories and ideas by connecting them with openly eugenic scholarship, including studies by Charles Davenport, Robert Yerkes, and many others (see prior chapter on eugenics).

However, Watson's behaviorism may have avoided being more directly associated with eugenics because Watson was dismissed from academia in mid-1920s for his research activities (description of which is found below). Following a scandal Watson was dropped from membership in all scholarly organizations (Buckley, 1989), including the eugenic ones (i.e., Watson's name was taken off eugenic organizational leadership rosters). He lost his prestigious post at Johns Hopkins, his editorial leadership positions in scientific journals, his research privileges at hospitals, and access to funding (Buckley, 1989). In reaction to his fall from grace, subsequent editions of Watson's (1930) behaviorism textbooks and other writings offer more critical views of all dominant perspectives in American psychology (e.g., he adamantly attacked "moral psychology" tradition of William James and Stanley G. Hall). Besides confronting these other dominant views, Watson (1930) appears to claim that old-fashioned, purely hereditarian perspectives in psychology later "grew up" or evolved, although he remained openly dedicated to eugenic-based based values and practices. Notably, Watson remained adamantly committed to using his behaviorist theories and methods to achieve utopian promises of socially engineering happy and efficient people.

Watson's Darwinism and the Sciences of Emotional Control

In his initial book on behaviorism entitled *Behavior: An Introduction to Comparative Psychology*, Watson (1914) outlined numerous ways that the field of psychology, in order to become a genuinely scientific endeavor, must move away from the study of subjectively experienced introspection or consciousness toward promises of the biological sciences, including eugenics. In a section on the *Hereditary Character of Certain Instinctive Acts and Traits*, Watson specifically praised eugenic research by Yerkes (see previous chapter) for having "*made the only contribution bearing directly upon the heredity of instinctive acts and traits. He [Yerkes] has recently tested the heritability of savageness, wildness, and timidity in certain strains of rats*" (p. 144). Watson highlighted this supposedly unquestionable proof of the heredity of "savageness, wildness, and timidity," noting that these negative emotional states among humans were also based on their inherited genetic endowments rather than the environment (p. 144). Distancing himself from other studies of "experimental evolution" (p. 148), Watson nevertheless openly embraced Darwinist hereditary and evolutionary theories, specifically research on human neurology and the brain. The brain, Watson asserted, was scientifically proven to posses hereditarily based "arcs" that influence and shape behavior: "special systems of [brain] arcs underlying instinctive activity are [hereditarily] predetermined in some way in the egg" (p. 151). Thus, after discussing differences among fowl and peas, Watson also declared:

> The important fact for our present purpose [discussing behaviorism] is that when the progeny of any cross are interbred among themselves, they produce in their progeny not only their own type, but also that of both their parents, and in quite definite proportions. *The characters do not lose their identity in hybrids but reappear unchanged in later generations and appear, moreover, in definite proportions which may be determined empirically.* (p. 153)

Discussing the works of Charles Darwin, Charles Davenport, and Robert Yerkes, Watson further promoted their belief that human differences, including human behavioral variances, are based on hereditarily acquired biological differences. Watson, like other eugenicists, emphasized that inborn characteristics in eugenically fit children must be shaped and managed during early childhood. It is in this space of early childhood adaptation, where instincts could be adapted, that Watson carved out the space for his behaviorist ideas.

Thus, after struggling with the dominant view that human difference is essentially inherited and driven exclusively by the Darwinist principle of survival of the fittest, Watson positioned behaviorism within the "habit formation" supported by hereditary endowments but still malleable enough to be shaped by behaviorist techniques. Moreover, after hundreds of pages of scientific argumentation, Watson claimed that his behavioral views fit well with dominant eugenic perspectives of human betterment and are justifiable by their evolutionary results: "habit [formation or behavior modification] reveals itself as being a positive factor in evolution" (p. 169).

In addition, Watson openly dismissed non-Darwinist evolutionary theories, especially Lamarckian ones, because they focused on the role of the environment in any evolutionary change. While Watson proclaimed Lamarck's ideas as unscientific, he praised the theory of germo-plasms central to all eugenic writings:

> The followers of Lamarck carried this theory to still further extremes, assuming that all characters acquired by the individual as the result of the action of environment were inherited... As soon as an attempt was made to verify the theory by experimental evidence, the strongest possible objection to it appeared the theory did not seem to work the tails might be cut from mice for many generations without reducing the size of the tails of the progeny; the strong arm of the blacksmith was not transmitted to his son. Then came Weismann's theory of the continuity of the germ-plasm which showed the difficulties in the way of the transmission of bodily characters to the germ cells. Lamarck's theory was practically dropped for many years. (p. 179)

Social Darwinism and eugenics were foundational to Watson's behaviorism. In subsequent writings, Watson begins to emphasize the role of behaviorism in eugenic visions of betterment for "civilized" groups.

In one of his other foundational books on psychology, *Psychology from the Standpoint of Behaviorism*, Watson (1919) promoted his psychological strategies as essential for the "civilized nations," who supposedly required help "*to teach us how to dwell together wisely and happily*" (p. vii). He attacked the early American psychology of the "interepectionists," who apparently sought to "halt a strong emotion in its course and describe where the 'sensation' are localized and determine what 'imagery' is present and whether the whole experience is 'pleasant' or 'painful,' etc." (p. viii). In contrast, Watson proposed psychology that must be based on "laboratory" studies and would be thus "objective" (p. viii), with the primary goal of "*the prediction and control of human action*" (p. ix). This statement is a direct echo of Yerkes (1923) in relation to centrality of eugenics to American psychology.

Watson (1919) also re-published Darwin's works on emotions in animals and humans, especially focusing his behaviorist work on the development of control over the supposedly problematic human emotions identified by Darwin as primitive: fear, anger, and lust. In Watson's view, these negative emotional states made people vulnerable to "feeble-mindedness," a key term denoting their genetic unfitness and a terrifying prospect, considering contemporary eugenic writings on feeble-mindedness (e.g., Goddard, 1911, 1917; Terman, 1916).

Biological heredity, including heredity of emotional states, played a central role in the development of behaviorism. According to Watson (1919), "an emotion is an hereditary 'pattern-reaction' involving profound changes of the bodily mechanisms as a hold, but particularly visceral and glandular systems" (p. 195). Watson repeatedly emphasized that the study of human experiences, especially human emotions, required empirical knowledge primarily drawn from "experimental zoology," "experimental biology," "neurology," and "animal behavior" (p. 196). Watson claimed that human emotional states were merely animal instincts, which could then be conditioned during early childhood and which became entrenched in adults as particular negative behavioral states: "so-called emotional reactions… [can be experimentally studied as] certain unconditioned stimuli arousing total bodily reactions called 'fear', 'rage', 'love', etc., can be substituted for just as in the simple reflex field" (Watson, 1935, p. 34):

> I feel reasonably sure that there are three different forms of emotional response that can be called out at birth by three sets of stimuli. Don't misunderstand me if I call these responses "fear," "rage" and "love."

> *Let me hasten to assure you that while I use the words fear, rage and love, I want you to strip them of all their old connotations. Please look upon the reactions we designate by them just as you look upon breathing, heart beat, grasping and other unlearned [hereditary] responses.* (p. 121)

Watson (1919, 1928, 1935) routinely discussed these “emotions” as entirely physiological states (adrenaline), visceral states (bodily reactions), and, of course, as animal instincts. These rhetorical methods for denying the reality of emotional states–by reducing them through new empirical linguistic strategies and theories to “reactions,” “reflexes” and so on–were a central concern of eugenic and Darwinist-fueled scientists. These negative emotions were claimed to have evolutionary dysgenic impact on human life. Thus, Watson (1935) specifically promoted behaviorism as a scientific psychological method designed to (finally) control all negative emotional states: “*The importance of early conditionings in building up bodily attitudes, especially on the emotional side, is almost undreamed of*” (p. 35).

Despite the changes in his academic status and, seemingly, some of his commitments to eugenics, Watson continued to discuss human emotional states in this same vein throughout his career. Consider the following passage from Watson’s (1935) revised key textbook, *Behaviorism*, which describes a human reaction of grief alongside quotes from his fellow psychologists:

> The neck is bent, the head hangs (‘bowed down’ with grief), the relaxation of the cheek- and jaw- muscles makes the face look long and narrow, the jaw may even hang open. The eyes appear large, as is always the case where the orbicularis muscle is paralyzed, but they may often be partly covered by the upper lid which droops in consequence of the laming of its own levator. “But this weakness of the entire voluntary motor apparatus (the so-called apparatus of ‘animal’ life) is only one side of the physiology of grief. Another side, hardly less important, and in its consequences perhaps even more so, belongs to another subdivision of the motor apparatus, namely, the involuntary or ‘organic’ muscles, especially those which are found in the walls of the blood-vessels, and the use of which is, by contracting, to diminish the latter’s calibre. These muscles and their nerves, forming together the ‘vaso-motor apparatus,’ act in grief contrarily to the voluntary motor apparatus. Instead of being paralyzed, like the latter, the vascular muscles arc more strongly contracted than usual, so that the tissues and organs of the body become anaemic. The immediate consequence of this bloodlessness is pallor and shrunkenness, and the pale color

> and collapsed features are the peculiarities which, in connection with the relaxation of the visage, give to the victim of grief his characteristic physiognomy, and often give an impression of emaciation which ensues too rapidly to be possibly due to real disturbance of nutrition, or waste uncompensated by repair. (p. 110)

Watson (1935) further continued to rely on the racial and evolutionary views of emotions common to eugenicists. In the revised *Behaviorism*, a chapter entitled *The Behaviorist's Approach to the Problem of Emotion* discussed optimal and non-optimal emotional states as related to individuals' race, age, intelligence level, and so forth:

> The negro down South whines and trembles at the darkness which comes with a total eclipse of the sun, often falling on his knees and crying out, begging the Deity to forgive him for his sins. These same negroes will not pass through graveyards at night. They cringe and shrink when charms and relics are shown. They will not burn wood which has been struck by lightning. In rural communities adults and children collect around the home as soon as dusk begins to fall. They often rationalize it by saying that they will get the "misery" from the night air. *Situations of the most ordinary kinds judged from our more sophisticated standpoint arouse the strongest kinds of emotional reactions in them.* (p. 113).

Building on eugenic attitudes, Watson's further linked "negative" emotional states such as "anger" and "temper" to such supposedly problematic social and cultural evils as murder, sexual fetishes, homosexuality, chemical dependency and sexual addictions (pp. 114–115). According to Watson, the behaviorist first and foremost "has to study emotional behavior genetically" (p. 116) but then has to recognize that many of these emotions are conditioned early and in their particular expression by parents, and therefore, could be shaped by behaviorist strategies toward optimal evolutionary fitness.

Scientific Pollyannaism and the Experiments on Infants and Young Children

In order to study these genetic, hereditary, and instinctive emotional tendencies, Watson (1935) described numerous ways that the "behaviorist" conducts "testing" on young children:

> *In order to get a picture of his emotional behavior, we have to test separation from mother. We have to test him with different and uncustomary foods, with strange people to feed him, with strange nurses to be with him, clothe him and put him to bed. We must rob him of his toy things he is playing with. We must let a bigger boy or girl bully him, must put him in high places, on ledges (making injury impossible he ever), on the backs of ponies or dogs.* (pp. 116–117)

Notably, Watson's (1935) claimed that experiments on infants and young children were necessary to locate the differences between supposed hereditary (i.e., genetic) and learned (i.e., behaviorally conditioned) emotional reactions (i.e., fear, anger, love). He also suggested that his behaviorist experiments offered ways to manipulate or control inherited negative emotional states while decreasing the amount of behaviorally conditioned expressions of these negative emotions (e.g., parental coddling leading to tantrums). Watson, whose experiments with human beings were carried out almost exclusively on infants and young children, routinely included such methods as loud banging noises, the exposure of children to fire or strange animals, severely constraining infants' movements, and so on. Among the more disturbing descriptions on these experiments in Watson's numerous books and articles are routine reports of direct and indirect "observations" and "experiments" in relation to "love," which Watson defined interchangeably as dependence, affection, and lust. In his *Behaviorism*, Watson (1935) described the following assumptions in relation to study of "love" in infants:

> Love: The study of this emotion in the infant is beset with a great many difficulties on the conventional side. Our observations consequently have been incidental rather than directly experimental. The stimulus to love responses apparently is stroking of the skin, tickling, gentle rocking, patting. The responses are especially easy to bring out by the stimulation of what, for lack of a better term, we may call the erogenous zones, such as the nipples, the lips and the sex organs. (p. 124)

These same descriptions of experiments on behaviorist manipulations of various supposedly hereditary responses in infants are described in Watson's (1919) *Psychology from the Standpoint of Behaviorism.* His studies on infants' "fear" included such strategies as "to suddenly remove from the infant all means of support," "loud sounds," "a sudden push or a slight shake" just as "infant is just falling asleep," and so on (pp. 199–200). In turn, infant's "rage" was studied through such methods as "hampering of the infant's' movements" in such a way that leads to infant "crying" and "screaming" to such a degree as to "often result in a disturbance so great that the experiment had to be discontinued for a time" (pp. 200–201). Lastly, experiments on "love" or sexual lust among infant research subjects by Watson involved "the original situation which calls out the observable love responses seems to be the stroking or manipulation of some erogenous zone, tickling, shaking, gentle rocking, patting, and turning upon the stomach across the attendant's knee" (p. 201).

Watson's focus on negative emotional or behavioral states and techniques for controlling or even eliminating them is central to behaviorism. In Watson's (1935) chapter on psychological development, *The Birth Equipment of the Human Being*, Watson discusses his scientific and experimental observations of "unlearned equipment," that is, humans' hereditary reactions, as opposed to their subsequent development and control. Crying, which Watson notes is one of the earliest human reactions, is described by him as a method by which infants and children supposedly manipulate the adults: "Crying as such very shortly becomes conditioned. The child quickly learns that it can control the responses of nurse, parents and attendants by the cry, and *uses it as a weapon ever thereafter*" (p. 477).

Moreover, as noted above, Watson, who together with another psychology leader Karl Lashley dedicated themselves also to the study of eugenic sexual hygiene films with titles such as *Fit to Win* (Watson & Lashley, 1920), believed that a lack of control over "love" or the need for affection could lead to sexually transmitted disorders, unfit relationships, and other evolutionary negative outcomes. Anger and fear in male children was also thought to lead, in adulthood, to such evils as refusing to be efficient workers or failing to become optimal military personnel.

The Myths and the Horrors of "Little Albert" Experiments

As we have seen, Watson's (1914, 1919, 1920, 1928) primary work focused on socially engineering human beings during their infancy and childhood. His infamous Little Albert experiments emerged as the foundational myth of behaviorism, despite the fact that the experiments were carried out on the neurologically compromised child of a wet nurse who worked under Watson's authority at a hospital, or the fact that "little Albert," who was terrorized in these experiments, was pulled out of the studies by his mother and was never "unconditioned" (Beck, Levinson, & Irons, 2009; Fridlund, Beck, Goldie, & Irons, 2012; Harris, 2011). Watson's works are filled with what could be described as sadistic experiments on infants and young children, many of whom Watson acknowledges to be orphans or children who were institutionalized under his care at a children's hospital. The Little Albert experiments were no exception. Watson conducted these experiments around the year 1920, alongside his student and soon-to-be wife R. Rayner, and continued to boast of them as triumphs of behaviorism in his publications throughout his career. In his revised *Behaviorism*, Watson (1935) recollected:

> we finally decided to experiment upon the possibility of building up fears in the infant and then later to study practical methods for removing them. We chose as our first subject Albert B, an infant weighing twenty-one pounds, at *eleven months of age*. Albert was the son of one of the wet nurses in the Harriet Lane Hospital. He had lived his whole life in the hospital. He *was a wonderfully "good" baby*. In all the months we worked with him we *never saw him cry until after our experiments were made!* (p. 128)

In the original publications about the study Watson and Rayner (1920) described why they selected this little boy as their Little Albert to be experimented on:

> He was on the whole *stolid and unemotional*. His stability was one of the principal reasons for using him as a subject in this test. We felt that we could do him relatively little harm by carrying out such experiments as those outlined below. (p. 1)

Moreover, they noted that "*No one had ever seen him [little Albert] in a state of fear and rage. The infant practically never cried*" (p. 2). In their description, Watson and Rayner detailed their experiments on the little boy, such as scaring him with loud banging noises, which were paired with presenting the little boy with toys. According to Watson and Rayner's own publications, these efforts initially made the little boy merely startled, although he was then described by them as whimpering and, later, as crying uncontrollably. According to historians, little boy's mother removed him from the studies before they could be completed, so it cannot be true that these experiments prove the effectiveness of behaviorist methods from "improving" emotional responses, as Watson and Rayner (1920) themselves confess: "unfortunately Albert was taken from the hospital the day the above tests [to condition fear] were made. Hence the opportunity of building up an experimental technique by means of which we could remove the conditioned emotional responses was denied us" (p. 15). Nevertheless, not only are the stunning abusive methods rarely questioned, but the mythologized implications of this study in the field remain broadly undisputed (Harris, 2011).

Albert's actual name was, most likely, Douglas Meritte, a neurologically compromised and visually impaired boy who died within decade of these experiments (Fridlund et al., 2012; Harris, 2011). Had Watson and Rayner (1920) been able to continue, his short life would have included the following, described here by the founder of behaviorism and his partner:

> We *should have tried out several methods*, some of which we may mention. (I) *Constantly confronting the child* with those stimuli which called out the responses in the hopes that habituation would come in corresponding *to "fatigue" of reflex* when differential reactions are to beset up. (2) By trying to "recondition" by showing objects calling out fear responses (visual) and *simultaneously stimulating the erogenous zones (tactual). We should try first the lips, then the nipples and as a final resort the sex organs.* (p. 16)

The Parenting Utopias and the "Dangers of Too Much Mother Love"

Among the main ideas widely propagated by Watson was that behaviorism as a parenting tool might solve all societal ills was, a belief which he spread not only in both books and more ephemeral forms of print media (Buckley, 1989). Thus, one of Watson's most lasting contributions to American culture was his popularization of behaviorism as scientific form of parenting advise. Throughout his career, Watson was involved in a number of efforts to influence parents, as in his work on a co-authored volume (Jennings, Watson, Meyer, & Thomas, 1917) entitled *Suggestions of Modern Science Concerning Education*. In this volume, Watson and colleagues argued that behaviorism and psychological strategies were needed because

> *Superior parents have no guarantee that their children will be [evolutionary] superior.* No one can predict the qualities that will arise from their combination, for millions of possibilities are equally open. Superior parents must watch and help their children with the same anxious care that others must use. *Of course we know that gifted parents are much more likely to produce gifted children, inferior parents inferior children.* (p. 15)

Watson and his scientific colleagues especially warn about the problematic role of intense negative emotions:

> All the details of our lives are examples of this, and particularly in childhood are the examples striking. *When the organism is taken up with intense emotion, particularly painful emotion, digestion stops, excretion stops, growth stops; respiration almost stops; thought of everything else stops; almost everything stops save that which ministers to the affair with which this emotion is connected.* (p. 25)

In this 1917 parenting manual they further insisted that scientific studies on both physiology and psychology produced empirical truths, which verified that positive emotions were always optimal whereas so-called negative emotions were detrimental to all aspects of human life:

> One of the most striking things in the development of modern physiology is its gradual recognition of the *great value of those pleasurable emotional states which may be classified together under the abused word "joy," and of the harmfulness of the opposite emotional states anxiety, sorrow, worry, fear, pain, and the like. The condition of happiness, of "joy," is that in which development is unhindered, and flourishing; in which the functions are proceeding harmoniously; while worry, fear, unhappiness, are the marks of the reverse condition of affairs; something is blocked and is going wrong.* (pp. 43–44)

Watson (1928) continued this scientific Pollyannaist advise in his most successful parenting book, entitled the *Psychological Care of Infant and Child*, which sold in the millions due to its scientific and therefore indisputable authority. Watson's book on behaviorist parenting not only became one of the most popular parenting manuals in the U.S., but continued to be promoted as empirically grounded and scientific until recently (Buckley, 1989). It is one of the strongest testaments to both the power of scientific Pollyannism, and the damage is has wrought.

In the introduction to *Psychological Care of Infant and Child*, Watson encourages parents to "produce" a child "who finally enters manhood so bulwarked with stable work and emotional habits that no adversity can quite overwhelm him" (p. 10). The book was "*dedicated to the first mother who brings up a happy child*" (dedication). Watson's celebrated parenting manual claimed to be based entirely on "scientific material" (acknowledgments). The book is filled with scholarly references and pictures of the brain and bodily organs, with empirical studies on animals and infants, and with numerous allusions to undisputed scientific authority of behaviorism and Watson himself.

Notably, this empirical parenting advice was claimed to be based on studies of traditional American families of the middle- to upper-classes. Watson's guidelines required the presence of stay-at-home mothers in addition to full-time paid "nurses" or caregivers. Because Watson insisted that close proximity to other children could result in over-dependency on other human beings as well as same-sex behavior, Watson maintained that each child must be housed, alone, in her or his own room. Watson's behavioral schedules included specific dietary recommendations closely resembling contemporary eugenicist regimens, which claimed that Nordic and Anglo-Saxon diets were superior to all others (Bashford & Levine, 2010; Codgell, 2010). Eugenic assumptions about race, gender, sexuality, social class and ethnicity, pervade Watson's supposedly neutral and objective manual.

Parents, specifically mothers, were warned that "*once a child's character has been spoiled by bad handling which can be done in a few days, who can say that the damage is ever repaired*" (p. 3). Watson further claimed that behavioral psychological advise was even more important that physiological childcare suggestions. He promised that his scientific advice was guaranteed to result in "*finer and happier children*," and was intended for "*parents [who] want their children to be happy, efficient and well adjusted to life*" rather than find themselves with a "*weakling, a petted, spoiled, sullen, shy youngster who would grow up a liar and a thief*" (pp. 5–6).

As noted above, by this time in his career (late 1920s), Watson had been dismissed from academia by his fellow eugenic psychologists (including from his Johns Hopkins post), all professional organizations, journal editorial boards, and the profession, and seemed to be questioning explanations of human behaviors which were exclusively heredity and genetics-first. However, eugenic values are clearly in evidence throughout his parenting manual, as for example when Watson refers to the Malthusian and Darwinian-Galtonian "overpopulation" problem and parrots the eugenic "slogan": "no more babies but better brought up babies" (p. 9). Watson further allies himself with eugenicists, as well as the middle- and upper-class American families, with openly eugenic proclamations, such as "*there are too many people in the world right now—too many people with crippled personalities—tied up with such a load of infantile carry-overs (due to faulty brining up) that they have no chance for happy lives*" (p. 9). In fact, it is the parents, according to Watson, who can improve on what an infant hereditarily brings with him or her, so that the child will "*grow into a happy person, wholesome and good natured, [or] whether he is to be a whining, complaining neurotic, an anger driven, vindictive, overbearing slave driver, or one whose every move in life is definitely controlled by fear*" (p. 45).

Watson's greatest emphasis in this book was on the "*the dangers of too much mother love*" (p. 69). Watson asserted that mothers' affection for their children was "*an instrument which can inflict a never healing wound, a wound which may make infancy unhappy, adolescence a nightmare, an instrument which may wreck our adult son or daughter's vocational future an their chances for marital happiness*" (p. 87). As in other eugenic writings, women carry the primary burden of being mothers of the race, on whose shoulders rested the evolutionary well-being of both their progeny and society at large.

Consistent with my assertions in regard to scientific Pollyannaism, all negative states in children's lives were presented by Watson as malicious and problematic. The methods employed by Watson to remove these negative emotional states should appear inhumane and shocking to a reader with any knowledge of childhood development. For example, Watson described a four-year girl who supposedly had "*temper tantrums*," refusing to eat food during meals she was offered. Watson boasted of his experiment on this child, which involved repeatedly dismissing caregivers close to the girl, and seeing to it "*that the mother should take a six-week's vacation*," leaving the child behind (p. 110). After this extensive Watsonian "time-out," Watson claimed that "a complete and speedy cure resulted" in that the little girl no longer displayed any negative reactions (p. 110).

Among other key advice provided in the book encouraged parents to schedule their children's lives from rising to sleeping, including bathroom breaks. Following the above experiment, Watson encouraged parents to remove themselves from children in any case of "tantrums" and recommended punishing children for undesirable behaviors with such methods as rapping rulers on their fingers. Watson insisted on minimizing any physical affection with the child (e.g., hugging or holding of children was prohibited) and forbade expressing open affection for the child, encouraging their early and complete independence from parents. Watson recommended quickly hiring and firing different nurses for children so that children never attached to any specific caregiver, and thus became dependent on that person or anyone else. According to Watson's parenting manual,

> *Let your behavior always be objective* and kindly firm. *Never hug and kiss them [children], never let them sit in your lap.* If you must, kiss them once on the forehead when they say good night. Shake hands with them in the morning. Give them a pat on the head if they have made an extraordinarily good job of a difficult task. (pp. 81–82)

Scientific Sadistic Pollyannaism: The Survivor Stories

Examples of Watson's sadistic experiments on infants and children are found throughout this book. After he was dismissed for his academic and laboratory posts, he seems to have made his own children, William and James, (i.e., "Billy" and "Jimmy," sons from his second marriage to Rayner), his primary text subjects, describing them throughout his work as behaviorist success stories. In one of his parenting book, Watson (1928) describes performing numerous experiments on his sons until one of them "*screams until he is black in the face*" (p. 88). He goes on to share his fantasies of various studies he wishes he could carry out on his sons and other children:

> *if now we could charge Billy's toys with electricity* so that he could play with them with impunity but so arrange affairs that Jimmy would get shocked with the current whenever he reached for Billy's toys, then Jimmy would soon learn to keep his hands off Billy's toys. But in real nursery life toys cannot be charged with electricity. (p. 89)

The violence—and long-term consequences—of Watson's methods are thus most clearly documented in the histories of his children. As noted earlier, Watson routinely experimented on his sons Billy and Jimmy, also applying his methods to the children of his first marriage, Polly and Johnny. Watson claimed publicly and often that his children were superlatively well-adjusted and emotionally healthy children (Buckley, 1989). In contrast, his children and even grandchildren later claimed that they were incredibly damaged by Watson's behaviorist parenting.

According to multiple biographies and interviews, Polly Watson, Watson's oldest daughter, grew up to a life of alcoholism and was regularly hospitalized for attempted suicides (Buckley, 1989; Hartley & Commire, 1990; Walker, 1990). Watson's second son, John, died of bleeding ulcers, which he attributed to the fact that his father's strict feeding schedule mandated a daily glass of orange juice for all infants and children over six months of age (Buckey, 1989). William Watson, the third son, attempted to distance himself as much as he could from his father by studying psychoanalysis (which Watson openly derided as the "voodooism") and by publishing scathing personal letters about his father's abusive experiments in *Life Magazine* (Buckley, 1989; Hannush, 1987; Walker, 1990). Billy (William), who was most likely the recipient of Watson's most intense experiments after Watson's disgraceful removal from academia, committed suicide in his 30s (Buckley, 1989; Hannush, 1987). It seems likely, based on Watson's open discussion of his experiments, that Billy was the recipient of not only stunning amount of emotional deprivation but also early sexual abuse by his own parents. Profoundly age-inappropriate sexual discussions were apparently commonplace in the Watson household, including adults discussing their sexual escapades in front of their young children or insisting that William and James must find "mistresses" by age ten (video interview with James Watson by Walker, 1990 in APA archives; Hartley & Commire, 1990).

Watson's youngest son, James, became among the most vocal critics of his father's abusive experiments and treatments. In public interviews, James described how his father's methods contributed to his and his siblings' many emotional, physical, and relational struggles (e.g., video interview with James Watson by Walker, 1990 in APA archives). James admitted coming very close to taking his own life, eventually entering into a program of treatment involving extensive psychoanalysis: appointments four times a week for over six years. James claimed that being in psychoanalysis not only saved his life, but specifically helped him recover from his father's behaviorism (interview with Walker, 1990). James remained very troubled by the impact of his father's behaviorism on others. In his 1990s interview, he said:

> I am concerned that so many lives may have been affected during his [John B. Watson's] teaching days and during his advocacy of behaviorism that may have had *very adverse affect on people from emotional point of view*... And it saddened me to think that in his zeal and in his interest in pushing the behavioristic philosophy as a child raising methodology that so many people could have been affected and probably were affected by it. *That it is a convenient way to raise kids but has a hell of a lot of devastating effects as an adult.*

Watson's granddaughter, the Hollywood actress and mental health advocate Mariette Hartley, daughter of Watson's oldest child Polly, was another victim of Watson's behaviorism. In her national bestseller *Breaking the Silence*, Hartley (written with Commire, 1990) decried her grandfather's "scientific" method, "Watson Master Plan" as a "debilitating inheritance" (p. 18). She recalled an obsessive emphasis on emotional self-control, on cleanliness, and on instilling guilt, supposedly designed to re-conditioning her undesirable emotions or behaviors. Hartley wrote that she grew up feeling "*very ashamed of big feelings*," which she believed led to her struggles with depression and suicide as well as her incapacity to use her anger to set boundaries in relationships, which exposed her to interpersonal violence (p. 117).

Among other details scrubbed from history to preserve behaviorism's reputation for scientific neutrality and efficacy is the fact is that Watson himself was never able to re-condition his own problematic behaviors: throughout his life he remained an alcoholic, terrified of the dark (i.e., he slept with bright lights on), obsessively clean and organized, fixated on documenting his own and his children's bowel movements, and phobic about driving cars and flying on airplanes (Buckley, 1989; Hartley & Commire, 1990; Walker, 1990).

Keeping the dirty secrets of Pollyannist sciences and scientists maintains the veneer that scientific Pollyannaism is a valid approach to understanding human experiences and to helping individuals supposedly live happy lives. As I detail in the following section on contemporary positive psychology, this pattern of evasiveness continues on today. Recovering this history is vital because the larger culture, like the discipline of psychology, seems to have forgotten the suffering perpetrated by empirical behaviorist methods in the name of socially engineering happy productive people. Such forgetting (or intentional sanitizing) of scientific Pollyannaism's history in American psychology, has allows it to develop new iterations, such as the contemporary Western positive psychology movement. Positive psychology, as the next chapter shows, is a direct descendent of behaviorism and another effort to establish the sciences of enforced happiness.

References

Bashford, A., & Levine, P. (Eds.). (2010). *The Oxford handbook of the history of eugenics*. New York: Oxford University Press.

Beck, H. P., Levinson, S., & Irons, G. (2009). Finding Little Albert: A journey to John B. Watson's infant laboratory. *American Psychologist, 64*(7), 605–614.

Buckley, K. W. (1989). *Mechanical man: John Broadus Watson and the beginnings of behaviorism*. New York: Guilford Press.

Cogdell, C. (2010). *Eugenic design: Streamlining America in the 1930s*. Philadelphia: University of Pennsylvania Press.

Eugenical News. (1916–1922). Monthly publication of the Eugenics Record Office, Cold Springs, NY. Retrieved on February 22, 2018 at https://babel.hathitrust.org/cgi/pt?id=coo.31924063788834.

Fridlund, A. J., Beck, H. P., Goldie, W. D., & Irons, G. (2012). Little Albert: A neurologically impaired child. *History of Psychology, 15*(4), 302–327.

Galton, F. (1869). *Hereditary genius: An inquiry into its laws and consequences*. New York, NY: Macmillan.

Goddard, H. H. (1911). The elimination of feeble-mindedness. *The Annals of the American Academy of Political and Social Science, 37*(2), 261–272.

Goddard, H. H. (1917). Mental tests and the immigrant. *Journal of Delinquency, 2*, 243–277.

Guyer, M. F. (1916). *Being well-born: An introduction to eugenics*. New York, NY: Bobbs-Merrill Company.

Hannush, M. J. (1987). John B. Watson remembered: An interview with James B. Watson. *Journal of the History of the Behavioral Sciences, 23*(2), 137–152.

Harris, B. (2011). Letting go of Little Albert: Disciplinary memory, history, and the uses of myth. *Journal of the History of the Behavioral Sciences, 47*(1), 1–17.

Hartley, M., & Commire, A. (1990). *Breaking the silence*. New York, NY: GP Putnam's Sons.

Jennings, H. S., Watson, J. B., Meyer, A., & Thomas, W. I. (1917). *Suggestions of modern science concerning education*. New York: Macmillan.

Terman, L. M. (1916). *The measurement of intelligence*. New York: Houghton Mifflin.

Walker, E. (1990). *Interview with James Watson*. Video recording retrieved from American Psychological Association Archives, Akron, OH.

Watson, J. B. (1914). *Behavior: An introduction to comparative psychology*. New York, NY: H. Holt.
Watson, J. B. (1919). *Psychology: From the standpoint of a behaviorist*. Philadelphia, PA: Lippincott.
Watson, J. B. (1928). *Psychological care of infant and child*. New York: W. W. Norton.
Watson, J. B. (1930). *Behaviorism* (Rev. ed.). New York, NY: W. W. Norton.
Watson, J. B. (1935). *Behaviorism* (Rev. ed.). New York, NY: W. W. Norton.
Watson, J. B., & Lashley, K. S. (1920). A consensus of medical opinion upon questions relating to sex education and venereal disease campaigns. *Mental Hygiene, 4*, 769–847.
Watson, J. B., & Rayner, R. (1920). Conditioned emotional reactions. *Journal of Experimental Psychology, 3*(1), 1–14. https://doi.org/10.1037/h0069608.
Yerkes, R. M. (1923). Eugenic bearing of measurements of intelligence. *The Eugenics Review, 14*(4), 225–229.

CHAPTER 6

Scientific Pollyannaism of Authentic Happiness, Learned Optimism, Flow and the Empirically Correct Positivity Ratios

The newest iteration of psychology that insists on a scientific Pollyannaism perspective of human experiences is so-called "positive" psychology. Developed in the U.S. and later exported throughout the world as a scientific and empirically valid method, positive psychology is a contemporary manifestation of the scientific Pollyannaism identified in this book. Specifically, this new movement in psychology, claiming to be exclusively empirical, data-driven, experimentally confirmed, and ideologically neutral, is another approach to psychology that minimizes or denies the role of social context in shaping human emotional experiences. Moreover, like eugenics and Watsonian behaviorism before it, positive psychology pathologizes "negative" emotional reactions, while placing the blame on the individual, and routinely shaming individuals into emotional compliance and increased behavioral self-control. Moreover, positive psychology bears many direct and indirect connections to American eugenics, and seeks to elevate its scientific by claiming that happiness is, to large extend, genetic and hereditary.

Terms and ideas created by eugenicists over 100 years ago, such a resilience or flow, are being once again re-introduced to the public by positive psychologists. According to Popenoe and Johnson's (1935) influential book on eugenics, resilience is supposedly the mark of individuals' advanced evolutionary fitness, minimizing the role of the environment or the impact of multiple traumas or access to care. For example, Popenoe and Johnson praised studies by Harvard University psychologist McDougall who drowned pregnant rats in an effort to verify that

O. Yakushko, *Scientific Pollyannaism*,
https://doi.org/10.1007/978-3-030-15982-5_6

rat's progeny either lacked or possessed inherited resilience when they too were purposefully drowned. In addition, as detailed by Lombardo (2011), the Tuskegee syphilis experiments were conducted precisely for purposes of detecting resilience to sexually-transmitted disorders by denying treatments to African American men who were infected with this disease. Popenoe and Johnson (1935) extolled efforts to deny treatments for any disease or disorder since people who survived on their own were supposed to possess more resilient genes; in contrast, those who lack such genetic endowments should be allowed to die off more quickly, without passing on their inferior genetic material to future generations. Likewise, eugenic-fueled promotion of Nordic diets by the cereal magnate Kellogg, used the term "flow" to designate particular characteristic only available to eugenically fit individuals who ate eugenically superior diets. Eugenic dieting strategies–like eating Kellogg's cereal–were said to cause the "flow" of evolutionary advanced physical, moral, emotional, and cognitive abilities (Cogdell, 2010). Neither resilience nor flow in these eugenic efforts were linked to the absence of oppression or superior access to resources: both characteristics stem solely from the individual and their genetic inheritance, in defiance of environmental obstacles.

Positive Psychology as the Reprise of Scientific Pollyannaism

Positive Psychology emerged as a distinct movement in late 1990s, drawing on many other scientific Pollyannaist efforts described earlier in this volume. However, positive psychology puts its own modern twist on this tradition by incorporating fetishized versions of Eastern religions (e.g., mindfulness), and "new age" terminology (e.g., authenticity, evolution of consciousness), and by exploiting lucrative business practices (e.g., large-scale sale of pop self-help positivity manuals). These efforts remain entwined with long-standing and problematic disciplinary practices in psychology, including tortuous experiments on laboratory animals, dubious claims to ideological neutrality, and an insistence on the universal, biological foundation of their views. Thus, although positive psychology gained its standing through the publication of numerous popular self-help books (e.g., Csikszentmihalyi, 1997; Fredrickson, 2009; Lopez, 2013; Lyubomirsky, 2008; Seligman, 2002, 2006, 2011; Seligman, Railton, Baumeister, & Sripada, 2017), its primary goal has been to legitimize itself to the public and within the academy as a form of science. According to Cabanas (2016),

> Positive psychologists, as well as self-help writers, counselors, motivational speakers, and coachers, play a prominent role within this industry of happiness by providing a multitude of happiness-based techniques for emotional and cognitive self-regulation. These techniques—ranging from those consisting in changing emotional styles, to those focused on making frequent positive self affirmations, training hope, practicing gratitude and forgiveness, developing resilience, cultivating optimism, or mastering mindfulness ...all promise individuals that they will succeed in expanding their self-governing abilities in order to increase performance, build positive and profitable relationships, reduce stress and anxiety, develop healthy habits, cope with risk and uncertainty, improve communicative abilities, rationalize everyday failures in a positive and productive manner, and so on. (pp. 471–472)

This new scientific Pollyannaism, like others before it, has so far succeeded in its goal: it has become immensely influential not just within the broader culture of happiness-seeking but in the field of psychology itself. Positive psychology has hailed itself as the "fifth force" in psychology, having been ushered officially into the discipline's top scientific journals almost immediately following a series of summits of American psychologists in the late 1990s. These were sponsored by the American Psychological Association (APA) and included APA leaders such as its CEO and its then president (Deiner, Kesebir, & Lucas, 2008; Seligman & Csikszentmihalyi, 2014; Seligman, Steen, Park, & Peterson, 2005), and other noted American psychologists from elite U.S. institutions who held leadership positions in APA.

The Exotic Resort Solutions to Re-creating Scientific Pollyannaism

According to histories positive psychologists provide about themselves, in late 1990s approximately 20 of these psychologists were invited to all-expenses-paid multi-week meetings at luxury resorts on the beach of Akumal, Mexico, funded by then-CEO of APA, R. Fowler (Sheldon, Frederickson, Rathunde, Csikszentmihalyi, & Haidt, 2000; Sheldon, Kashdan, & Steger, 2010). These meetings produced the Akumal Manifestos, which outlined methods for establishing positive psychology as a genuine psychological science (e.g., publication in top journals, gaining funding, hiring leading statisticians) and as a cultural product (e.g., selling positive psychology to the public, the educational system, and the government). A smaller group of positive psychology's leaders, together with Fowler and Seligman (then President of APA), also held meetings in the Grand Cayman islands, which produced the taxonomy of positive psychological outcomes (Cayman Taxonomy Meeting, 1999).

The rationale psychology leaders provide for what they claim is the new field or movement within psychology disparages other mental health scholarship and practices for being too negative and focusing too much on illnesses, suffering, and various human problems rather than on health, well-being, and human strengths (Deiner et al., 2008; Lopez & Gallagher, 2009; Seligman et al., 2005; Seligman & Csikszentmihalyi, 2014). Positive psychology leader Martin Seligman (2002, 2006) has attacked contemporary psychology for being influenced by theories such as psychoanalysis and Marxism because, according to Seligman, these make wrong or anti-scientific focus on human social context and seek to change "the unchangeable."

The disciplinary power of these individuals cannot be underestimated. Seligman (2002, 2006, 2011) openly describes using his position as president of the APA to promote positive psychology. As noted, R. Fowler, who funded the initial positive psychology meetings in Mexico and Caymans, was then the APA's CEO and Editor-in-Chief of *The American Psychologist*, the APA's main publication. Thus, shortly after the initial meeting at Akumal, Mexico, Seligman and Csikszentmihalyi (2000) published an article describing positive psychology as a new "fifth force," equal to and following in the footsteps of such traditions in psychology as psychoanalysis, behaviorism, humanistic psychology and multiculturalism.

Torture and the Contemporary Scientific Pollyannaism

It is worth nothing that a number of positive psychology's key tenets, including learned helplessness and the location of attributions (i.e., internal locus of control versus external one), were derived from Seligman and his colleagues' torture of animals. Seligman's (1975) book entitled *Helplessness: On Depression, Development, and Death* describes his development of the concept of learned helplessness from the torture of animals, especially dogs. Seligman's (2002, 2006, 2011) subsequent writings routinely include a defense of his torture of dogs: this work had to be done for the sake of scientific development. For example, in his book *Learned Optimism* Seligman (2006) describe experiments that resulted in what appears to be animal suicides: "*There was no way I could ethically give trauma to other human beings. This seemed to leave only experiments with animals*" (p. 21). Seligman further explained that together with his co-researchers he "put the dogs through the very process that the behaviorists say will make them super-helpless" (p. 26), which involved electric shocks, high-pitched sounds that distressed dogs and other such torturous strategies. These experiments on tortured animals, Seligman claimed, show how human beings seek to regain said self-control at all costs. He theorizes that if individuals blame their environment or others for their difficulties, they learn to become helpless.

In his initial book on learned helplessness, Seligman (1975) extends his theories to explain human social differences. Among other things, Seligman claims that "welfare system" must be abolished because it supposedly "adds to the uncontrollability" of people who receive it (p. 161). According to Seligman's theories, any social aid from the external environment "*undermines the dignity of its recipients because their actions do not produce their own source of livelihood*" (p. 161). Thus, in this book Seligman also argues that African Americans' anger at White Americans stemmed from their learned helplessness as recipients of welfare, which encouraged their supposedly external attributions (i.e., blaming racism for their circumstances rather than themselves). "Learned helplessness" and "internal attributions" theories are foundational to positive psychology as a contemporary form of scientific Pollyannaism.

Scientific justifications for the torture of animals (i.e., learned helplessness), were also used to justify the recent involvement of psychologists in the torture of human beings. Specifically, Seligman, Fowler and many other American psychologists were engaged in secret collaborations with the CIA to develop enhanced interrogation (i.e., torture) techniques applied to supposed terrorists (The Independent Report, 2015). The Independent Report (2015) was created by a legal group at the request of APA after psychologists' involvement in "enhanced interrogations" was revealed by whistleblowers. This report detailed how Seligman's work on learned helplessness was integrated by psychologists who designed torture techniques:

> In addition, Hubbard, Mitchell and other CIA psychologists [key individuals involved in development and facilitation of torture of detainees considered terrorists] met with *former APA President Martin Seligman at his home to fully understand the psychological theory of "learned helplessness,"* a theory that Mitchell and others at the CIA were clearly incorporating into the CIA interrogation program. Seligman and Matarazzo [leader of U.S. interrogation programs] also spoke at the SERE training academies where Mitchell and Jessen [psychologists directly implicated in design and delivery of torture] had been instructors, with Seligman doing so at Hubbard and Mitchell's request. (p. 44)

This report also noted Seligman's long history of claiming that science is somehow a-political and non-ideological, and that psychology's ethical code should not acknowledge social environment and social categories (e.g., race, ethnicity) in ethical decision-making. In his comments on the Ethical Code for Psychologists, Seligman complained that psychologists tend to "confound the political leanings of many of the members, with what is known scientifically" (p. 117). The report also highlighted Seligman's repeatedly denials of direct involvement with or knowledge of the practices of torture. In contrast, whistleblower-psychologists noted that many of the meetings about enhanced interrogations occurred at Seligman's private home, and that Seligman subsequently received large grants from the Department of Defense:

> Critics also allege that the University of Pennsylvania's Positive Psychology Center, founded by Seligman, received a $31 million sole source contract from DoD in 2010 *because of assistance Seligman provided to the government with its counter-terrorism efforts. Seligman said that this contract was awarded because there were no competing entities who had the same experience in training and research on the topic of positive psychology, and there was an urgent need for a program in positive psychology to help returning troops.* (p. 164)

Specifically, Seligman's (2011) *Flourish: A Visionary New Understanding of Happiness and Well-Being* and a special issue of the *American Psychologist* both included descriptions of the program for which Seligman received DoD funding, called the Comprehensive Soldier Fitness Program (Seligman & Fowler, 2011). However, while the *American Psychologist* (Seligman & Fowler, 2011) and the Independent Report (2015) both list the monetary figure granted by the military for this program at approximately $30 million U.S. dollars, the amount claimed by Seligman (2011) in *Flourish* became $130 million.

Seligman's (2002, 2006, 2011) publications are filled with boastful descriptions of his numerous grants, which supposedly demonstrate the veracity and authority of his positive psychology. However, Seligman himself admits that many of these grants were acquired from close personal connections, as, for example, a $1.5 million grant from his father-in-law, supposedly give to support the study of genocides. This grant appeared to result in a book, co-edited by Seligman, entitled *Ethnopolitical Warfare: Causes, Consequences, and Possible Solutions* (Chirot & Seligman, 2001), in the introduction to which Seligman proclaimed that since he does not study social issues, his only contribution was to introduce the volume, in which he stated:

> The only silver lining I can see in the horrors of the 20th century is that the *N* [number of genocides] is now large enough to ask scientific questions, questions of prediction and prevention and about movement from one stage to another. (p. xv)

Citing the escape of one of his close collaborators' family from the Pogroms, Seligman ends his preface to this book on ethnopolitical warfare with references to "the dawn of a peaceful era," which apparently can be brought about by psychologists "isolating the casual variables that move societies toward genocide or toward reconciliation" (p. xvi).

This Pollyannaist vision of torture and genocide was also foundational to the development of experiments on post-traumatic growth, applied to U.S. military personnel with funding received by Seligman from the Department of Defense. The Comprehensive Soldier Fitness program was based on the premise that engaging in combat or war can be psychologically fruitful; according to the creators of this program, their specific goal was "*to increase the number of soldiers who derive meaning and personal growth from their combat experiences*" (Cornum, Matthews, & Seligman, 2011, p. 6).

This program was discontinued by the Department of Defense within few years over justifiable concerns about its ethics, as well as the recognition that it was not actually based on any scholarly evidence, but merely on positive psychology's vague and general claims to empiricism, which I term in this book scientific Pollyannaism (Soldz, 2016). After the revelations of the Independent Report (2015), moreover, the APA discontinued any support for psychologists engaged in the torture of human beings, re-enforcing its own ethical standards of beneficence and care by forbidding any member of the profession to engage in such heinous acts.

This shadowy history of positive psychology does not appear in any of its many handbooks, books and journals. Instead, positive psychology continues to promote itself as a salvific and pure empirical force in psychology. Seligman's (2011) *Flourish*, which is based entirely on the now-defunct Comprehensive Soldier Fitness program, continues to be sold to the unsuspecting public.

Positive psychology historians continue to assert that their approach has been revisionary "rounding out" psychology from its unduly negative thrust, reducing or removing scholarly disagreements, and has been instrumental in "giving psychology away" by offering "new" information to "normal people" as well as attracting "more talent to psychology" through an exclusive commitment to statistical "observation and experiment" (Lopez & Gallagher, 2009, pp. 3–5). It promotes itself as a "fifth force" within psychology, equal in scope to such monumental influences as psychoanalysis, behaviorism, humanistic psychology and multiculturalism (Deiner et al., 2008; Seligman et al., 2005; Seligman & Csikszentmihalyi, 2014).

Building a New Religion from the Sciences of Happiness

Seligman, the field's principal leader and founder, began publishing and promoting books on positivity targeted towards "normal people," but also in order to create lucrative contracts with businesses, governments, the military as well as via online positive coaching services (Ehrenriech, 2009). According to Seligman's (2002, 2006) books, with titles like *The Learned Optimism* and *Authentic Happiness*, positive psychology was also the promotional development product encouraged by his editor, who believed (probably correctly) that Seligman's writings on tortured animals and people (i.e., his learned helplessness studies) were not as marketable to the general public. In his introduction to *Learned Optimism* Seligman (2006) quoted his agent Richard as saying: "I pray you'll write a book about this [positivity]. They make religion out of this stuff!" (p. iii). Seligman (2006) goes on to complain about psychology's exclusive focused on "victims" who were apparently living in the "negative" life spheres (p. xi). In contrast, he proposed a psychology for those who, like him, needed "to go from plus two to plus seven" (Seligman, 2006, p. xi).

Consistent with earlier versions of Scientific Pollyannaism, positive psychology's focus remains on demonizing negative emotional states and enforcing the requirement of positivity in order to be considered mentally healthy. Being positive emerges here as a skill that can be acquired through the techniques of positive psychology, and mental health now requires more than supposed freedom from disordered emotions (i.e., sadness, anger) but the perpetual presence of positive ones. According to Seligman (2011),

> *the skills of enjoying positive emotion ... are entirely different from the skills of not being depressed, not being anxious, and not being angry.* These dysphorias get in the way of wellbeing, but they do not make well-being impossible; nor does the absence of sadness, anxiety, and anger remotely guarantee happiness. The takeaway lesson from positive psychology is that positive mental health is not just the absence of mental illness. ... *Positive mental health is a presence: the presence of positive emotion.* (p. 182)

The promise of positive psychology, then, is both to ensure control over one's negative emotional states in order to "*unlearn pessimism*," and then to replace those emotions with positive ones, using "*skills of looking at setbacks optimistically*" (Seligman, 2006, p. 13). These definitions are exact replicas of Pollyanna's glad games (Porter, 1913), expressed in new scientific terms and backed by new empirical data.

Seligman (2006) further explained his reasons for creating positive psychology, in contrast to all other types of psychologies that focus on aiding human beings who suffer:

> Psychology now seemed half-baked to me. The half that was fully baked was devoted to suffering, victims, mental illness, and trauma. Psychology has worked steadily and with considerable success for fifty years on the pathologies that disable the good life, which make life not worth living. (p. iii)

It is striking how easily these accusations against other forms of psychology and psychologists became accepted by both the field and the public. Certainly, the history of enforced happiness, shaping social and professional values, plays central role in this new turn to scientific Pollyannaism where human suffering is not only denied but openly maligned. This attack on psychology as a field, which, like medicine, is dedicated to helping people and communities heal, is especially eye-opening. These claims that psychology's efforts "disable the good life" are alarming, just as in the eugenic era of American psychology, where experiments on infants and animals claimed to produce utopian happy futures of self-controlled people while denying their social realities. It is useful to consider what would happen if a parallel move in the field of medicine was taken, in which treatment of physical illnesses would not only be proclaimed as a "half-baked" attempt but would also be blamed for making people sick.

Positive psychology makes open, extensive and exclusive use of scientific Pollyannaism. It claims that positive psychology is required for societal well-being, targeting parents and educators with promises of new generations of well-behaved children and large corporations with promises of happy, productive workers. Their theories are declared to exist outside any cultural norms or social values and disavow any need to promote change on a structural level: positive psychology routinely claims that individual and social problems will be solved when people learn to control themselves and to think or behave in "correct," positive ways (Deiner et al., 2008; Lopez, 2013; Lopez & Gallagher, 2009; Lyubomirsky, 2008; Seligman & Csikszentmihalyi, 2014; Seligman & Fowler, 2011; Seligman et al., 2005; Sheldon et al., 2000; Sheldon et al., 2010). Diener (2009a), one of the most celebrated scholars of "happiness," who is primarily known for his widely publicized annual tables of supposedly happiest places, states,

> Positive psychology emphasizes not only the actualization of the individual, but development within the framework of his or her contributions to other people and the world. Thus, *our discipline is poised to answer questions that are pivotal to building healthier societies.* (p. 8)

According to Biswas-Diener, Linley, Govindji, and Woolston (2011), positive psychology I claims to be the "force for social change" (p. 410) because it supposedly views human conditions "beyond money" (p. 412), by developing "strength based organizations" through research on positive managers, by recognizing "high producers", by noting "achieving" schools (p. 413), and by tackling "poverty through enabling human talent and potential" without changing the environment (p. 413). Lopez (2013), who has authored multiple scholarly books on positivity, and has written for the popular press such works as *Making Hope Happen*, also led the Gallop's Clifton Center on Human Strengths, which promoted positivist ideas in U.S. schools: dreaming big and having hopeful attitude was all the child needed for future success.

"Top-Notch Research" of Positive Psychology

Positive psychology's claims to validity are based on the claim, not only that its methods are scientific, but that it is somehow more scientific than other psychology sciences. Individual scholars promoting positivity are often touted as coming from leading academic institutions and being funded by top funding groups. Positive psychologists' popular media sites and publications highlight their academically impressive yet accessible personas (e.g., Dr. Optimism, Dr. Happiness). Self-help books by these psychologists include titles such as Lyubomirsky's (2008) *The How of Happiness: A Scientific Approach to Getting the Life You Want* and Fredrickson's (2009) *Positivity: Top-Notch Research Reveals the 3 to 1 Ratio that Will Change Your Life.*

Moreover, positive psychologists' academic status and access to professional publications have resulted in an explosion of scientific-sounding volumes, filled with graphs, data, fMRI pictures, genetics, evolutionary psychology justifications and more: *The Oxford Handbook of Positive Psychology, Journal of Happiness Studies, Journal of Positive Psychology, Handbook of Positive Psychology, Making Hope Happen, Positive Psychology in Practice, Positive Psychological Assessment, Handbook of Hope,* and *Handbook of Positive Behavior Support* are only a very few of their titles. Even mainstream psychology journals have begun to publish entire special issues on positive psychology (Joseph & Murphy, 2013; Lopez et al., 2006; Magyar-Moe & Lopez, 2008; Magyar-Moe, Owens, & Scheel, 2015; Robbins & Friedman, 2008; Wong, 2011).

Positive psychologists claim that their turn to positivity was motivated by their abhorrence of supposed negativity in their discipline. In his book *Flourish*, Seligman (2011) explains that for him and other positive psychologists, helping people who suffer became a "drag":

> I have spent most of my life working on psychology's venerable goal of relieving misery and uprooting the disabling conditions of life. *Truth be told, this can be a drag. Taking the psychology of misery to heart – as you must when you work on depression... trauma, and the panoply of suffering that makes up psychology-as-usual's primary material—can be a vexation to*

> *the soul… psychology-as-usual does not do much for the well-being of its practitioner.* If anything changes in the practitioner, it is a personality shift toward depression. (p. 1)

Therefore, Seligman claimed, "*the people who work in positive psychology are the people with the highest well-being I have ever known*" (p. 2). There's a lot to be said about this attitude towards psychology, but what I want to highlight here is what statements like this leave out. Specifically, positive psychology has been entirely silent about the fact that one of its leading voices, the author of almost all the handbooks of positive psychology, promoter of ideas that hope is all one needs, committed suicide in 2016. Shane Lopez' suicide remains basically unacknowledged: with an exception of an obscure obituary by his colleague, all other online and printed documents about Lopez refuse to acknowledge that one of the most published and celebrated positive psychologists took his own life. According to a eulogy by Krieshok (2016), Lopez' colleague at the University of Kansas,

> Many of you may not know that a little over two years ago Shane fell suddenly into a very deep depression [during these years and until his death Lopez produced numerous optimistic TED talks and publications on positive psychology and hope]. I had lunch with him one day, and he was his regular, normal, healthy, chipper self. When I saw him two weeks later he was so depressed, I spent the night with him and [his wife] at their house because I was worried for his safety. I have worked around depression for many years, but his was unlike anything I had ever seen, and it came on so suddenly, as if he had been struck by lightning. If you ever wondered about depression being a bio-chemical event in the brain, Shane's experience is living evidence that it is. (p. 4)

Lopez's death is a tragedy—he died in his mid-40s, a husband and father to an teenage son (Krieshok, 2016). His suicide provides glimpses into how much he must have suffered despite his many strengths and accomplishments, including in promotion of positivity. If Lopez did suddenly develop the kind of bio-chemical depression Krieshok claims, it would have been uncommon in the extreme by all psychological and psychiatric standards. It is far more likely that Lopez had been depressed for some time and hid it from the public, as Krieshok seems also to be doing, in order to sell positive psychology as the cure for all psychological ills, all the while struggling with a debilitating depression (e.g., Lopez, 2013;

Lopez, Pedrotti, & Snyder, 2018). If even the most celebrated and apparently well-adjusted positive psychologists can succumb to depression that leads to suicide, how effective can his ideology of unmitigated positivity be at producing happiness and mental health? How can we believe his philosophy that "all you need is optimism and control over your thoughts"? And how can the public evaluate positive psychologists' credibility if they are denied basic facts.

In addition to authoring major textbooks and self-help books on positivity and hope, Lopez led Gallop's Clifton Human Strength Institute. None of the websites, including the Gallop Clifton Strengths Institute, which continues to sell positivity to children and educational institutions, mention Lopez' suicide.

Positive psychology's main emphasis remains on assuring the public that paying attention to any negative aspect of life undermines human health and success. According to Seligman's (2002) *Authentic Happiness*:

> Insufficient appreciation and savoring of the good events in your past and overemphasis on bad ones are the two culprits that *undermine serenity, contentment, and satisfaction*. There are two ways of brining these feelings about the past well into the region of contentment and satisfaction. Gratitude amplifies the savoring and appreciation of the good events gone by, and *rewriting history for forgiveness loosens the power of the bad events to embitter* (and actually transforms bad memories into good ones). (p. 70)

Scientific Pollyannaism Efforts to Discredit All Other Forms of Psychology

Positive psychology routinely links depression and suicide to other theoretical approaches, especially psychoanalysis, while positive psychology and its parent theory of cognitive-behaviorism are described as invariable salvific for all. Seligman (2002, 2006, 2011) has consistently claimed that depression is merely episodic and can be managed through few brief positive coaching sessions, and seeking other forms of treatment, such as psychoanalysis, leads to suicide. His *Learned Optimism* Seligman (2006) warns against psychoanalysis, which he claims was scientifically invalid, mercenary, and erroneously focused on treatment of depression and other mental conditions that cause suffering (i.e., it focuses on complex subjective and social origins of human experiences). According to Seligman,

> Dutifully incorporating this insidious bit of nonsense [psychoanalytic views Seligman caricatures] into their treatment of patients, the Freudians urged depressives to let all their emotions hang out—*with the common result of increased depression and even suicide.* (p. 71)

Moreover, Seligman explained:

> For all its hold over the American (particularly in Manhattan) imagination, I have to say that this view [psychoanalytic view that depression requires treatment] is preposterous. It dooms its victim to years of one-way conversation about the murky, distant past in order to overcome a problem that usually would have gone away by itself in a matter of months. *In more than 90 percent of cases, depression is episodic: It comes and then it goes.* (p. 11)

Humanistic traditions in psychology are similarly maligned as completely ineffectual, because unscientific, in treating mental illnesses like depression. According to Seligman and Csikszentmihalyi (2000),

> Unfortunately, *humanistic psychology did not attract much of a cumulative empirical base*, and it spawned myriad therapeutic self–help movements... However, one legacy of the humanism of the 1960s is prominently displayed in any large bookstore: The "psychology" section contains at least 10 shelves on crystal healing, aromatherapy, and reaching the inner child for every shelf of books that tries to uphold some scholarly standard. (p. 7)

Instead, Seligman has created a rival self-help empire, peddling his own self-help books filled with tests and references to individual scientific studies, which apparently distinguish positive psychology as the exclusively scientific and thus highly effective "*new science of personal control*" (p. 15). Seligman (2011) especially disparages therapy, stating that "In general, talk therapy techniques all share the property of being difficult to do, *no fun at all*, and difficult to incorporate into your life. ... By contrast, *try this next positive psychology exercise. It is fun to do and self-maintaining once you catch on*" (p. 48). Women are encouraged to be more like men in order not to get depressed—they supposedly ruminate or think too much about their lives instead of focusing on action, like men (Seligman, 2002).

The newest iterations of positive psychology focus on resilience and so called post-traumatic growth in response to problematic past or present experiences. Thinking exclusively about one's happy, positive future is, supposedly, the empirically valid path to a good life. According to Seligman et al. (2017) the experimental, evolutionary, and neuropsychological sciences support the claim that a human being must train to be a Homo Prospectus, a person who only focuses on rosy hopeful future. Promoting their new book entitled *The Homo Prospectus*, Seligman and colleague (2017) summarize this view: "*Homo prospectus... doesn't dwell on the past: There's nothing he can do about it. He became Homo sapiens by learning to see and shape his future, and he is wise enough to keep looking straight ahead*" (n.p.). This new positive psychology contribution is filled with Darwinist-inspired musings about "cave men" and animals, promoting in its introduction that "*in the game of life, life must win every moment of every day, while death has to win only once*" (p. 9). Because death supposedly "wins" when our "batteries run out" (p. 10), we are told we must a enact a "reshaping of how we understand all of the key processes of mind" in order to achieve "effectiveness and efficiency in using energy... at a premium" (p. 10). This and other of their publications give evolutionary adaptive reasons to become a Homo Prospectus, claiming that laboratory (i.e., caged) animals, especially "mice and rats," possess "cognitive maps" which apparently make them prospective or future-oriented, positive living beings (p. 23).

Again evoking large scale experimental studies, Seligman et al. (2017) book proclaimed that humans themselves must never think about morbid things like death. This assertion is based on a study conducted in Chicago, in which their participants recorded that thoughts of death and dying constituted approximately 1% of their cognitive self-records. What is not discussed in their promotion of this study is what part of Chicago the sample was drawn from. In contrast, the study by Geronimus, Bound, and Colen (2011) noted the tremendously high mortality rates among African Americans in many parts of Chicago where death is witnessed routinely by all the members of community. Denials of death are a privilege afforded by those who do not need to face realities of death, injury, or violence daily. Focusing on rosy pictures of the future while denying realities of violence remains central to scientific Pollyannaism.

Funding of New Scientific Pollyannaism

Whereas greater number of scholars have began to expose positive psychology and its values (e.g., Friedman & Brown, 2018; Held, 2004, 2018; Nickerson, 2018; Yakushko, 2018; Yakushko & Blodgett, 2018), it is journalists such as award-winning Barbara Ehrenreich (2009) in her *Bright-Sided*, which documented the mercenary trends that underlie positive psychology as a movement. Promises of producing happy children, workers, or military personnel by leading Western academics via their new scientific methods and technologies lead to lucrative contracts. Moreover, leading conservative funders appear to be especially interested in backing studies of resilience and optimism for the struggling populace. According to one of the most recent works by Seligman et al. (2017) (i.e., *Homo Prospectus*) positive psychology was especially sought out by the Templeton Foundation. In his introduction to *Homo Prospectus*, Seligman described:

> Enter the Eagle Scouts of philanthropy: the John Templeton Foundation… by 1996 I had been a supplicant for 40 years and my knees were almost work out. Then I became President of the American Psychological Association and suggested that *psychology turn it attention to what makes life worth living, rather than just what impedes the good life. Something odd began to happen. Donors came to me. One of these was the Templeton Foundation.* Shortly after my election, I got a warm letter from Jack Templeton, an accomplished neurosurgeons and the head of the Foundation, offering to hold a fest-schrift in my honor… the Foundation's executive staff appeared in my living room. (p. xiii)

Notably, Templeton Foundation has been noted as one of the far-right or socially conservative U.S. foundations. Ehreneich (2007), a leading U.S. investigative journalist, in her article entitled *John Templeton's Universe* stated that "*the right-wing philanthropist is pushing the phony science of positive psychology to numb Americans into smiley-faced acquiesce to the status quo*" (online). Ehrenreich documented that John Templeton, Jr., praised by Seligman for his personal attention and generosity, was in fact also associated with many other far-right political groups with names such as the Freedom's Watch and Let the Freedom Ring (i.e., foundations that supported current wars in the Middle East and conservative evangelical Christian political candidates). According to Williams' (2015) report on Templeton foundation, the far-right political and religious agendas, funded by this group, focus on such topics as "free will and self-control" ($4.5 millions) or evolutionary study of the "human origins" ($4.9 millions). Foundation's largest grants are consistent with far-right and politically conservative agendas, such as the ideologically-grounded studies of the "foundational questions in evolutionary biology," or "research on unlimited love," or "accelerating progress at the interface of positive psychology and neuroscience" (Waldrop, 2011). The most current webpage for Templeton Foundation (2019) notes that in addition to funding studies on "the science and the big question," its focus is on funding research on "character virtue and development," "individual freedom and free markets," "exceptional cognitive talent and genius," "genetics" and "faith-based family planning" (online). Currently, John Templeton Jr. also funds such groups as the Foundation for Individual Right in Education (FIRE), an organization that promotes far-right racist and sexist ideologies in educational institutions, claiming their supposed right to "free speech" and decrying "political correctness" (Sleeper, 2016, online). According to the Source Watch (2019), an organization that traces funding to its causes, Templeton foundation and its leaders have supported primarily far-right, nationalist, and socially conservative individuals (e.g., election of George Bush, Wisconsin governor Scott Walker) and causes (e.g., war in Iraq). This and other funders of positive psychology or scientific Pollyannaism efforts have supported many causes that produce profound suffering while being supportive of ideologies that deny social oppression.

The Magic of "It's All in Your Head" Versus the Sciences of Real Human Experiences

The history of positive psychology's funding should lead us to question how oppression and inequality are represented in positive psychology. It is also important to note that the funding sources of supposedly neutral scientific studies have been likely to hide or deny contrary evidence and alternative explanations. In my prior contributions to scholarship on positive psychology in *The Journal of Humanistic Psychology* (Yakushko & Blodgett, 2018) and *Psychotherapy and Politics International* (Yakushko, 2018) I have discussed alternative or contradictory findings and critical theories related to positive psychology and its origins. I further highlight that scholars in many fields, including education, medicine, and business, have noted the lack of scientific corroboration for positive psychology's problematic claims about their own fields. I note that numerous studies in psychology itself indicate that many claims made by positive psychology are simply false. I especially comment about positive psychology's efforts to minimize and deny social context, including racism, sexism, or poverty.

For example, in his *Learned Helplessness*, ignoring the disproportionate effects of the hurricanes on racial minority groups, Seligman (2006) shared the following idea for what he termed an "ideal" experiment:

> The ideal experiment would have been something like this: to test everyone in a small town on the Gulf Coast of Mississippi for depression and explanatory style and then wait for a hurricane to hit. After the hurricane passed, *we'd go see who lay there passively in the mud and who got up and rebuilt the town.* (pp. 77–78)

Csikszentmihalyi (2001) in his highly popular book *Finding Flow* similarly condemns people who are so weak as to be influenced by circumstance. In his words, "it is easier to doubt that life makes sense if one is born deformed, poor, and oppressed" (p. 234) but, Csikszentmihalyi assures readers throughout the book, none of these experiences should hamper individuals because it is up to an them to achieve flow regardless. Csikszentmihalyi (1997) shamed his Western readers for not flowing or being positive:

> This general malaise is not due directly to external causes. Unlike so many other nations in the contemporary world, we can't blame our problems on a harsh environment, on widespread poverty on the oppression by the foreign occupying army. *The root of the discontent is internal, and each person must untangle them personally, with his or her own power.* (p. 12)

For Csikszentmihalyi's (1997), it is good for individuals to not question oppressive social norms, because hard work and self-denial teaches human beings to flow. Women's capacity to do-it-all (i.e., maintain the household, their children, and their husband's well-being as befit a traditional happy housewife) is claimed to be central to their flow capacity. In contrast, these women's husbands, Csikszentmihalyi asserted, do not develop flow because after working all day at a factory, they seek to "forget the dullness of the day with beer and camaraderie… more beer in front of the TV, a brief skirmish with the wife" (p. 149).

Instead of questioning these oppressive norms, positive psychologists routinely warn against attending to issues of social justice and social context as being terrible and detrimental to one's positive mental health. Specifically, acknowledging racism or sexism by expressing anger about these forms of oppression is viewed as a significant barrier to positive psychological health. Seligman's (2002) explained the dire problems that arise when "*contemporary American demagogues who play the race card, invoking reminders of slavery ... at every opportunity, create the same vengeful mindset in their followers*" (p. 76). In fact, Seligman (2002, 2006, 2011) consistently warns that any attention on changing one's environment, either for oneself or others, sets individuals up to have an external locus of control and, thus, diminish their own sense of self-control, making them learnedly helpless.

Instead, positive psychologists claim that racism and other forms of oppression will disappear when people pursue their own happiness. Fredrickson (2009) in her self-help book on "positivity ratios," claimed that racists are merely unhappy people and that making racists happy will apparently reduce and even remove their racism. In her words, positive psychology research shows that "*racial differences – seem to melt away when our hearts are warmed by positivity*" (p. 68). Conversely, Csikszentmihalyi (1997) warned that those individuals who lack "goals and rules for intense flow experiences" are at risk to "*become fundamentalist Christians, or Muslims, or communists*" (p. 238). Thus, happy flowing people are also apparently free of prejudice and social malice as well as uninhibited by cultural or socio-political commitments.

Happy Hateful States

Denials of social context and oppressive environment are embedded in many positive psychology studies. In an era following the vitally important multicultural movement in psychology, which occurred in 1990s, positive psychologists routinely refer to cultural values in vague and general terms, while emphasizing that their Western values, research, and practices are, in fact, universal. For example, Pedrotti, Edwards, and Lopez (2009) claim that positive psychology offers a "culture-free perspective" (p. 50). Peterson and Seligman (2004) stated, after surveying what appear to be the most conservative and fundamentalist versions of world religions, that positive psychology fosters a set of human strengths congruent with universal human values. Numerous empirical efforts focus on world-wide testing and evaluation of happiness and optimism, rating varied groups, countries, states, and demographically different communities on their levels of positivity based on Eurocentric assessments (Diener, 2009b; Fischer & Chalmers, 2008).

Thus, another example of positive psychology's sanitization of culture and society is found in the studies by Deiner and colleagues on differences in happiness (e.g., Deiner, 2009b). As noted above in relation to Gallup's Clifton Strength Institute, which employs positive psychologists to promote positivity to children and educational institutions, Gallup has put considerable amount of money and effort towards promotion of happiness and positivity concepts. Their 2017 report bemoans data that paints a "bleak picture of the well-being of Americans" (online). However, they stated that "despite the national downturn," Americans supposed authentic positivity is evident in the increase of regular exercising and abstinence from smoking cigarettes. All the U.S. states are then ranked against each other based on the self-reported happiness of its populace. In the 2017 Gallop report, "South Dakota claimed the top spot, with a well-being score of 64.1 out of 100 possible points" (online). What Gallup happiness studies appear to ignore is the other findings and facts, easily available online.

Specifically, according to a South Dakota state governmental flyer by South Dakota Suicide Prevention (2018), the state has the 13th highest rate of completed suicide, with suicide being the 2nd cause of death among adults ages 15–34, with that rate being 2.3 times higher among Native American residents. Data by the Center for Disease Control (2019) showed that South Dakota, "the happiest state in America" for 2017, rose in 2018 to being the 7th highest for completed suicides among the 50 U.S. states. Previously, according to a CNN report by Sutter (2014), based on FBI data, "The state with the second-highest rate of reported rape, behind Alaska, is South Dakota, with a rate of 70 per 100,000" (online). On the other hand, according to the reports by the Daily Beast (2011), which draws its data from multiple state and federal reports of hate crimes and discrimination reports, South Dakota was listed 39th out of 50 on measures of tolerance. Reading these reports, we have to question who actually is happy in the state of South Dakota or any other state with given the highest happiness rankings. What do positive psychology's assessments of happiness, optimism, and well-being truly report on, and for whom? Examination of other states which have been "empirically proven" as the happiest produces similar results: the state of New Hampshire (3rd on happiness in 2017 report) has the highest rates of deaths from the drug overdose (Center for Disease Control, 2018). North Dakota has rates of suicides, rape and tolerance similar to South Dakota (Center for Disease Control, 2019; The Daily Beast,

2011). Colorado, Utah, and Hawaii are also among these happy states with high rates of suicide (Center for Disease Control, 2019). The popularized promotions of happy states in the media and positive psychology literature seem to entirely omit this other data.

And its not just violence, suicides or drug epidemics that escape calculations of human happiness. Among the most openly dismissed social struggles is poverty. Positive psychologists routinely claim that money or poverty have nothing to do with happiness (Csikszentmihalyi, 1997; Fredrickson, 2009; Lyubomirsky, 2008; Seligman, 2002, 2006, 2011). Frequently, positive psychological writings give Pollyannaish representations about the state of American and the Western economy. For example, in his *Authentic Happiness* Seligman (2002) claims: "In the low-unemployment economy America has been enjoying for twenty years, the majority of young people emerging from college have considerable choice about their careers" (p. 174). Therefore, Seligman claims, those who do not succeed economically or in their careers in such a universal time of prosperity and ease are unhappy pessimists and have only themselves to blame because, in his words, "*pessimists are losers on many fronts*" (p. 178).

Shaming the poor for trying to find more happiness through acquisition, particularly through buying the lottery tickets (i.e., known as "tax" on the poor) is commonplace in positive psychology writings (Deiner & Seligman, 2004; Seligman, 2002, 2006). Chaning any circumstance of one's personal life is openly discouraged, because it is only the individual's attitude towards life that makes a difference to personal flow, authentic happiness, positivity, and flourishing. Thus, according to Sonja Lyubomirsky (2008), one of the leading positive psychology scholars, frequently appearing in popular media outlets such as the *Time* magazine or the American Association of Retired Persons (AARP): "If you're unhappy with your job, your friends, your marriage, your salary, or your looks, the first step you should take towards reaching greater lasting happiness is to *put those things aside in mind for now*" (p. 52).

These scientific Pollyannaist ideas about ignoring one's economic conditions are not just published in scientific journals or positive psychology pop self-help books. During 2018 the National Public Radio routinely advertised podcasts from a positive psychology center that encouraged positivity by chiding radio listeners for wanting to find more happiness with a winning lottery ticket. These publicly-funded radio podcasts supposedly delivery "*research-based tips for a meaningful life*" (PRI, 2019, online). Moreover, numerous other positive psychologists routinely insist that their indices of personal happiness should become the "new measures of prosperity" in contrast to all other measures such as the actual income or other measures of well-being, such as health and access social services (Seligman, 2011, p. 96). Relatively poor nations like Bhutan, as the next section will show, are regularly and erroneously used as token evidence that poverty does not matter. Meanwhile most of the empirical data collected by positive psychology is derived from wealthiest nations and wealthiest individuals on earth, with their conclusions skewed as a result.

Winning the "Glad Games" by Ethnocentric Nationalism and Late Stage Capitalism

Since the happiest nations on earth, according to positive psychologists, also happen to be the wealthiest, the rhetoric of positive psychology appears almost exclusively aimed at these richest industrialized countries on earth, rather than the poor or marginalized world communities. According to Seligman (2011), "*the wealthy nations of the world—North America, the European Union, Japan, and Australia— are at a Florentine moment: rich, at peace, enough food, health, and harmony. How will we invest our wealth? What will our renaissance be?*" (p. 237). Many studies on supposed positivity differences between national groups appear on nationalist and White supremacy group websites such as the American Renaissance (Southern Poverty Law Center, 2019). According to the American Renaissance's (2019) description of their own activities and focus:

> Race is an important aspect of individual and group identity. Of all the fault lines that divide society—language, religion, class, ideology—it is the most prominent and divisive. Race and racial conflict are at the heart of some of the most serious challenges the Western World faces in the 21st century. The problems of race cannot be solved without adequate understanding. Attempts to gloss over the significance of race or even to deny its reality only make problems worse. Progress requires the study of all aspects of race, whether historical, cultural, or biological. This approach is known as *race realism*. (online)

In addition to ads for "WhiteDate for European Singles," "Hate Hoax" and "Anti-Trump Hate" maps, the American Renaissance website (2019) is dedicated to summarizing numerous scholarly contributions by "race realist" psychologists, including those on the happiness achievable through racial segregation and reclamation of cultural White supremacy. For example, the 2017 re-posted summary of studies by evolutionary psychologists Kanazawa and Li (2015) on racial homogeneity and happiness, published in the *Journal of Research in Personality* claimed that:

> *Recent developments in evolutionary psychology suggest that living among others of the same ethnicity might make individuals happier and further that such an effect of the ethnic composition on life satisfaction may be stronger among less intelligent individuals.* Data from the National Longitudinal Study of Adolescent Health showed that White Americans had significantly greater life satisfaction than all other ethnic groups in the US and this was largely due to the fact that they were the majority ethnic group; minority Americans who lived in counties where they were the numerical majority had just as much life satisfaction as White Americans did. Further, *the association between ethnic composition and life satisfaction was significantly stronger among less intelligent individuals. The results suggest two important factors underlying life satisfaction and highlight the utility of integrating happiness research and evolutionary psychology.* (online)

While their study seems to suggest that less intelligent people prefer ethnic similarity, the findings nevertheless celebrated the overall happiness of these individuals, which was supposedly threatened by diversity.

Furthermore according to studies, noted on the American Renaissance website, the "*Danish DNA*" is a "*key to happiness*" (PhysOrg, 2014, online). Moreover, MacInnis, Busseri, Choma, and Hodson's (2013) Canadian study is used on the American Renaissance webpages (Jacobs, 2013) to argue that, according to research, "*extreme conservatives make happier people*" (online). Jacobs (2013) summarizes this study's results for the American Renaissance readers:

> *On the general level, greater generalized authoritarianism was clearly related to greater subjective well-being,*" the researchers write. "The association suggests that *generalized authoritarianism may be 'good' for the self.*" (online)

Another posting on their website by Eatson (2006) similarly summarized that "*diversity*" can "*make us unhappy*" (online). The American Renaissance website claims, moreover, that happiness is assuredly the genetic trait of racially "superior" groups. Citing evidence from research by neuropsychologists, the American Renaissance celebrated the discovery of the predominately Caucasian Pollyanna gene: gene named ADRA2b, which supposedly "processes negative emotions positively:"

> The ADRA2b deletion variant appears in varying degrees across different ethnicities. Although roughly *50 per cent of the Caucasian population studied by these researchers in Canada* carry the genetic variation, it has been found to be prevalent in other ethnicities. For example, one study found that just *10 per cent of Rwandans* carried the ADRA2b gene variant. (Science Daily, 2015, online)

When critiqued for myopic focus on the privileged people of privileged nations, positive psychologists bring up one, single example of a non-wealthy and non-European country: the Kingdom of Bhutan (Biswas-Diener et al., 2011; Seligman, 2011). Recent books on positive psychology use the Kingdom of Bhutan and its Domestic Happiness Product to demonstrate the global and supposedly multicultural nature of positive psychology (Biswas-Diener et al., 2011). But nowhere in their writings these positive psychology scholars note that Kingdom of Bhutan has the worst rates of gender violence in its region, and that it has been implicated in horrific human rights violations against its own minorities, or that its people are commanded by their king to claim to be happy (Iyer, 1990; Pulla, 2016).

Positive psychology is peppered with incomplete representations of happiness data. Seligman's (2002, 2006, 2011) many contributions routinely provide partial information that is either based on a single case (e.g., Bhutan or "the golden girl") or references large-scale statistical data about happy countries and states with a skewed sample (see comments above). Scientific Pollyannaist rhetoric by positive psychologist presents itself as applying to all human beings. In contrast, their popular self-help books, such as Seligman's (2006), are invariably pitched to what appear to be the wealthiest individuals: his many varied scales of authentic happiness, optimism, locus of control and so forth typically contain questions such as "Your stocks make you a lot of money" and "You fall down a great deal while skiing" (pp. 33–39). Happiness, Seligman assures his readers, makes the person happy, healthy, and wealthy: "*Happy people, furthermore, have better health habits, lower blood pressure, and feistier immune system than less happy people*" (p. 40). These are not only stunning over-statements but, in fact, entirely inaccurate: many studies show opposite occurrences for individuals who deny their negative emotional states. Medical scholars have shown that positive psychological ideologies have profoundly detrimental influences on people with physical illnesses, especially life-threatening conditions such as cancer (Coyne, Stefanek, & Palmer, 2007; Coyne & Tennen, 2010; Palmer, Stefanek, Thombs, & Coyne, 2010; Stefanek, Palmer, Thombs, & Coyne, 2009; Sumalla, Ochoa, & Blanco, 2009; Yakushko & Blodgett, 2018).

It is not only health that is guaranteed to people following contemporary scientific Pollyannaism of positive psychology: happy people, it is claimed, also get elected to political offices. Seligman (2006) claims:

> *When optimists run for office, they are more apt to be elected than pessimists are. Their health is unusually good. They age well, much freer than most of us from the usual physical ills of middle age. Evidence suggests they may even live longer.* (p. 5)

According to Keith (2017), Donald Trump's primary personal and religious adherence is to "positive thinking" ideology of positive thinking gurus such as the infamous Vincent Peale (online). In the *Politico* report by Kruse (2017), Trump's success is related to the over-abundance of positive psychological self-help literature consumed by Americans:

> Self-help is a multibillion-dollar business. Airport shelves groan under the weight of how-to and pick-me-up books churned out by writers who all are essentially Peale progeny. The industry is prevalent in American culture to the point that it has spawned its own sub-group of critics who dismiss it as silly at best and dangerous at worst. (online)

Kruse's article on Trump and his followers' adherence to positive thinking and positive psychological propaganda includes questions posed to positive psychology guru Diener and his obfuscating responses:

> "There is a lot to like in the idea of power of positive thinking," Ed Diener, one of the country's leading researchers of happiness, told me, "but of course it must be grounded in a degree of realism." And where's that dividing line? The dividing line, Diener said, "is when the delusions become dysfunctional." And where is that? (online)

Kruse comments on Deiner's confusing and misleading response: would a nuclear war threat be finally enough, Kruse wonders. It seems that contemporary politicians and politics are fueled by positive psychology scientific Pollyannaism narratives. These views permit them to attack any person or view for being "negative" as well as to lie by elevating their own perspective as supposedly a positive view. Donald Trump is a confirmation of positive psychology sciences. From referring to Hillary Clinton as a "nasty woman" to declaring that he had the largest inauguration crowd to ending his 2017 State if the Union address with a typical positive psychology slogan "We must think big and dream even bigger" and promising greatness, Trump is a prototypical example of scientific Pollyannaism (Brody & Lamb, 2018).

Science that contradicts positive psychologists also exists, although it is minimized and marginalized in Western contemporary psychology. Pérez-Álvarez (2013) summarized empirical research studies that show that individuals who self-identified as "happy" were also more likely to be "conceited, selfish" and even "sad," when valuing or seeking personal happiness as a goal (p. 213). I also note in my other publications (e.g., Yakushko, 2018; Yakushko & Blodgett, 2018), that numerous studies in medicine, education, business, and psychology indeed contradict the scientific Pollyannaism research published under the guise of positive psychology (e.g., positive people give less to charity; more optimistic high school students have greater academic failure rates and higher depression during their college years).

Raising Pollyannas: The Sciences of Making Children Orphan Their Feelings

Another specific target of contemporary Scientific Pollyannaism are children, their parents and their educational systems. While focusing on children become a source of lucrative grants from the government and private institutions (e.g., Clifton Strength Institute at Gallop), positive psychology has found an easy target for their sciences by concentrating on overburdened parents and educational systems. For example, Miller (2008) noted that educational institutions, using the rhetoric of positive psychology, enforce preferences for every student to be a "cheerful, outgoing, goal-driven, status-seeking extravert" (p. 591). As noted in other chapters, focus on controlling children's and parental lives through control over their emotional lives was the hallmark of other scientific Pollyannaism efforts such as eugenics and behaviorism.

Contemporary positive psychology's Akumal (i.e., Mexico resort) Manifesto (Sheldon et al., 2000) included numerous mentions of educational systems and children. Moreover, Seligman (2007) produced a separate book for parents entitled *The Optimistic Child*, in which he claimed that U.S. had fallen behind many other Western countries on measures of happiness, and that this pessimism was directly related to parents' and teachers' lack of scientifically grounded positive treatment of children. Similarly, in his initial pop self-help contribution entitle *Authentic Happiness* Seligman (2002) decried:

> *While you are coping with tantrums, pouts and whines, it is very easy to overlook the fact that your young children have a lot of positive emotions. Like puppies, little kids are... cute, playful, and sunny. It is not until late childhood an early adolescence that stony indifference, chilly torpor, and the pall of dysphoria set in.* (p. 209)

Just like behaviorist John B. Watson (1928), Seligman (2006) represents children's distress or "negative" emotions as "tantrums" and "whining," and their expressions of non-positive emotions as tactics to manipulate their parents: "*The infant can now bawl whenever he wants his mother. He badly overuses this new power*, until it stops working" (p. 6). In fact, Seligman (2006) claims that the root of society's problems can be found in "*intelligent devoted parents producing fragile spoiled children*" (p. 15).

Mythic Evolutionary Origins of Pollyannaism

Positive psychology uses the typical strategies of scientific Pollyannaism: deploying "empirical" claims to justify the status quo while endorsing a particular ideology that equates positivity with goodness and success with personal character or genetics. Indeed, one of positive psychology's patterns, which mark its direct connections to eugenics, can be found in its continued claims that happiness is, in large part, evolutionary and genetic. Evolutionary psychology is often included in explanations of human differences in happiness (Seligman, 2006; Seligman et al., 2017), and, in turn, evolutionary psychologists promote positive psychology scholarship and views (Buss, 2000; Pinker, 2018). According to Buss' (2009) claims, which offer contemporary iterations of ultra Darwinism that focuses on the survival of the fittest groups with control over females and resources, evolutionary psychology provides needed insights into human happiness. According to Buss (2000), this evolutionary link to happiness is found in mythologized accounts of how human beings move from stage of evolution to another. To summarize varied contemporary evolutionary research on happiness, Buss (2000) shared the following review of studies in the conclusion to his article on evolution and positivity:

> Individual difference(s) in dispositional happiness appear moderately heritable… Comprehensive theories of human happiness will have to explain adaptively patterned phenomena such as *why winners of competitions* experience a hedonic and hormonal boost… and why *women's feelings of well-being appear to peak during the late follicular phase of the ovulatory cycle*, when fertility and chance of conception are maximal. (p. 22)

This statement links evolutionary psychology with the neo-Darwinist idea that those who are winners in the competition to survive are the happiest or that women are happiest when they breed. In reading these scientifically sounding proclamations, recall that evolutionary psychology is in fact a direct descendent from the eugenic scientific organizations in the U.S. (Gould, 1996; Tucker, 1996; Yakushko, 2019). Moreover, numerous scholars from fields such as biology and anthropology, from which evolutionary psychology claims to draw facts, have disowned evolutionary psychology as a pseudo-science that refuses actual evidence, essentially as a new iteration of racist and sexist forms of social Darwinism (Gould, 1996; Grossi, Kelly, Nash, & Parameswaran, 2014; Kamin, 2012; Lewontin, Rose, & Kamin, 1984; Oikonnen, 2013; Rose & Rose, 2010; Ruti, 2015; Yakushko, 2019).

When evolutionary psychology discusses happiness in scholarly publications, a confusing set of ideas are presented: negative emotions (i.e., anger) seem to be essential for human evolutionary survival in that they aid in destroying all others in fight for dominance. Precipitously, these evolutionary sciences are followed by assurances that since humanity has achieved the new evolutionary peaks of greatness these supposedly primitive adaptive mechanisms (i.e., anger) are no longer needed or valuable (Buss, 2000; Fredrickson, 2013).

One of the newest contributions to the public readership by positive psychologists, *Homo Prospectus* (Seligman et al., 2017), is filled with allusions to evolution and Darwinist interpretations of animal behavior.

Multiple references are made to works of many behavioral geneticists (i.e., a field stemming from eugenics), including Dawkins, which leads the authors to claim that selfishness toward others is merely evolutionary, and that humans' happy state of mind is based on exclusive care of those they perceive as being genetically similar to themselves (i.e., happiness is secured by racial and demographic homogeneity). Seligman et al. (2017) re-state that human beings should merely accept that "creatures will make sacrifices and accept risks so as *to benefit others who share our genes*" and no one else (p. 151).

Lastly, the academic dominance of positive psychology is routinely connected to academic evolutionary psychology. For example, Yale University has boasted of hosting the largest single class filled with undergraduates who are eager to study positive psychology (Science Friday, 2018), much as it once boasted of housing the largest and most noted academic eugenics laboratory with a focus on "human betterment" (e.g., *Eugenical News,* 1916–1922). In the National Public Radio weekly show called Science Friday (2018) entitled *What Makes Your Brain Happy?*, the instructor of the "largest in their history" Yale university positive psychology class was introduced as "Laurie Santos [who] studies primate cognition—and teaches about the psychology of happiness" (online). In her interview, Santos claimed that her laboratory studies on caged monkeys apparently proved that if individuals do not have any care about their past or future, the person is supposedly finally free to live in the present with unalloyed happiness, optimism, and even mindfulness. This use of animals, usually selectively picked animals, whose conditions are ignored (i.e., minimizing that they are caged and mutilated for studies), is a signature feature of scientific Pollyannaism. The use of select animals (i.e., caged laboratory rats or patriarchally-organized primates) as models for human behavior is a touchstone of scientific Pollyannism. To remind the reader, Yerkes (1907) and Watson (1914, 1919) tortured animals to produce what they believed were accurate descriptions of human experience, as well as to develop techniques for socially engineering well-behaved humans (i.e., "comparative psychology"). A recent example animal-based studies of comparative psychology is a study of zoo primates, which found that "subjective well-being" was genetically based as well as related to "dominance" over others (Weiss, Adams, Widdig, & Gerald, 2011, p. 1141).

Evolutionary psychology, as an iteration of eugenic psychology, has been revived and celebrated once again in positive psychology. In his

Authentic Happiness, Seligman (2002) openly promoted evolutionary psychology perspectives, especially neo or fundamentalist Darwinist re-introduction of evolutionary psychology to the public by Wright's (1994) *The Moral Animal*. Seligman praised this book, stating it "was the most important book on science he [Seligman] has ever read" (p. 254). Wright's book, in addition to promoting Darwinism in relation to human differences and human experiences, made many such statements as:

> *a female, in sheerly Darwinian terms, is better off mating with a good rapist, a big, strong, sexually aggressive male; her male offspring will then be more likely to be big strong, and sexually aggressive… and therefore prolific. So female resistance [to rape] should be favored by natural selection [primarily] as a way to avoid having a son who is an inept rapist.* (p. 52)

Indeed, scientific Pollyannaism, whether in studies of "happy states" such as South Dakota (i.e., state with second highest rate of completed rapes in the nation) or countries such as Bhutan (i.e., a country with the worst record on sexual violence in its region), can openly dismiss sexual violence while promoting the achievements of positivity (see above). A growing number of concerned scholars have noted that gender stereotyping, sexist assumptions, and heteronormative values are as central to evolutionary psychology writings (McKinnon, 2006; Ruti, 2015) as they are to positive psychology narratives (Yakushko, 2018). Nevertheless, these critiques do not appear in any of positive psychology scholarship or pop self-help contributions. In contrast, positive psychology publications assert that questioning or fighting external factors such as sexism or racism leads to dire mental health defects and mental illness (Yakushko, 2018; Yakushko & Blodgett, 2018).

Happiness Is (Once Again) Mostly in Your Genes

Among their "scientific" reasons for suppressing negative feelings and not making trouble is the assurance that non-positive emotional states can reveal biological or heritable problems. As I noted above, scientific Pollyannaism features prominently on White supremacy websites such as the American Renaissance, with claims that those who posses "Danish DNA" (i.e., Nordic White superior genes) hold the "key to happiness" (PhysOrg, 2014). The idea that happiness has a genetic foundation is also promoted throughout contemporary positive psychology literature, as for example, Pluess's (2015) edited collection entitled *Genetics of Psychological Well-Being*: The Role of Heritability and Genetics in *Positive Psychology*. Famed positive psychologists routinely claim that approximately 50% of differences in human happiness are genetic (i.e., inherited, biological), which incidentally is the same ratio used by scholars to describe genetic racial differences in intelligence: Rushton and Jensen (2005) claimed that these statistical ratios prove African Americans lack intelligence possessed by Whites.

Seligman (2002) openly promotes research into the genetic superiority and inferiority of racial groups, such as the work of Thomas Bouchard at the University of Minnesota Twin and Adoption Studies. Bouchard's work was funded by an organization identified as one of the most racist contemporary organizations–the Pioneer Fund (Southern Poverty Law Center, 2019). Bouchard (1996) claimed to have used twin and adoption studies (i.e., a method developed by eugenicists such as Terman and Thorndike) to declare that not only intelligence but also human personality features like optimism are derived from racially determined hereditary factors. Bouchard's work is featured heavily in justifications of White supremacy, whether in books like David Duke's (1999) *My Awakening* or in science-focused publications by White supremacy groups like the American Renaissance. For example, in the 2011 version of the re-published articles by Jared Taylor (2011) entitled *Genetics, Personality, and Race*, these scientific studies are used to assert that

> Although it is difficult to evaluate personality, and the political pressures against racial comparisons are enormous, a certain amount of data has nevertheless come to light. For example, it is well known that criminals typically have lower IQs than non-criminals. *The lower average intelligence of blacks and Hispanics as compared to whites and Asians doubtless explains much of the differences in crime rates.* (online)

The American Renaissance's articles describe Taylor Bouchard's and colleague's data—including studies published in the *American Psychologist*, the flagship scientific journal of the APA—as central contributors to their white supremacist views:

> The study of identical twins therefore suggests that heredity accounts for much more of our personalities and characteristics than even geneticists had thought possible. As Dr. Bouchard puts it, "the vast majority

> of psychological traits are influenced to some degree by genetic factors." Personality testing of twins has led him to conclude that although environment has a clear effect on personality, even such things as religious fervor, political convictions, gregariousness, and moral integrity appear to be 40 to 50 percent determined by heredity. (online)

Bouchard's work appears in highly popular and well-promoted positive psychology publications. In his *Authentic Happiness*, Seligman (2002) routinely dismisses the role of the environment in shaping human personality, supporting his claim with "careful research from the University of Minnesota [Bouchard's Pioneer Fund funded studies on twins and adoption, which] shows that there is a *personality trait of good cheer and bubbliness (called positive affectivity)*, which, it turns out, *is highly heritable*" (p. 33). Thus, "heredity" continues to feature prominently in interpretations of human emotional experiences, including supposedly positive and negative reactions to life circumstances (Seligman, 2011, p. 104).

The "Hard" Sciences Behind Contemporary Scientific Pollyannaism

Positive psychology has legitimized itself primarily by repeating, over and over, that is based on "literally hundreds of studies" and "in tests of hundreds of thousands of people," producing findings that were purportedly "discovered in the laboratories and clinics" and "rigorously validated" (Seligman, 2006, p. 5). In one of the many handbooks of positive psychology Simonton (2011) declared that exclusively quantitative, experimental studies were the hallmark of positive psychology in contrast to other, apparently more humanistic ways of studying humanity:

> Although the humanistic psychologists tended to emphasize human virtues and strengths, their research was most prone to be qualitative and even holistic–more akin to human sciences than to the natural sciences. In contrast, positive psychologists have investigated many of the same topics using psychometric, experimental and survey methodologies. (p. 451)

Another *Oxford Handbook of Methods in Positive Psychology* (Ong & van Dulmen, 2006) claimed that positive psychologists "avoid the 'soft' label" (p. vi) as scientists at all costs. In contrast to supposedly other "soft" sciences, authors assert "quite simply, the only viable future for positive psychology is for it to become 'hard' sciences" through the concerted effort to utilize "latest in technologies," "fMRI scans," "genetics," and "multiple methodological techniques" by avoiding even "self report questionnaires" because their "days... are over" (p. vi).

Because positive psychology has much in common with positivity-oriented religions and philosophies (e.g., Vincent Peale's ideology, which is central to Donald Trump's views, or the Prosperity Gospel promoted by evangelical pastors like Joel Osteen), it actively seeks to distinguish itself from these movements by establishing its scientific credentials. For example, Lopez and Galllagher (2009) vehemently denied that positive psychology has anything to do with such positive-promoting, think-good-thoughts-and-be-wealthy-healthy-and-great ideas as those found in the popular self-help book *The Secret*. In *Learned Optimism* Seligman (2006) claimed that "Far from being the creations of boosters or of the popular media, these skills [his positive psychology strategies] were discovered in the laboratories and clinics of leading psychologists an psychiatrists and then rigorously validated" (p. 5). The majority of pop positive psychology books evoke their empirical bases through their rhetoric and by advertising it on the front-cover, such as Lyubomirsky's (2008) *The How of Happiness: A Scientific Approach to Getting the Life You Want*, Fredrickson's (2009) *Positivity: Top-Notch Research Reveals the 3 to 1 Ratio that Will Change Your Life* or Shane Lopez et al.'s (2018) *Positive Psychology: The Scientific and Practical Explorations of Human Strengths.*

However, a significant amount of research also offers findings that discount or entirely contradict positive psychology assumptions (Held, 2004, 2018; Pérez-Álvarez, 2013; Yakushko & Blodgett, 2018). One recent such example is Fredrickson's (2009, 2013) broaden-and-build theory, supposedly based on empirically derived positivity ratios (i.e., how many positive to negative thoughts are needed to broaden and build on one's positivity toward supposed flourishing). Fredrickson ignores and minimizes these critiques, continuing to promote her positive psychological ideas as supposedly valid. Nickerson's (2014) review of Fredrickson's scholarship showed that:

> Fredrickson's (2013) [her article in the *American Psychologist* entitled *Updated Thinking on Positivity Ratios*] insistence is not warranted, by first noting that there was a mismatch between Fredrickson and Losada's (2005) theory and the data used to test it, then describing the

> methodological and statistical problems of Fredrickson and Losada's (2005) empirical study [published in the *American Psychologist]* that invalidate its results, and, finally, demonstrating that Fredrickson (2013) has not interpreted correctly the results of the seven other studies that she cited as providing substantial empirical evidence. (p. 305)

Nickerson continued that not only does

> *there exists no tipping point [Fredrickson's theory] between nonflourishing and flourishing, or no nonlinear relation between the positivity ratio and well-being*, but, rather, that no convincing evidence has yet been presented for such. This lack of evidence suggests that continued investigation into the possible existence and values of critical minimum and maximum positivity ratios, as urged by Fredrickson (2013), is likely to prove a fool's errand. (p. 306)

In the analysis of Brown, Sokal, and Friedman, (2013), Fredrickson's ratio reflects a form of wishful thinking rather than anything approximating genuine science. Moreover, Brown, Sokal, and Freidman (2014) come to the following conclusion of positive psychology's "science" as exemplified in Fredrickson's work:

> Since its advent as a relatively new subdiscipline, positive psychology has claimed superiority to its precursor, the subdiscipline of humanistic psychology, in terms of supposedly both using more rigorous science and avoiding popularizing nonsense. The debunking of the critical positivity ratio demonstrates that positive psychology did not live up to these claims, and this has important implications, which are discussed in terms of "romantic scientism" and "voodoo science." (pp. 239–240)

In summary, the values, the ideologies, the methods, and professional strategies of positive psychology are consistent with many other iterations of scientific Pollyannaism in the American academic tradition. Positive psychology perpetuates the demonization of negative emotional states and the refusal to acknowledge social factors. In turn, biological, personal "superiority" is celebrated as foundational to the capacity for self-control and therefore crucial for the cultivation of perpetual optimism. These "empirical" claims are, once again, validated to a popular audience by parading elite degrees and complex scientific narratives, a rhetorical and ideological strategy that, taken together, I call scientific Pollyannaism.

References

The American Renaissance. (2019). *About us*. Retrieved on January 14, 2019 from https://www.amren.com/about/.

Biswas-Diener, R., Linley, P. A., Govindji, R., & Woolston, L. (2011). Positive psychology as a force for social change. In K. M. Sheldon, T. B. Kashdan, & M. F. Steger (Eds.), *Designing positive psychology: Taking stock and moving forward* (pp. 410–418). New York: Oxford University Press.

Bouchard, T. J. (1996). Galton lecture: Behaviour genetic studies of intelligence, yesterday and today: The long journey from plausibility to proof. *Journal of Biosocial Science, 28*(4), 527–555.

Brody, D., & Lamb, S. (2018). *The faith of Donald J. Trump: A spiritual biography*. New York, NY: HarperCollins.

Brown, N. J., Sokal, A. D., & Friedman, H. L. (2013). The complex dynamics of wishful thinking: The critical positivity ratio. *The American Psychologist, 68*(9), 801–813.

Brown, N. J., Sokal, A. D., & Friedman, H. L. (2014). Positive psychology and romantic scientism. *The American Psychologist, 69*(6), 636–637.

Buss, D. M. (2000). The evolution of happiness. *American Psychologist, 55*(1), 15–23.

Buss, D. M. (2009). The great struggles of life: Darwin and the emergence of evolutionary psychology. *American Psychologist, 64*(2), 140.

Cabanas, E. (2016). Rekindling individualism, consuming emotions: Constructing "psytizens" in the age of happiness. *Culture & Psychology, 22*(3), 467–480.

Cayman Taxonomy Meeting. (1999). Retrieved on January 14, 2019 from https://ppc.sas.upenn.edu/opportunities/conference-archives.

Center for Disease Control. (2018). *Drug overdose mortality by state*. Retrieved on January 14, 2019 from https://www.cdc.gov/nchs/pressroom/sosmap/drug_poisoning_mortality/drug_poisoning.htm.

Center for Disease Control. (2019). *Suicide mortality by state*. Retrieved on January 14, 2019 from https://www.cdc.gov/nchs/pressroom/sosmap/suicide-mortality/suicide.htm.

Chirot, D. E., & Seligman, M. E. (Eds.). (2001). *Ethnopolitical warfare: Causes, consequences, and possible solutions*. Washington, DC: American Psychological Association.

Cogdell, C. (2010). *Eugenic design: Streamlining America in the 1930s*. Philadelphia: University of Pennsylvania Press.

Cornum, R., Matthews, M. D., & Seligman, M. E. (2011). Comprehensive soldier fitness: Building resilience in a challenging institutional context. *American Psychologist, 66*(1), 4–11.

Coyne, J. C., Stefanek, M., & Palmer, S. C. (2007). Psychotherapy and survival in cancer: The conflict between hope and evidence. *Psychological Bulletin, 133*(3), 367–394. https://doi.org/10.1037/0033-2909.133.3.367.

Coyne, J. C., & Tennen, H. (2010). Positive psychology in cancer care: Bad science, exaggerated claims, and unproven medicine. *Annals of Behavioral Medicine, 39*(1), 16–26. https://doi.org/10.1007/s12160-009-9154-z.

Csikszentmihalyi, M. (1997). *Finding flow: The psychology of engagement with everyday life*. New York: Basic Books.

The Daily Beast. (2011). *List of the most tolerant and the least tolerant states*. Retrieved on January 14, 2019 from https://www.thedailybeast.com/ranking-the-most-tolerant-and-least-tolerant-states.

Diener, E. (2009a). Positive psychology: Past, present, and future. In S. J. Lopez & S. R. Snyder (Eds.), *Oxford handbook of positive psychology* (pp. 7–11). New York: Oxford University Press.

Diener, E. (Ed.). (2009b). *The science of well-being: The collected works of Ed Diener*. New York, NY: Springer Science & Business Media.

Deiner, E., Kesebir, P., & Lucas, R. (2008). Benefits of accounts of well-being–For societies and for psychological science. *Applied Psychology: An International Review, 57*(Suppl. 1), 37–53. https://doi.org/10.1111/j.1464-0597.2008.00353.x.

Diener, E., & Seligman, M. E. (2004). Beyond money toward an economy of well-being. *Psychological Science in the Public Interest, 5*(1), 1–31.

Duke, D. E. (1999). *My awakening: A path to racial understanding*. Convington, LA: Free Speech Press.

Easton, M. (2006). Does diversity make us unhappy? *The American Renaissance*. Retrieved on January 14, 2019 from https://www.amren.com/news/2006/06/does_diversity/.

Ehrenreich, B. (2007). John Templeton's universe. *The Nation*. Retrieved on January 14, 2019 from https://www.thenation.com/article/john-templetons-universe/.

Ehrenreich, B. (2009). *Bright-sided: How the relentless promotion of positive thinking is undermining America*. New York, NY: Metropolitan Books.

Fischer, R., & Chalmers, A. (2008). Is optimism universal? A meta-analytical investigation of optimism levels across 22 nations. *Personality and Individual Differences, 45*(5), 378–382.

Fredrickson, B. (2009). *Positivity: Top-notch research reveals the 3 to 1 ratio that will change your life*. New York, NY: Three Rivers Press.

Fredrickson, B. L. (2013). Updated thinking on positivity ratios. *American Psychologist, 68*(9), 814–822. https://doi.org/10.1037/a0033584.

Fredrickson, B. L., & Losada, M. F. (2005). Positive affect and the complex dynamics of human flourishing. *American Psychologist, 60,* 678–686. https://doi.org/10.1037/0003-066X.60.7.678.

Friedman, H. L., & Brown, N. J. (2018). Implications of debunking the "Critical Positivity Ratio" for humanistic psychology: Introduction to special issue. *Journal of Humanistic Psychology, 58*(3), 239–261.

Geronimus, A. T., Bound, J., & Colen, C. G. (2011). Excess black mortality in the United States and in selected black and white high-poverty areas, 1980–2000. *American Journal of Public Health, 101*(4), 720–729.

Gould, S. J. (1996). *The mismeasure of man*. New York, NY: W. W. Norton & Company.

Grossi, G., Kelly, S., Nash, A., & Parameswaran, G. (2014). Challenging dangerous ideas: A multidisciplinary critique of evolutionary psychology. *Dialectical Anthropology, 38*(3), 281–285.

Held, B. S. (2004). The negative side of positive psychology. *Journal of Humanistic Psychology, 44*(1), 9–46.

Held, B. S. (2018). Positive psychology's a priori problem. *Journal of Humanistic Psychology, 58*(3), 313–342.

Independent Review Report. (2015). *American Psychological Association*. Retrieved on October 5, 2016 from https://www.apa.org/independent-review/APA-FINAL-Report-7.2.15.pdf.

Iyer, V. R. K. (1990). *Human rights and human wrong*. Ann Arbor: University of Michigan Press.

Jacobs, T. (2013). Study: Extreme conservatives make happier people. *The American Renaissance*. Retrieved on January 14, 2019 from https://www.amren.com/news/2013/07/study-extreme-conservatives-make-happier-people.

Joseph, S., & Murphy, D. (2013). Person-centered approach, positive psychology, and relational helping: Building bridges. *Journal of Humanistic Psychology, 53*(1), 26–51.

Kamin, L. J. (2012). *The science and politics of IQ*. New York, NY: Routledge.

Kanazawa, S., & Li, N. P. (2015). Happiness in modern society: Why intelligence and ethnic composition matter. *Journal of Research in Personality*. Retrieved on January 14, 2019 from https://www.amren.com/news/2017/12/happiness-modern-society-intelligence-ethnic-composition-matter/.

Keith, T. (2017). How positive thinking helped propel Trump to presidency. *NPR All Things Considered Report*. Retrieved on January 14, 2019 from https://www.npr.org/2017/01/19/510628862/how-positive-thinkinghelped-propel-trump-to-the-presidency.

Krieshok, T. (2016). *Eulogy for Shane Lopez*. Retrieved on April 1, 2019 from http://www.people.ku.edu/~tkrieshok/Lopez_eulogy.pdf.

Kruse, M. (2017). The power of Trump's positive thinking. *The Politico*. Retrieved on January 14, 2019 from https://www.politico.com/magazine/story/2017/10/13/donald-trump-positive-thinking-215704.

Lewontin, R. C., Rose, S., & Kamin, L. J. (1984). *Not in our genes: Biology, ideology, and human nature*. New York, NY: Pantheon.

Lombardo, P. A. (Ed.). (2011). *A century of eugenics in America: From the Indiana experiment to the human genome era.* Bloomington: Indiana University Press.

Lopez, S. J. (2013). *Making hope happen: Create the future you want for yourself and others.* New York, NY: Simon & Schuster.

Lopez, S. J., & Gallagher, M. W. (2009). A case for positive psychology. In S. J. Lopez & S. R. Snyder (Eds.), *Oxford handbook of positive psychology* (pp. 3–6). New York: Oxford University Press.

Lopez, S. J., Magyar-Moe, J. L., Petersen, S. E., Ryder, J. A., Krieshok, T. S., O'Byrne, K. K., … Fry, N. A. (2006). Counseling psychology's focus on positive aspects of human functioning. *The Counseling Psychologist, 34*(2), 205–227.

Lopez, S. J., Pedrotti, J. T., & Snyder, C. R. (2018). *Positive psychology: The scientific and practical explorations of human strengths.* Thousand Oaks, CA: Sage.

Lyubomirsky, S. (2008). *The how of happiness: A scientific approach to getting the life you want.* New York, NY: Penguin.

MacInnis, C. C., Busseri, M. A., Choma, B. L., & Hodson, G. (2013). The happy cyclist: Examining the association between generalized authoritarianism and subjective well-being. *Personality and Individual Differences, 55*(7), 789–793.

Magyar-Moe, J. L., & Lopez, S. J. (2008). Human agency, strengths-based development and well being. *Biennial Review of Counseling Psychology, 1,* 157–175.

Magyar-Moe, J. L., Owens, R. L., & Scheel, M. J. (2015). Applications of positive psychology in counseling psychology: Current status and future directions. *The Counseling Psychologist, 43*(4), 494–507. https://doi.org/10.1177/0011000015581001.

McKinnon, S. (2006). *Neo-liberal genetics: The myths and moral tales of evolutionary psychology.* Chicago, IL: Prickly Paradigm Press.

Miller, A. (2008). A critique of positive psychology—Or 'The new science of happiness'. *Journal of Philosophy of Education, 42*(3/4), 591–608. https://doi.org/10.1111/j.1467-9752.2008.00646.x.

Nickerson, C. A. (2014). No empirical evidence for critical positivity ratios. *The American Psychologist, 69*(6), 626.

Nickerson, C. A. (2018). There is no empirical evidence for critical positivity ratios: Comment on Fredrickson (2013). *Journal of Humanistic Psychology, 58*(3), 284–312.

Oikkonen, V. (2013). *Gender, sexuality and reproduction in evolutionary narratives.* London, UK: Routledge.

Ong, A. D., & van Dulmen, M. H. (Eds.). (2006). *Oxford handbook of methods in positive psychology.* New York, NY: Oxford University Press.

Palmer, S. C., Stefanek, M. E., Thombs, B. D., & Coyne, J. C. (2010). Psychological intervention and survival: Wishing does not make it so–Letter. *Clinical Cancer Research*. https://doi.org/10.1158/1078-0432.CCR-10-1703.

Pedrotti, J. T., Edwards, L. M., & Lopez, S. J. (2009). Positive psychology within a cultural context. In S. J. Lopez & S. R. Snyder (Eds.), *Oxford handbook of positive psychology* (pp. 49–57). New York: Oxford University Press.

Pérez-Álvarez, M. (2013). Positive psychology and its friends: Revealed. *Papeles del Psicólogo, 34*(3), 208–226.

Peterson, C., & Seligman, M. E. P. (2004). *Character strengths and virtues: A handbook and classification*. New York, NY: Oxford University Press.

PhysOrg. (2014). Danish DNA could be key to happiness. *The American Renaissance*. Retrieved on January 14, 2019 from https://www.amren.com/news/2014/07/danish-dna-could-be-key-to-happiness.

Pinker, S. (2018). *Enlightenment now: The case for reason, science, humanism, and progress*. New York: Penguin.

Pluess, M. (Ed.). (2015). *Genetics of psychological well-being: The role of heritability and genetics in positive psychology*. New York, NY: Oxford University Press.

Popenoe, P., & Johnson, R. H. (1935). *Applied eugenics* (2nd ed.). New York: Macmillan.

Porter, E. (1913). *Pollyanna*. Boston, MA: Colonial Press.

Pulla, V. (2016). *The Lhotsampa people of Bhutan: Resilience and survival*. New York, NY: Palgrave.

Robbins, B. D., & Friedman, H. (2008). Introduction to our Special Issue on Positive Psychology. *The Humanistic Psychologist, 36*(2), 93–95.

Rose, H., & Rose, S. (2010). *Alas poor Darwin: Arguments against evolutionary psychology*. New York: Random House.

Rushton, J. P., & Jensen, A. R. (2005). Wanted: More race realism, less moralistic fallacy. *Psychology, Public Policy, and Law, 11*(2), 328–336. https://doi.org/10.1037/1076-8971.11.2.328.

Ruti, M. (2015). *The age of scientific sexism: How evolutionary psychology promotes gender profiling and fans the battle of the sexes*. Toronto, ON: Bloomsbury.

Science Daily. (2015). How your brain reacts to emotional information is influenced by your genes. *The American Renaissance*. Retrieved on January 14, 2019 from https://www.amren.com/news/2015/07/how-your-brain-reactsto*emotional-information-is-influenced-by-your-genes/.

Science Friday. (2018). *What makes your brain happy?* National Public Radio segment recorded on July 13, 2018. Retrieved on April 1, 2019 from https://www.sciencefriday.com/segments/what-makes-your-brain-happy/.

The Science of Happiness. (2019). Research-based tips for a meaningful life. A co-production with the Greater Good Science Center at UC Berkeley. *The Public Radio International*. Retrieved on January 14, 2019 from https://www.pri.org/programs/science-happiness.

Seligman, M. E. (1975). *Helplessness: On depression, development, and death*. New York, NY: W.H. Freeman/Times Books/Henry Holt & Co.

Seligman, M. E. (2002). *Learned optimism: How to change your mind and your life*. New York, NY: Vintage.

Seligman, M. E. (2006). *Authentic happiness: Using the new positive psychology to realize your potential for lasting fulfillment*. New York, NY: Simon & Schuster.

Seligman, M. E. (2007). *The optimistic child: A proven program to safeguard children against depression and build lifelong resilience*. New York, NY: Houghton Mifflin Harcourt.

Seligman, M. E. (2011). *Flourish: A visionary new understanding of happiness and well-being*. New York, NY: Simon & Schuster.

Seligman, M. E., & Csikszentmihalyi, M. (2014). *Positive psychology: An introduction*. New York, NY: Springer.

Seligman, M. E., Railton, P., Baumeister, R. F., & Sripada, C. (2017). *Homo prospectus*. New York, NY: Oxford University Press.

Seligman, M. E., Steen, T. A., Park, N., & Peterson, C. (2005). Positive psychology progress: Empirical validation of interventions. *American Psychologist, 60*(5), 410–421.

Seligman, M. E. P., & Csikszentmihalyi, M. (2000). Positive psychology: An introduction. *American Psychologist, 55*(1), 5–14.

Seligman, M. E. P., & Fowler, R. D. (2011). Comprehensive soldier fitness and the future of psychology. *American Psychologist, 66*(1), 82–86.

Sheldon, K. M., Frederickson, B., Rathunde, K., Csikszentmihalyi, M., & Haidt, J. (2000). *Positive psychology manifesto*. Retrieved on October 5, 2016 from http://www.positivepsychology.org/akumalmanifesto.html.

Sheldon, K. M., Kashdan, T. B., & Steger, M. F. (Eds.). (2010). *Designing positive psychology: Taking stock and moving forward*. New York: Oxford University Press.

Simonton, D. K. (2011). Positive psychology in historical and philosophical perspective: Predicting its future from the past. In K. M. Sheldon, T. B. Kashdan, & M. F. Steger (Eds.), *Designing positive psychology: Taking stock and moving forward* (pp. 447–454). New York: Oxford University Press [Orig. 2010].

Sleeper, J. (2016). The conservatives behind the campus free speech crusade. *The American Prospect*. Retrieved on April 1, 2019 from https://prospect.org/article/conservatives-behind-campus-'free-speech'-crusade.

Soldz, S. (2016). The comprehensive soldier fitness program: Discontinued and misrepresented positive psychology. In S. Soldz, & O. Yakushko (Co-chairs), *Ethics of social justice/Social justice of ethics: Implications for psychology and psychologists*. Symposium presented at the meeting of the American Psychological Association, Denver, CO.

The Source Watch. (2019). *John Templeton, Jr.* Retrieved on January 14, 2019 from https://www.sourcewatch.org/index.php/John_Templeton,_Jr.

South Dakota Suicide Prevention. (2018). *Suicide Factsheet.* Retrieved on January 14, 2019 from http://doh.sd.gov/documents/statistics/SuicideFactsheet.pdf.

Southern Poverty Law Center. (2019). *Fighting hate/extremist files: The American Renaissance.* https://www.splcenter.org/fighting-hate/extremist-files/group/american-renaissance.

Stefanek, M. E., Palmer, S. C., Thombs, B. D., & Coyne, J. C. (2009). Finding what is not there. *Cancer, 115*(24), 5612–5616.

Sumalla, E. C., Ochoa, C., & Blanco, I. (2009). Posttraumatic growth in cancer: Reality or illusion? *Clinical Psychology Review, 29*(1), 24–33.

Sutter, J. D. (2014). List: States where rape is most common. *CNN Report.* Retrieved on January 14, 2019 from https://www.cnn.com/2014/02/03/opinion/sutter-alaska-rape-list/index.html.

Taylor, J. (2011). Genetics, personality, and race. *American Renaissance.* Retrieved on January 14, 2019 from https://www.amren.com/news/2011/07/genetics_person/.

Templeton Foundation. (2019). *Funding Areas.* Retrieved on January 14, 2019 from https://www.templeton.org/funding-areas.

Tucker, W. H. (1996). *The science and politics of racial research.* Carbondale: University of Illinois Press.

Waldrop, M. K. (2011). Religion: Faith in science. *Nature, 470*, 323–325. https://doi.org/10.1038/470323a. Retrieved on April 1, 2019 from https://www.nature.com/news/2011/110216/full/470323a.html.

Watson, J. B. (1914). *Behavior: An introduction to comparative psychology.* New York, NY: H. Holt.

Watson, J. B. (1919). *Psychology: From the standpoint of a behaviorist.* Philadelphia, PA: Lippincott.

Watson, J. B. (1928). *Psychological care of infant and child.* New York: W. W. Norton.

Weiss, A., Adams, M. J., Widdig, A., & Gerald, M. S. (2011). Rhesus Macaques (Macaca Mulatta) as living fossils of hominoid personality and subjective well-being. *Journal of Comparative Psychology, 125*(1), 72–83.

Williams, T. (2015). What makes Templeton tick and just how scary is this place. *The Inside Philanthropy.* Retrieved on January 14, 2019 from https://www.insidephilanthropy.com/home/2015/1/6/what-makes-templetontick-and-just-how-scary-is-this-place-a.html.

Wong, P. T. (2011). Reclaiming positive psychology: A meaning-centered approach to sustainable growth and radical empiricism. *Journal of Humanistic Psychology, 51*(4), 408–412.

Wright, R. (1994). *The moral animal: The new science of evolutionary psychology.* New York: Pantheon Books.

Yakushko, O. (2018). Don't worry, be happy: Erasing racism, sexism, and poverty in positive psychology. *Psychotherapy and Politics International, 16*(1), e1433.

Yakushko, O. (2019). Eugenics and its evolution in history of western psychology: A critical archival review. *Psychotherapy and Politics International*, online.
Yakushko, O., & Blodgett, E. (2018). Negative reflections about positive psychology: On constraining the field to a focus on happiness and personal achievement. *Journal of Humanistic Psychology*. https://doi.org/10.1177/0022167818794551.
Yerkes, R. M. (1907). *The dancing mouse: A study in animal behavior*. New York, NY: Macmillan.

CHAPTER 7

On Being Pollyanna About Sciences

Throughout the history of the sciences of enforced happiness, described in this book, it has been common for proponents of these ideas to promote them as absolutely true because they are "scientific" and produced by "scientists." Shaming individuals for following their "feel-good" or "bleeding heart" responses (e.g., human rights concerns, care for children when they are distressed) rather than adhering to supposedly scientifically derived and empirically validated strategies (e.g., eugenic policies, psychological treatments with focus on control) has also been a prevailing strategy. In this brief chapter I will examine such practices under the umbrella term, "scientism," as well as focus on the intentional use of ideologically-informed sciences that nevertheless promotes themselves as socially neutral, apolitical, or culture-blind. These forms of science or scientism contribute to various forms of social violence, including not only the "epistemological violence" inherent in the propagation of their truth-claims, also their methodological practices, and the impact of both their processes (e.g., impersonal data collections) and findings on lives of the individuals and communities they target (Teo, 2008, 2010).

The Discovery of Scientism

Scientism is defined as an ideological movement which champions the use of purportedly objective empirical tools in the promotion of socio-politically normative values (Bannister, 1991; Sorell, 2013; Stenmark, 2018; Williams & Robinson, 2014). Scholars who study the

O. Yakushko, *Scientific Pollyannaism*,
https://doi.org/10.1007/978-3-030-15982-5_7

rise of scientism point to the Enlightenment era as the moment when sciences become a tool of cultural and political control, intentionally used in service of the powerful (Olson, 2008; Sorell, 2013; Stenmark, 2018; Williams & Robinson, 2014). Contemporary writers on scientism often use the "evolutionary" sciences as an explanatory touchstone: according to Sorell (2013),

> *Scientism is the belief that science, especially natural science, is the most valuable part of human learning—much the most valuable because it is much the most authoritative, or serious, or beneficial.* Other beliefs related to this one may also be regarded as scientific, e.g. the belief that science is the *only* valuable part of human learning, or that the view that is always good for subjects that do not belong to science to be placed on scientific footing. (p. 4)

According to Stenmark (2018), although scientism is likely as old as science itself, contemporary iterations have become a significant social force, especially in Western societies. In his view, this rise is due to a cultural requirement that moral questions be posed and answered by scientists rather than religious or cultural authorities. Stenmark asserted,

> These scientific discoveries are believed to be the greatest intellectual advanced of the twentieth century and to have profound impact on our self-view; we have to start all over again *to describe and understand ourselves in terms alien to our intuitions. Some of these scientists also believe that contemporary science, with the recent development of evolutionary biology, can even tell us how we morally ought to live and what we ought to value in life.* (p. 3)

In contemporary discussions, the term "scientism" has come to imply two different trends. One of them is reflected in inaccurate or inappropriate use of the sciences to fit specific ideological causes (Bannister, 1991; Sorell, 2013; Stenmark, 2018). For example, the studies discussed in the previous chapter—backed by the Pioneer Fund, and featured in White supremacy publications (e.g., Duke's 1999 *My Awakening* or articles posted on the American Renaissance website)—reflect this intentional use of science to pursue a racist agenda. This form of scientism was certainly central in large-scale eugenic studies such as the Army Mental Tests (Brigham, 1923; Yerkes, 1920), which openly embraced social Darwinist eugenic agenda of "racial betterment." To remind the reader, not only did this study of nearly two million military recruits produce stunningly racist, Anti-Semitic, and xenophobic results, it was grounded in eugenic strategies and produced by openly eugenic promoters (e.g., Yerkes advertised for testing technicians for this study in multiple eugenic journals; all of the scholars involved in it are listed as leaders of varied American eugenic organizations) (*Eugenical News*, 1916–1922; Gould, 1996; Smith, 1985; Tucker, 1996; Zenderland, 2001).

The term "scientism" is also used to describe the selective use of scientific epistemological values and tools (e.g., methodologies and strategies) to meet specific ideological goals. Specifically, this form of scientism insists that the paradigms of the natural sciences are the most or the only appropriate methods for the study of human beings and human life (Bannister, 1991; Williams & Robinson, 2014). According to Sorrell (2013), "*Scientism is a matter of putting too high a value on natural science in comparison with other branches of learning or culture*" (p. 1). Blackburn (2005) further defined scientism as a "pejorative term for the belief that the methods of natural science, or the categories and things recognized in natural science, form the only proper elements in any philosophical or other inquiry" (pp. 331–332).

The intention of scientism throughout history has been not only to elevate sciences to the status of religion (e.g., build "temples of reason") but also to shape individual and social behavior (Stenmark, 2018; Williams & Robinson, 2014). For example, in his study of the long history of scientism, Sorell (2013) cites scientific encyclopedia entries by Diderot, an Enlightenment thinker, in which he sought not only to systematically organize and display scientific findings but also use knowledge so that "our children, becoming better instructed, *may become at the same time more virtuous and happy*" (p. 176). Sorell further showed that many Western philosophers viewed scientific pursuit as directly linked to various aspects of human happiness leading to such claims as:

> Theoretical science contributes to a culture of skill, taking the satisfaction of human desires more efficient, and therefore helping us to become happy. Practical science—the system of morality—contributes to a culture of discipline. It tells us what ends we ought to pursue and also which of our policies of action are consistent with those ends. *Trying to live by this science is what makes us worthy to be happy.* (p. 74)

The question remains, is scientism truly a form of science, even if ideologically driven? Stenmark (2018) argues that the results and interpretations made of scientism-fueled sciences do not meet the standards of what is considered genuine scientific endeavor because "Scientism typically is a combination of certain scientific theories and a particular ideology or world view, namely naturalism or materialism… [which themselves] are not scientific but philosophical theories" (p. 4). Sorell (2013) further argued that any scientific claim that asserts absolutist empiricist claims likely reflects scientism. Thus, Sorell posited the following five features of fundamentalist or rigid scientific/scientistic empiricism:

> (1) science is united; (2) there are not limits to sciences; (3) science has been enormously successful at prediction explanation and control; (4) the methods of science confer objectivity or scientific results; and (5) science has been beneficial to human beings. (p. 4)

In contrast, scholars of scientism describe the inaccuracy of these claims and their deliberately misleading application in the social, political, and individual spheres of human life (Sorell, 2013; Stenmark, 2018).

No forms of science, especially the sciences that study human beings, function outside of human philosophies and worldviews. Scientific Pollyannaism, along with other forms of sciences that claimed to be neutral (e.g., "race realism," evolutionary psychology), is marked by the assertions that their sciences are above ideology, are impartial and universal. Scientific Pollyannaist scholars routinely declare that their sciences are the truth and cannot be biased. In short, this requirement that a person be a Pollyanna about scientific Pollyanist claims to be non-ideological and absolutely "true," is most likely a form of scientism. Scientism itself in turn requires scientific Pollyannaism.

Scientific or Scientistic Pollyannaism from *The Hammer of Witches* to "Race Realism"

In the various iterations of scientific Pollyannaism described in this book, science and scientists are elevated to paragons of absolute truth and knowledge. Although the *Malleus Malificarum* (*The Hammer of Witches*) relied on predominately Biblical justifications for demonization of certain emotional states and people who display them, its theological claims were always justified by the available scientific knowledge. In addition to philosophers such as Socrates, Aristotle, Plato or Seneca, the *Malleus* referred to the available biological sciences of the time (e.g., distribution of blood humors). As noted in a section on eugenics, eugenic scientists presented their sciences of "racial betterment" as both exact and impartial. For example, Galton (1869) in his book, *Hereditary Genius: An Inquiry Into Its Laws and Consequences*, dismisses challenges to his attempts to define human differences as hereditary and biological, distancing his own beliefs from other uneducated and supposedly unscientific "pretensions of natural equality":

> I have no patience with the hypothesis occasionally expressed, and often implied, especially in tales written to teach children to be good, that babies are born pretty much alike, and that the sole agencies in creating differences between boy and boy, and man and man, are steady application and moral effort. *It is in the most unqualified manner that I object to pretensions of natural equality*. The experiences of the nursery, the school, the University, and of professional careers, are a chain of proofs to the contrary. (p. 14)

Galton (1907) routinely attacked anyone who refused the "proven" truth of his eugenic sciences by claiming that their objections stemmed either from ignorance or obstinate refusal to learn:

> I propose now to speak of those fundamental principles of the laws of Probability that are chiefly concerned in the newer methods of Biometry, and consequently of Eugenics. Most persons of ordinary education seem to know nothing about them, not even understanding their technical terms, much less appreciating the cogency of their results. This *popular ignorance so obstructs the path of Eugenics* that I venture to tax your attention by proposing a method of partly dispelling it. Let me first say that no one can be more conscious than myself of the large amount of study that is required to qualify a man to deal adequately with the mathematical methods of Biometry, or that any man can hope for much success in that direction unless he is possessed of *appropriate faculties and a strong brain*. On the other hand, I hold an opinion likely at first sight to scandalize biometricians and which I must justify, that the fundamental ideas on which abstruse problems of Probability are based admit of being so presented *to any intelligent person as to be grasped by him, even though he be quite ignorant of mathematics*. (p. 15)

As noted earlier, Karl Pearson, a eugenicist and founder of the field of statistics, similarly shamed individuals for their refusal to follow eugenic sciences rather than their feel-good humane responses to marginalized groups. In his *National Life from the Standpoint of Science* Pearson (1905) claimed that his eugenic statistical work was "powerful" in its "effect on the mind of a true scientific education, which enables a man or woman to form *judgments freed from individual bias*" (p. 107). Throughout this work he shamed his readers, including for "romantic sympathy for the Red Indian" (p. 25) while praising "America" for the genocide against the indigenous peoples as supposedly "masterful human progress following the inter-racial struggle" (p. 25).

Evans (1931), who led the American Eugenic Society's Committee on Formal Education, stated that eugenics, in contrast to other approaches, was a "*method of direct scientific observation rather than methods of second-hand or hearsay evidence*" (p. 29).

Another eugenicist, a Harvard psychologist, and two-time president of the American Psychological Association Robert Yerkes (1923) further argued that without its scientific foundation eugenics, like other disciplines or social phenomena, would not be as successful. The sciences, especially psychological sciences, Yerkes assured the both academic and broader community, would provide irrefutable proof for eugenic values and practices. In his words,

> *Eugenics needs accurate and reasonably complete description of human behaviour as partial basis for methods of control.* It may look to psychology hopefully for accurate descriptions of traits of mind and their expressions in action, for measurements of the manifold features of intellect, feeling, will, temperament, character-in fine for the scientific description of the human personality. (p. 226)

In the Introduction to the Army Mental Test summary by Princeton psychologist and later developer of the Scholastic Apperception Test (SAT) Brigham (1923), entitled *A Study in American Intelligence*, Yerkes encouraged the readers to explicitly trust eugenic scientific findings. As noted earlier, these Army Mental Tests provided numerous statistical graphs and summaries with claims of the irrefutable empirical evidence of "the marked intellectual inferiority of the negro" (p. 190), data to "disprove the popular belief that the Jew is highly intelligent" (p. 190), proof that "the average intelligence of our immigrants is declining" (p. 197) and "the recent immigrants [Southern Europeans, Irish, Slavic] are intellectually closer to the negro than to the native born white sample" (p. 199). Thus, Yerkes proclaimed: "*It behooves us to consider their [the Army Mental Test findings'] reliability and their meaning, for no one of us as a citizen can afford to ignore the menace of race deterioration or the evident relations of immigration to national progress and welfare*" (p. viii).

Eugenicists claimed that happiness would stem from adherence to scientific eugenic advice. Melendy (1914), a medical scholar who produced the voluminous *Science of Eugenics and Sex Life*, filled her book not only with numerous references to scientific studies as well as images of the brain and other human organs. She also routinely connected human difficulties with failure to follow eugenic guidelines. In her chapter entitled *Science the Friend of Love*, Melendy declared

> The quarrels, separations and divorces now of such frequent occurrence would be unheard of if all about to marry would be guided by judgment and science, which are the true friends, not the foes, of happy love. Now, youths and maidens, I adjure you with all the emphasis of my lifelong dealing with humanity on this subject, to be guided by your own carefully-studied ideals in making a life-choice!... *Equip your mind with these principles of science, so vital to your future happiness.* (p. 215)

As noted before, John B. Watson (1914, 1919, 1928) routinely shamed readers about their unwillingness to accept his scientific behavioral experiments and conclusions, warning of dire consequence by those who do not adhered to his scientific advice. In his introductory books on behaviorism Watson (1914, 1919) justified the torture of caged animals for his studies and chided his audience for their squeamish attitudes about their treatment. His 1928 book, co-written with his student and mistress-turned-wife Rosalie Reyner, *Psychological Care of Infant and Child*, became one of the first national best-sellers on parenting, selling over 100,000 copies in the first few months of its publication (Buckley, 1989). Dedicated to "*the first mother who brings up a happy child*," it emphasized the use of "scientific material" and "experimental work."

In the introduction, Watson decried that "*parents—mother especially—resent still more strenuously any [scientific] advice or instructions on how to care psychologically for their children*" (p. 3). As noted above in a section on Watson and behaviorism, the basis for his "advice and instruction" were sadistic experiments on young children, including his own children. Decrying the state of the country and the state of parenthood, Watson declared "there are undoubtedly more scientific ways of bringing up their children which will probably mean finer and happier children" (p. 5). His science-based admonitions included statements such as "won't you then remember when you are tempted to pet your child that mother love is a dangerous instrument" (p. 87).

Using science to justify ideology has remained central to Western academic practice, even after eugenic-based racism and anti-Semitism fell out of vogue, with the result that scientific Pollyannaism has continued in contemporary psychology. Notably, even after the exposure of the eugenic foundations of Nazi policies, eugenics and other racist and sexist sciences remained dominant in Western psychology. H. E. Garrett, president of the American Psychological Association in 1946 and psychology professor at Columbia University, remained committed to hereditary biological explanations of human differences and was instrumental in developing the branch of eugenic and Darwinist psychology re-branded as "behavioral genetics" (Tucker, 1996). Garrett was among a number of psychologists who took the witness stand to provide empirical support for maintaining racial segregation of schools in the *Brown v. Board of Education* hearings (Tucker, 1996). He also served as the director of the racist and eugenics-focused Pioneer Fund and contributed to such White Supremacy publications as the *White Citizen Gazette.* Garrett's (1961) article entitled *The Equalitarian Dogma* using terms such like "dogma," to describe supposedly "politically correct" (i.e., non-scientific) scholarly work that supported human rights, which supposedly denied scientific truth. Garrett is among many such scholars who shamed his colleagues and the public for their commitment to human rights and equality (Guthrie, 2004; Tucker, 1996; Yakushko, 2019). Garrett's work also stands in stunning juxtaposition to the multiple UNESCO (1969) proclamations, signed by leading world scientists after the end of the World War II, which applied UNESCO human rights protocols to scientific inquiries, particularly targeting the oppressive scientific myths used to justify racial inequality (e.g., genetic bases of racial group differences).

The Pioneering Funding of Scientific Racist Pollyannaism

Nevertheless, in the sciences just as in the rest of society, oppressive values and violent epistemologies persist (Bergman, 2014; Black, 2003; Chase, 1980; Tucker, 1996; Yakushko, 2019). Eugenic organizations in the U.S. have re-branded themselves. For example, the American Eugenics Society changed its name to the Society for the Study of Social Biology (Social Biology, 1973), which continued to produce Darwinist and eugenicist evolutionary "sciences," especially on racial difference (e.g., E. O. Wilson's 1975 *Sociobiology*). The American Breeder's Association's section dedicated to genetic eugenic studies (*American Breeders Magazine: A Journal of Genetics and Eugenics*, 1912), renamed itself as the field of behavioral genetics (see Whitney, 1999, description of behavioral genetics in his introduction to Duke's 1999 *My Awakening*). Moreover, the Pioneer Fund, named one of the most notorious racist contemporary organizations by the Southern Poverty Law Center (2019), has been actively funding eugenic, racist, xenophobic and sexist studies since 1930s. It is notable that this organization, funded by far-right philanthropists, does not endow politicians, media personalities or cultural icons. The Pioneer Fund's primary mission has been to financially support scientists. Its success in legitimizing eugenics, racism, sexism, xenophobia and other forms of social violence with "scientific" facts and data is remarkable, as its clandestine power in the academy itself. According to its website, the Pioneer Fund (2013) is

> a not-for-profit foundation established in 1937 to advance the scientific study of *heredity and human differences*. Named to honor the early pioneers who built America, our mandate is to *support pioneering research in those fields*. We solicit contributions, which we use to fund vital research projects into the basis and correlates of *human ability and diversity*, and for the dissemination of that research to the public… Even in that period, the Pioneer Fund helped keep alive the naturalist perspective by supporting vital research in:
>
> - Behavioral Genetics
> - Intelligence
> - Social Demography
> - Group Differences – Sex, Social Class, and Race.

> Through our grants program, The Pioneer Fund has *changed the face of the social and behavioral sciences by restoring the Darwinian-Galtonian perspective to the mainstream in traditional fields such as anthropology, psychology, and sociology, as well as fostering the newer disciplines of behavioral genetics, neuroscience, evolutionary psychology, and sociobiology.* The Pioneer Fund's biosocial approach recognizes no fixed boundaries between disciplines, only different questions to be asked and answered. The research we support *looks at our evolutionary past (human origins), our present (individual and group differences), and our future (the impact of technology and globalization on human ecology and demography).* (online)

Recipients of the Pioneer Fund include Hans Eysenck (British psychologist who worked to prove that not only intelligence but also personality characteristic such as optimism are inherited and differ by race); Linda Gottfredson (American psychologist studying the heredity of intelligence, criminality, and other factors; an open opponent of affirmative action); Arthur Jensen (American intelligence researcher and psychologist who promoted the inferiority of non-White groups based on their intelligence); Thomas Bouchard (American psychologist whose behavioral genetic twin studies insist on the biological foundations for racial differences in both intelligence and personality characteristics such as optimism); Richard Lynn (British psychologist who promotes intellectual and personality inferiority of racial minorities); J. Phillipe Rushton (Canadian psychologist who claimed that racial difference in intelligence are evolutionary and related to size of genitalia and brain), and many other Western scholars (see Pioneer Fund website, for more information). Many of these individuals have been and continue to be published in leading psychology journals and are interviewed as expert authorities by media on various subjects (e.g., Rushton was featured by CNN as an expert on intelligence). Many of them present both at scientific conferences and at meetings of organizations such as the American Renaissance, a White supremacy think-tank. Rushton (2002), in his laudatory history of the Pioneer Fund, stated that the "mission" of this organization has been

> To conduct or aid in conducting study and research *into the problems of heredity and eugenics in the human race generally and such study and such research in respect to animals and plants as may throw light upon heredity in man, and…research and study into the problems of human race betterment [eugenics] with special reference to the people of the United States.* (p. 258)

One of the Fund's recipients, Lynn (2007), continues to publish a tremendous amount of racist "race realism" research, such as a lengthy article, included on the American Renaissance website, about the empirical proof that Black and African American people are distinguished from other "races" by their "psychopathic personality" (online). These scientists routinely claim that their scientific work represents the truth, a truth they claim is only deniable by wrong-headedly denied by the feel-good politically-correct followers of equality and social justice, inside the academia and out. They are supported by conservative financial backers such as Templeton (see information about Templeton and FAIR in the previous chapter). Calling themselves "race-realists" and "gender feminists" (i.e., promoters of different-but-equal beliefs), these scholars routinely present themselves being persecuted for their supposed commitment to scientific truth (Garrett, 1961; Gottfredson, 1994a, 1994b, 2005; Hunt, 1999; Itzkoff, 1994; Lynn, 2001a, 2001b; Pinker, 2002, 2018; Whitney, 1997, 1999).

Scientific Eugenic Utopias in Contemporary Psychology

Many of the scientists connected to varied versions of scientific Pollyannaism continue to offer utopian visions of happiness, apparently based on empirical formulations. One such "study" was made by Raymond Cattell, a noted statistics scholar and a member of multiple contemporary eugenic societies (American Eugenics Society, 2015; Gottfredson, 1994a; Whitney, 1997). Cattell (1987) penned a racist eugenic book entitled *Beyondism*: Religion from Science. Discussing his ideas for the *Beyondist* foundation's newsletter, Cattell further extolled eugenics as a salvific path to universal happiness, as a "human substitute for natural selection" (in Mehler, 1997, p. 154). He then attacked individuals who questioned eugenics, proclaiming that only "uneducated people" associated eugenics with "what Hitler did," while the truly intelligent thinker will recognize that "*Hitler actually shared many values of the average American*" such as "family values," and Hitler's turning "evil in his militarism and his treatment of Jews," should not lead "*a rational person… calling all his [Hitler's] attitudes mistaken*" (in Mehler, 1997, p. 154). National and individual happiness and well-being, Cattell claimed, were the primary reasons why Hitler pursued his idea of purifying the German nation. These ideas are echoed in the writings of other contemporary defenders of eugenics such as Herrnstein and Murray (1996) and Pinker (2002, 2018).

How Pollyannas Become Enlightened Through Sciences

Another recent work of Scientific Pollyannaism asking for blind faith in Western sciences while claiming to be the only source of happiness, is found in the work of evolutionary psychologist Steven Pinker. Pinker's views on the supposedly salvific nature of science, coupled with his shaming of those who question him, have been promoted in several other popular books such as Hunt's (1999) *The New Know-Nothings: The Political Foes of the Scientific Study of Human Nature*. The most recent contribution by Pinker (2018)—*Enlightenment Now: The Case for Reason, Science, Humanism, and Progress*—is a continued anthem to Western scientism. In his book Pinker proclaimed that while everything else has supposedly failed (e.g., religion, politics, culture, humanities), it is Western science and scientists who have brought on the evolution of everything good in society, singularly responsible for humanities' current progress marked by greatest health, happiness, and prosperity for all.

Pinker's hereditarian and biologizing views are masked by numerous proclamations that he is not a far-right ideologue including inspirational quotes from Beatles, Bill Gates, and Barak Obama. In this and other books such as his *Blank Slate* (2002) Pinker routinely represents himself as a progressive liberal "gender feminist" (see discussion of different-but-equal gender perspectives in this book) while mixing sciences of physics, technology or medicine with social sciences of human difference. Under this guise Pinker openly promotes many racist and sexist scholars of the past (e.g., Galton, E. O. Wilson) and present (e.g., Pioneer Fund recipients such as Gottfredson, Jensen, Rushton). Resistance to racist and sexist (supposedly) scientific works, such as to Herrnstein and Murray's (1996) *The Bell Curve* or to Thornhill and Palmer's (2000) *Rape: A Natural History*, is decried by Pinker as an example of "anti-scientific" efforts to justify feel-good "social justice dogmas" that fly in the face of scientific truths.

In his quest to make readers into Pollyannas about sciences, Pinker provides numerous examples designed to question reader's own subjective perceptions and require them to blindly replace those beliefs with (supposedly) data-based "facts." According to Pinker (2018), "the worldview that guides the moral and spiritual values of a knowledgeable person today is the worldview given to us by science" (p. 394) because "science has granted us the gifts of life, health, wealth, knowledge, and freedom" (p. 386). Such stunningly false statements should be recognized as profoundly ahistorical (e.g., science and scientists have been complicit in many violations of human and animal welfare), yet Pinker and others like him (e.g., Cattell, 1987; Hunt, 1999) continue to promote visions of happy utopias based on "sciences." Thus, in his book *Enlightenment Now* Pinker (2018) claimed that the humanity has finally evolved to be the healthiest and happiest (although most of Pinker's data appears to be focused on U.S. and Europe), ignoring the fact that, once again, these assertions are based on large scale data that privilege the Western majorities while minimizing minority experience as exceptions to their perfectly bell-shaped data. For example, Pinker maintained that the U.S. is the least racist it has ever been, but that anti-scientific media, which refuses to only focus on data Pinker supplied, falsely create the public impressions that racism is prevalent. This coverage of racial violence and abuses, Pinker claimed, is just sensationalism and social justice propaganda. He suggested that the media should stick to presenting only scientific "facts" (i.e., large scale empirical results), which would in turn assure the public that racism is the thing of the past.

Any evidence to the contrary is dismissed by Pinker as non-scientific "dogma," and critical reviews of such data or histories are attacked as being against the sciences, "enlightenment" and progress. Pinker's book is itself, ironically, a "feel-good" inspirational read, despite being filled with impressive scientific terms, references to numerous scientific studies, and extensive reliance on confusing double-negatives. The veneer of systematic and comprehensive scientific summaries, provided by Pinker, hide his ideologies (e.g., exclusive focus on biological genetic and universal determinants of human social differences; promotion of eugenics, "race realism," and different-but-equal gender theories).

The overall point of this new call for being Pollyanna about sciences appears designed to develop a new public capacity to deny and ignore social realities. Under the guise of being pro-scientific, Pinker requires his readers to become anti-intellectual. Pinker, like other scholars mentioned in this section, represent their scientific work as universal, neutral, non-biased, a-contextual, and, most importantly, based on large amounts of data. Except that mythologized accounts of history are required to support their views. Specifically, evolutionary theorists or scholars base many of their theories (e.g., Rushton's evolution of intelligence,

Kanazawa's "Savannah principle," or Buss' "mate killing mode") on mythologized accounts of Pleistocene (cave men) times. Other evolutionary theories, such as paternal investment theory (Buss), are grounded on a pick-and-choose selection of animal behaviors. A general assumption made by many evolutionary and behavioral genetics scholars, which is not supported by actual anthropological scientific evidence, insists that violent patriarchy is universal and biological (e.g., studies on rape as evolutionary natural sex supposedly common among both humans and animals). Pinker, who promotes all of these theories to the public, naturally glosses over the fact that numerous scientists have not only questioned but dismissed these "sciences" as, in fact, unscientific and ideological. Instead, Pinker attacks any critics as being driven by "dogmas" of social justice and human equality.

Nevertheless, an unsuspecting reader, even if slightly familiar with this scholarship, would have an enormously difficult time sifting through the scholarship Pinker thrusts on his readers in his lengthy books. His assertions are interspersed with numerous graphs and data descriptions as well as inspirational quotes, all while chiding both readers on the Right and the Left for being unscientific. Pinker's own racism, and the racism of the scholars he celebrates (e.g., Galton, E. O. Wilson, L. Gottfredson, Herrnstein & Murray) is excused by his self-proclaimed liberalism. The scientific sexism Pinker espouses in his books and talks—as, for example, his belief that women are, on average, biologically incapable of producing scientific work or that "typical" rape is not a form of violence—are explained away by his supposed commitment to what he calls "gender" ("non-equality" or "different-but-equal") feminism. While he rebukes those on the political Right for being too religious or denying evolution, he equally attacks the media, the Left, progressive students, "anti-science humanities," and even the UN for being "anti-scientific." According to Pinker (2018), the humanities are mired in "dogmas" of "political correctness" and are too negative and pessimistic, which could be corrected if humanities finally embraced the leading role of "natural" sciences,

> The humanities have yet to recover from the disaster of postmodernism, with its defiant obscurantism, self-refuting relativism, and *suffocating political correctness.* Many of its luminaries—Nietzsche, Heidegger, Foucault, Lacan, Derrida, the Critical Theorists--are *morose cultural pessimists* who declare the modernity is odious… [and that] Western civilization is circling down the drain… With such a cheery view of the world, it's not surprising

> that humanities often have trouble defining a progressive agenda for their own enterprise… [whereas] a consilience with science offers the humanities many possibilities for new insight. (p. 406)

These branches of human knowledge that are not to be trusted because they are too emotionally negative and glum (i.e., bad sciences) in contrast to other ones (i.e., natural biological silences), which are characterized as cheery, positive, hopeful, and salvific. Branding scholars and students for their commitment to social justice as angry and nasty, is another hallmark of Pinker's (2002, 2018) arguments, as for example: "non-leftist speakers are frequently disinvited after protests or drowned out by jeering mobs" (Pinker, 2018, p. 373). Pinker's (2002) *The Blank Slate* makes it clear that these "non-leftist speakers" specifically include Herrnstein & Murray, who in fact continue to promote their racist eugenic *The Bell Curve* across U.S. campuses. Throughout this and his other works Pinker especially decries the rise of what he calls the "social justice dogma" of human equality and social justice in Western academy. Pinker declares,

> When a creed [social justice focus on human equality] becomes attached to an in-group, the critical faculties of its members can be disabled, and there are reasons to think that has happened within swaths of academia. In *The Blank Slate* (updated in 2016) I showed how *leftist politics had distorted the study of human nature*, including sex, violence, gender, childrearing, personality, and intelligence. (p. 403)

Indeed, these attacks by Pinker reflect what other scholars have termed the rise of anti-intellectualism, which often masks itself, as in Pinker's writings, with scientific or scientistic rhetoric. For example, Giroux (2011) specifically highlighted the role of evolutionary theories with focus on "survival-of-the-fittest," such as the "economic Darwinism," in contributing to the "disappearing intellectual" (p. 163). The "leftist politics" to which Pinker disparaging alludes in his books are political, cultural, and scientific efforts to acknowledge the foundational influence of injustice, racism, and oppression in shaping human society and the lives of individuals. It is these intellectual scholarly commitments that Pinker attacks while he re-establishes human hierarchies that privilege white people, the wealthy, males and other groups whose access to power has made them to healthiest, happiest survivors in the evolutionary race.

Thus, Pinker (2002) argues that social stereotypes are accurate, because they are based on data:

> with some important exceptions, stereotypes are in fact *not* inaccurate [translate Pinker's commonly used double-negative to "stereotypes are accurate"] when assessed against objective benchmarks such as census figures… *people's stereotypes are generally consistent with the statistics*, and in many cases their bias is to *underestimate the real differences between sexes or ethnic groups.* (p. 204)

Pinker's (2002) further asserted that the affirmative action should be abolished because "the benefits of a racially diverse workspace and campuses are [wrongly] thought to outweigh the costs of *discriminating against whites*" (p. 148) and that affirmative action make its recipients unhappy and unsatisfied because they cannot succeed in these fields because of their lack of correct genes (citing evidence from the Pioneer Fund supported Linda Gottfredson). Pinker (2002) also routinely promotes what is considered a racist use of the sciences to claim that "racial differences [in intelligence and character] are *largely adaptations to climate*" (p. 143), views which were promoted by original eugenicists (e.g., Darwin, Galton) as well as contemporary racist scholars (e.g., Rushton, Jensen, Herrnstein & Murray) and White supremacists (e.g., David Duke). These scholars are regularly cited and openly celebrated in Pinker's books. Pinker's views on gender differences include claims that rape is not a form of violence, stating that those who insist that "*rape-is-not-sex [another Pinker double-negative] doctrine will go down in history as an example of extraordinary popular delusion and the madness of crowds*" (Pinker, 2002, p. 362) or that "*rape is rooted in a feature of human nature, such as that men want sex across a wider range of circumstance than women do*" (Pinker, 2002, p. 164). Moreover, Pinker (2002), who remains an ardent supporter of the former Harvard University president Larry Summers, dismissed for making misogynistic remarks in relation to women's scholarly capabilities, repeatedly justifies Summers' claims with statements such as that "*males and females do not have interchangeable minds*" in regard to their capabilities (p. 351). He further argues that women are not represented in sciences because most women are genetically precluded from producing scientific work (i.e., Summer's argument, which he supposedly based on behavioral genetics studies).

Not surprisingly, eugenics itself is routinely extolled in Pinker's books: "*if people differ genetically in intelligence and character, could we selectively breed for smarter and nicer people?*" (Pinker, 2002, p. 152) and that "*if races, for example, turn out to have any biological reality*, or if the Indo-Europeans really were a conquering tribe—*we would not want to concede that Nazism was so wrong after all*" (Pinker, 2002, p. 155). In his newest work, Pinker (2018) restates that the rejection of eugenics is based on "anti-scientific propaganda" (p. 400). Pinker (2002, 2018) celebrates Galton (eugenics), E. O. Wilson (i.e., eugenic continuation of racism evolutionary views in sociobiology), the eugenic supporters Herrnstein & Murray (i.e., *The Bell Curve*) as well as many other scientists, noted for their production of scientific racism or sexism, and defends them as misunderstood or unfairly maligned.

Another of Pinker's books, *Better Angels of Our Nature: Why Violence Has Declined* (Pinker, 2011), engaged in further stunning discussions and misinterpretations of history that elevate wealthy European males as paragons of morality and evolutionary goodness while claiming that the poor and racial minorities worldwide remain at primitive savage levels of violence. In this book, Pinker made such statements as "the European decline of violence was spearheaded by a decline of *elite* violence. Today, statistics from every Western country show that the overwhelming majority of homicides and other *violent crimes are committed by people in the lowest socioeconomic classes*" (p. 82). Such striking pronouncements erases the legally sanctioned forms of violence perpetrated by the upper classes of Western civilizations against the poor in the form of punishment. Pinker then moves on to compare the "rate of death in warfare in nonstate and state societies," primarily celebrating the low rates of "battle" and "war" deaths in twentieth century Western societies versus wars listed in areas which had been colonized by European powers during nineteenth and early twentieth century (p. 53). These racist, imperialist comparisons by Pinker are smoothed over by assurances to Western readers that wealthy Western men (i.e., evolutionary advanced groups) have decreased their violence in contrast to evolutionarily lower groups (i.e., Darwin's original argument about the evolutionary superiority of the Europeans). At no point does Pinker seem to reflect on either the violence of colonialism, which created genocides in areas these wealthy Europeans invaded, nor does he seem to recognize that Western wealthy men created multiple means of widespread human annihilation, such as weapons of mass destruction. In Pinker's scientific Pollyannaist musings on violence, it is the "Western males" who supposedly represent the "better angels of our nature" (title).

Thus, it is not surprising that, in his latest homage to the West and its evolutionary superiority, Pinker defends eugenic racist studies, such as the Tuskegee syphilis experiments, as merely a "*one-time failure to prevent harm to a few dozen people with the prevention of hundreds of millions of deaths per century in perpetuity*" (Pinker, 2018, p. 401). The problem, according to Pinker (2018), is that "many on the left encourage identity politicians and social justice warriors who downplay individual rights in favor of equalizing the standing of races, classes, and genders" (p. 31). Never mind the science showing that all politics are "identity politics" or studies showing that the criticism of efforts to create a more equal and just world reflect implicit or aversive (unconscious) racism (Dovidio & Gaertner, 2004; Lipsitz, 2006). Having argued for biological, universal differences in identity, especially in terms of gender and race, Pinker, like other ideologues, then attack the "identity politics" of social justice. This stunning move is common in works by Pinker and others who decry efforts to achieve human equality, but rarely questioned. Shaming individuals and groups for their support of social justice with terms like "equalitarian dogmas," "identity politics" or feel-good "snowflakes" who embrace "suffocating political correctness," remains central to contemporary far-right politics and sciences.

Thus, Pinker calls on readers to replace recognition of contemporary forms of social violence (e.g., rape, racist use of intelligence testing) with "scientific facts" about individual biological characteristics (i.e., the evolutionary need to spread one's genes through rape; the cave-man myth of climate differences leading to differences between races and genders). Instead, individuals are required to accept that Darwinist versions of evolution are indisputable, and that its pinnacle has been achieved today purely through work by Western scientists, most of whom are European White men. In fact, curiously for the purpose of this book, Pinker (2018) decries that while "people tend to see their own lives through rose-colored glasses," they become negative when they "change the question from the people's *lives* to their *society,* and *they transform from Pollyanna to Eeyore*" (p. 40). This summary seems to characterize Pinker's efforts: to literally encourage Pollyannaism about the world and, especially about certain forms of Western sciences and scientism.

Hopeful Sciences of White Supremacy and White Nationalism

Outside of the formal academic sciences, groups that promote human inequality and social oppression make use of academic findings to support their agendas and claims. White supremacist and misogynist websites are filled with references to studies that claim to have used scientific methods to prove that racial, gender, and national inequalities are in fact based in "real" differences (see the American Renaissance website as an example). Many scholars supporting far-right ideologies can be found on what constitutes the contemporary Intellectual Dark Web, routinely bemoaning the need to hide their "true scientific" work because they are being persecuted by social justice and human equality dogmatists. As noted above, whereas these scientists' exclusive focus is on dividing human beings based on their identity (e.g., race, gender) and using these identities as key variables of difference in their large data set studies, they are the most vehement attackers of what they call "Identity Politics," which they identify with "dogmas" of social justice and equality. While promoting racist and sexist ideologies, they complain about being silenced by political correctness.

An example of white supremacists using science to imagine Pollyannist utopias can be found in one of the most infamous contemporary White supremacy books: David Duke's (1999) *My Awakening: A Path to Racial Understanding*. Duke, a KKK leader and noted racist, filled his book with psychological science, especially the evolutionary and intelligence-focused works examined throughout this book. Duke's book chapters have titles like "A Question of Intelligence," "Heredity and Environment," "Race and Intelligence," "The Roots of Racial Differences," "The Evolution of Race," and "The History of Race." His claims present themselves as empirically backed, supported by citations of Darwin, Galton, Jensen, Rushton, Gottfredson, Bouchard, Lynn, Buss, Murray & Herrnstein and many others. According to Duke:

> *In truth, an incredibly harsh environment over many thousands of years is precisely what made our people what we are.* Before civilization, Nature pitilessly killed those individuals and groups who did not have the genetic fitness to survive. *Over thousands of generations Nature gradually elevated Western man until he finally broke the bounds of his environment*

> *and literally created a new one called civilization.* Its creation brought about both his greatness as expressed in its organization, form, and beauty, but also the seeds of his downfall, for civilization begins a process that chips away at the best genes. *The bounty created by civilization made survival far less dependent on intelligence, foresight, self-discipline and courage*...While the genetic elite found their greatest satisfaction in achievement and the luxuries of wealth and power, the lowly found it almost exclusively in sex. And while the brave and fittest went off to war to bleed, the cowardly and incompetent stayed home to breed. Finally, when civilized nations conquered lesser peoples, they brought their captives home as slaves with whom they gradually interbred. Ultimately, their slave's strands of DNA became entwined with that of their masters. *All these factors destroyed the genetic vitality of the civilization.* (p. 454)

Thus, Duke's "White strategy for victory" included scientific Pollyannaist plans:

> *Every awakened White person becomes an Aryan*, a racially conscious White person dedicated to our survival and evolutionary advancement... *Our real strength can only come from our utter dedication to the truth, the whole truth, and nothing but the truth.* That truth can be hard, it can be costly, it can generate our persecution from those who cannot stand its light, *but truth, utter truth, is the only possible path to our eventual victory.* (p. 470)

Duke ends his book with another evocation to biology, evolution, and the scientific truth: "We speak the truth because it is in our genes to do so. We speak the truth for our survival.... Let the revolution begin" (p. 477).

Notably, the introduction to Duke's book was written by G. Whitney, an American psychologist and one-time president of the American Behavioral Genetics Association, who promoted the book's scientific veracity and accuracy. In his introduction, Whitney proclaimed:

> As a scientist who specializes in the field of Behavioral Genetics, I must tell you that I have gone over David Duke's considerable data on genetics and race and find it in line with the latest scientific discoveries and knowledge in this area. His grasp of this area of research is quite remarkable for having a degree in History rather a doctorate in the biological disciplines. (p. 5)

Whitney introduction gives a rather stunning insight into the world of racist and sexist views inside the discipline of psychology while also explaining how these scholars hide behind their titles and scholarship. Views of these scholars are summarized in his introduction to *My Awakening*, in which Whitney reflects:

> David Duke's awakening is presented here in three interconnected major themes of his *discoveries of honest truths that are politically incorrect. One of his honest truths is that from a thorough immersion in modern science he became convinced that racial egalitarianism is the scientific equivalent of the flat-Earth theory.* He rejects the smear of "racist" while maintaining that the *true data are very different from those that most of us have been led to believe.* A second of his sets of honest truths is that a *powerful and cohesive self-serving group has promoted a dishonest and hypocritical version of egalitarianism that is inimical to the interests of Western Christian Civilization.* He rejects the smear of "anti-Semite" while maintaining that the true data are very different from those that most of us have encountered through the mass media. (p. 2)

This stunning summary of beliefs by scientists, purported to be based on scientific "truths," is far from singular or rare. Being a Pollyanna about science has been commonplace for a very long time. Atrocities connected to racist sciences, included the Holocaust, Apartheid, Jim Crow laws, colonial violence and more (Bashford & Levine, 2010; Guthrie, 2004; Lombardo, 2011; Tucker, 1996; Yakushko, 2019). Misogynistic science, especially in contemporary evolutionary psychology scholarship, continue to maintain their sexist narratives in regard to women's sexuality or intellectual capacities, often fueling social beliefs and practices that confine women to a single role—a happy housewife and a willing breeder (McKinnon, 2006; Ruti, 2015).

On Racist "Shameful Sciences" and the Empirical "Pretext" for Patriarchal "Happiness"

Among the scholars Pinker repeatedly condemns is Frantz Fanon, who Pinker mocks as an "eco-pessimist" and a "prophet of doom." Fanon, a psychoanalytic clinician and founder of anti-colonial movements, documented the impact eugenic sciences on Black Africans during the European colonization of Northern Africa the 1950s and 1960s. Fanon's books are not happy or in any way Pollyannaish. Fanon (1959) detailed profound violence exerted by racism and colonialism toward African peoples, including through use of sciences. He recorded the impact of such scientific "facts" used by colonialists as claiming that Black Africans were unintelligent, violent, and impulsive. In his *Black Skin, White Masks* Fanon (1959) stated

> This is how they have been able to tell themselves that "*the black man makes all the animals behave like a lower order of human intelligence*, the kind that the Negro himself can understand. The black man naturally feels that he is in closer touch with the "lower animals" than with the white man, who is so far superior to him in every respect..." Others have advanced the theory, with straight faces, that these stories are not reactions to the conditions imposed on the Negro in the United States but are simply survivors of Africa. Wolfe gives us the clue to such interpretations: On the basis of all the evidence, Br'er Rabbit is an animal because the Negro must be an animal; the rabbit is an outlander because the Negro must be branded as an *outlander down to his chromosomes. Ever since slavery began, his Christian and democratic guilt as a slave-owner has led the southerner to describe the Negro as an animal, an unchangeable African whose nature was determined as protoplasm by his "African" genes. If the black man found himself relegated to the Limbo of mankind, he was the victim not of Americans but of the organic inferiority of his jungle ancestors.* (p. 174)

Fanon also discussed the more insidious science of behavioral genetics, which supposedly proved that Blacks possessed genes of "cannibalism" as well as predisposition for "slavery" (p. 121). Fanon's observations of the social and emotional malice of what he termed "*shameful science*" serve as a crucial counterpoint to sanitized versions of Western sciences described above (p. 121). Fanon (1959), reflecting on these sanitized Pollyannaish books of scientific facts about Black people, recalled:

> In the first chapter of the history that the others have compiled for me, the foundation of cannibalism has been made eminently plain in order that I may not lose sight of it. *My chromosomes were supposed to have a few thicker or thinner genes representing cannibalism. In addition to the sex-linked, [inferiority of women to men] the scholars had now discovered the racial linked [inferiority of Black people to White]. What a shameful science!* But I understand this "psychological mechanism." For it is a matter of common knowledge that the mechanism is only psychological. Two centuries ago I was lost to humanity [via scientific narratives], I was a slave forever. (p. 120)

As Fanon noted, long before developing "scientific proof" of the inferiority of non-White peoples, scientists and scholars provided numerous proofs of female inferiority. Earlier in this book I described the mass genocide of women accused of witches, showing that the associated demonization of women and control exerted over their bodies and emotions were based on scientific claims of their inferiority to males. Darwin's writings, highlighted in this book, preserved the perceived validity of these views in contemporary science, passing down sexist science to future generation, as in claims Pinker's "gender feminism" (2002, 2018). Before Fanon, Simone De Beauvoir (1949) questioned the use of science to promote sexism, including through the sciences of positivity foisted on women due to their supposed biological position as breeders and housewives. In her book, the *Second Sex* De Beauvoir, stated:

> In proving woman's inferiority, the anti-feminists then began to draw not only upon religion, philosophy, and theology, as before, *but also upon science – biology, experimental psychology*, etc. At most they were willing to grant '*equality in difference*' to the other sex. *That profitable formula is most significant; it is precisely like the 'equal but separate' formula of the Jim Crow laws aimed at the North American Negroes. As is well known, this so-called equalitarian segregation has resulted only in the most extreme discrimination.* The similarity just noted is in no way due to chance, for whether it is a race, a caste, a class, or a sex that is reduced to *a position of inferiority, the methods of justification are the same*. (p. 8)

De Beauvoir continued to analyze the impact of these sciences on women's lives, with special focus on writings claiming that women are happier in inferior positions:

> If we survey some of the works on woman, we note that one of the points of view most frequently adopted is that of the public good, the general interest; and one always means by this the benefit of society as one wishes it to be maintained or established. For our part, we hold that the only public good is that which assures the private good of the citizens; we shall pass judgment on institutions according to their effectiveness in giving concrete opportunities to individuals. But we do not confuse the idea of private interest with that of happiness, although that is another common point of view. Are not women of the harem more happy than women voters? Is not the housekeeper happier than the working-woman? *It is not too clear just what the word happy really means and still less what true values it may mask. There is no possibility of measuring the happiness of others, and it is always easy to describe as happy the situation in which one wishes to place them*. (p. 11)

It is these efforts to "measure the happiness of others" in order to "describe as happy the situation in which one wishes to place them" that precisely constitute scientific Pollyannaism. According to de Beauvoir, "*in particular those who are condemned to stagnation are often pronounced happy on the pretext that happiness consists in being at rest*" (p. 11). De Beauvoir's critique is among many efforts, inside and outside of academia, to examine and name the oppressive nature of scientific Pollyannaism and its position in service of maintaining social status quos.

References

American Breeders Magazine: A Journal of Genetics and Eugenics. (1912). Washington, DC: American Breeders Association.

American Eugenics Society. (2015). *Members, officers, and directors activities database.* Retrieved on June 9, 2019 at https://ia801305.us.archive.org/25/items/AMERICANEUGENICSSOCIETYMEMBERS/AMERICAN%20EUGENICS%20SOCIETY%20MEMBERS.pdf.

Bannister, R. C. (1991). *Sociology and scientism: The American quest for objectivity, 1880–1940.* Chapel Hill: University of North Carolina Press.

Bashford, A., & Levine, P. (Eds.). (2010). *The Oxford handbook of the history of eugenics.* New York: Oxford University Press.

Bergman, J. (2014). *The Darwin effect: It's influence on nazism, eugenics, racism, communism, capitalism & sexism.* Green Forest, AR: New Leaf Publishing Group.

Black, E. (2003). *War against the weak: Eugenics and America's campaign to create a master race.* New York: Four Walls Eight Windows.

Blackburn, S. (2005). *The Oxford dictionary of philosophy.* Oxford, UK: Oxford University Press.

Brigham, C. C. (1923). *A study of American intelligence.* Princeton, NJ: Princeton University Press.

Buckley, K. W. (1989). *Mechanical man: John Broadus Watson and the beginnings of behaviorism.* New York: Guilford Press.

Cattell, R. B. (1987). *Beyondism: Religion from science.* New York: Praeger.

Chase, A. (1980). *The legacy of Malthus: The social costs of the new scientific racism.* Urbana-Champaign: University of Illinois Press.

De Beauvoir, S. (1949). *The second sex* (H. M. Parshley, Trans., 1974). New York: Vintage.

Dovidio, J. F., & Gaertner, S. L. (2004). Aversive racism. *Advances in Experimental Social Psychology, 36,* 4–56.

Duke, D. E. (1999). *My awakening: A path to racial understanding.* Convington, LA: Free Speech Press.

Eugenical News. (1916–1922). Monthly publication of the Eugenics Record Office, Cold Springs, NY. Retrieved on February 22, 2018 at https://babel.hathitrust.org/cgi/pt?id=coo.31924063788834.

Evans, W. S. (1931). *Organized eugenics*. New Haven, CT: American Eugenics Society.

Fanon, F. (1959/2008). *Black skin, white masks*. San Francisco, CA: Grove Press.

Galton, F. (1869). *Hereditary genius: An inquiry into its laws and consequences*. New York, NY: Macmillan.

Galton, F. (1907). *Probability: The foundation of eugenics*. London, UK: Clarendon Press.

Garrett, H. E. (1961). The equalitarian dogma. *Perspectives in Biology and Medicine, 4*, 480–484.

Giroux, H. A. (2011). The disappearing intellectual in the age of economic Darwinism. *Policy Futures in Education, 9*(2), 163–171.

Gottfredson, L. S. (1994a). Egalitarian fiction and collective fraud. *Society, 31*(3), 53–59.

Gottfredson, L. S. (1994b). The science and politics of race-norming. *American Psychologist, 49*(11), 955–963.

Gottfredson, L. S. (2005). Suppressing intelligence research: Hurting those we intend to help. *Destructive trends in mental health: The well-intentioned path to harm* (pp. 155–186). London: Routledge.

Gould, S. J. (1996). *The mismeasure of man*. New York, NY: W. W. Norton & Company.

Guthrie, R. V. (2004). *Even the rat was white: A historical view of psychology*. Upper Saddle River, NJ: Pearson Education.

Herrnstein, R. J., & Murray, C. (1996). *The bell curve*. New York: Simon & Schuster.

Hunt, M. (1999). *The new know-nothings: The political foes of the scientific study of human nature*. New Brunswick, NJ: Transaction.

Itzkoff, S. W. (1994). *The decline of intelligence in America: A strategy for national renewal*. Westport, CT: Greenwood Publishing Group.

Lipsitz, G. (2006). *The possessive investment in whiteness: How white people profit from identity politics*. Philadelphia, PA: Temple University Press.

Lombardo, P. A. (Ed.). (2011). *A century of eugenics in America: From the Indiana experiment to the human genome era*. Bloomington, IN: Indiana University Press.

Lynn, R. (2001a). *Eugenics: A reassessment*. New York: Praeger.

Lynn, R. (2001b). *The science of human diversity: A history of the Pioneer fund*. Lanham, MD: University Press of America.

Lynn, R. (2007, July). *Race and psychopathic personality*. American Renaissance. Retrieved at https://www.amren.com/news/2008/08/race_and_psycho/.

McKinnon, S. (2006). *Neo-liberal genetics: The myths and moral tales of evolutionary psychology.* Chicago, IL: Prickly Paradigm Press.
Mehler, B. (1997). Beyondism: Raymond B. Cattell and the new eugenics. *Genetica, 99*(2–3), 153–163.
Melendy, M. R. (1914). *The science of eugenics and sex life.* New York: W. R. Vansant.
Olson, R. (2008). *Science and scientism in nineteenth-century Europe.* Urbana-Champaign: University of Illinois Press.
Pearson, K. (1905). *National life from the standpoint of science.* London: Adam and Black.
Pinker, S. (2002). *The blank slate: The modern denial of human nature.* New York: Penguin.
Pinker, S. (2011). *The better angels of our nature: The decline of violence in history and its causes.* New York, NY: Penguin.
Pinker, S. (2018). *Enlightenment now: The case for reason, science, humanism, and progress.* New York: Penguin.
Rushton, J. P. (2002). The Pioneer Fund and the scientific study of human differences. *Albany Law Review, 66,* 207–262.
Ruti, M. (2015). *The age of scientific sexism: How evolutionary psychology promotes gender profiling and fans the battle of the sexes.* Toronto, ON, Canada: Bloomsbury Publishing.
Smith, J. D. (1985). *Minds made feeble: The myth and legacy of the Kallikaks.* Rockville, MD: Aspen.
Social Biology. (1973). A new name society for the study of social biology (Formerly the American Eugenics Society). *Social Biology, 20*(1), 1.
Southern Poverty Law Center. (2019). *Fighting hate/extremist files: The American Renaissance.* https://www.splcenter.org/fighting-hate/extremist-files/group/american-renaissance.
Sorell, T. (2013). *Scientism: Philosophy and the infatuation with science.* London, UK: Routledge.
Stenmark, M. (2018). *Scientism: Science, ethics and religion.* New York, NY: Routledge.
Teo, T. (2008). From speculation to epistemological violence in psychology: A critical-hermeneutic reconstruction. *Theory & Psychology, 18*(1), 47–67.
Teo, T. (2010). What is epistemological violence in the empirical social sciences? *Social and Personality Psychology Compass, 4*(5), 295–303.
The Pioneer Fund. (2013). Highlights of Pioneer Fund research and grants. Retrieved on June 15, 2018 at https://web.archive.org/web/20130103005545/http://www.pioneerfund.org:80.
Thornhill, R., & Palmer, C. T. (2000). *A natural history of rape.* Cambridge, MA: MIT Press.

Tucker, W. H. (1996). *The science and politics of racial research*. Carbondale: University of Illinois Press.
UNESCO. (1969). *Four statements on the race question*. Paris, France: The United Nations Publications. Retrieved on April 1, 2019 at http://refugeestudies.org/UNHCR/UNHCR.%20Four%20Statements%20on%20the%20Race%20Question.pdf.
Watson, J. B. (1914). *Behavior: An introduction to comparative psychology*. New York, NY: H. Holt.
Watson, J. B. (1919). *Psychology: From the standpoint of a behaviorist*. Philadelphia, PA: Lippincott.
Watson, J. B. (1928). *Psychological care of infant and child*. New York: W. W. Norton.
Whitney, G. (1997). Raymond B. Cattell and the fourth inquisition. *The Mankind Quarterly, 38*(1 & 2), 99–124.
Whitney, G. (1999). Introduction. In D. E. Duke (Ed.), *My awakening: A path to racial understanding* (pp. 2–11). Convington, LA: Free Speech Press.
Williams, R. N., & Robinson, D. N. (Eds.). (2014). *Scientism: The new orthodoxy*. London, UK: Bloomsbury Publishing.
Wilson, E. O. (1975). *Sociobiology: The new synthesis*. Cambridge, MA: Harvard University Press.
Yakushko, O. (2019). Eugenics and its evolution in history of western psychology: A critical archival review. *Psychotherapy and Politics International*, online.
Yerkes, R. M. (Ed.). (1920). *The new world of science: Its development during the war*. New York, NY: Century Company.
Yerkes, R. M. (1923). Eugenic bearing of measurements of intelligence. *The Eugenics Review, 14*(4), 225–229.
Zenderland, L. (2001). *Measuring minds: Henry Herbert Goddard and the origins of American intelligence testing*. New York: Cambridge University Press.

CHAPTER 8

Critics and Critiques of Scientific Pollyannaism

The Over-Emotional "Shrew" Who Socrates Could Not "Break"

The greatest of Hellenistic philosophers to promote happiness (i.e., good life) through rationality—Socrates–used his wife Xanthippe as an example of damaged, mutilated, and irrational humanity. According to dialogues attributed to Socrates, he married her as a personal challenge:

> It is the example of the rider who wishes to become an expert horseman: "None of your soft-mouthed, docile animals for me," he says; "the horse for me to own must show some spirit" in the belief, no doubt, if he can manage such an animal, it will be easy enough to deal with every other horse besides. And that is just my case. I wish to deal with human beings, to associate with man in general; hence my choice of wife. *I know full well, if I can tolerate her spirit, I can with ease attach myself to every human being else.* (Socrates speech cited in Xenophon, app. 400 BCE)

Thus, Xanthippe, Socrates' wife, came to symbolize the negativity of nagging wives, which even the great philosopher could not break. She became the subject of numerous paintings and writings over a millennia of Western history, often showing her dumping the urine pot on Socrates or appearing at his public suicide with their small children, begging Socrates to protect his family instead of condemning them to exile or death by his actions (see Xenophon *Symposium*). Xanthippe became so

O. Yakushko, *Scientific Pollyannaism*,
https://doi.org/10.1007/978-3-030-15982-5_8

infamous in the Western imagination as a shrewish and over-emotional female that British thinker and poet Robert Graves (1960) was lead to produce an essay entitled *The Case for Xanthippe*. In it, Graves discussed how the stereotype of Xanthippe as a melodramatic, complaining shrew is characteristic of a problematic cultural binary. Graves specifically juxtaposed "masculine" rationality (i.e., goodness) to qualities attributed to femininity, such as emotion and intuition (i.e., badness). Graves argued that such split was profoundly damaging to the culture and to individuals living in it, and especially harmful to poetic expression, artistic creativity, and the possibility of compassionate relationships.

Chesterton on Scientific Eugenics as "Our Happy Holiday in the Land of Nonsense"

Another example of resistance to scientific Pollyannaism is found in G. K. Chesterton's early-twentieth-century critiques. Chesterton (1922) wrote an influential response to contemporary eugenics, entitled *Eugenics and Other Evils*, describing the problems that arise from directing the upper classes to seek perpetual happiness at the expense of the poor and the marginalized, calling eugenics "*a modern craze for scientific officialism and strict social organization*" (p. 2). Chesterton especially held eugenics accountable for its "*silver-tongued rhetoric about purer motherhood and a happier posterity*" (p. 3), which, in his view, were responsible for socially abusive views and practices. Noting that eugenic efforts to produce and extoll scientific Pollyannaism were based on the writings of ancient Greek philosophers as well as Chesterton's own contemporaries, like George Bernard Shaw, he discussed the ways in which eugenics had become a "creed," embraced by scientists, politicians, and liberal social leaders alike (p. 11). According to Chesterton, the term "feeble-minded" was invented to be applied to all those individuals that society and individuals saw as unpleasant or as incapable of meeting societal expectations, so that the privileged could avoid addressing adverse conditions such as poverty:

> Indeed, the first definition of "feeble-minded" in the Bill [British eugenics bill such as the eugenic Lunacy Laws] was much looser and vaguer than the phrase "feeble-minded" itself. It is a piece of yawning idiocy about "persons who though capable of earning their living under favourable circumstances" (as if anyone could earn his living if circumstances were directly unfavourable to his doing so), are nevertheless "incapable of managing their affairs with proper prudence." (p. 21)

Chesterton argued that the birth of eugenics as a social "evil" was bound to occur when societies become consumed by a state of anxiety, in which individuals and groups engage in mass defensive strategies and loose the ability to distinguish between varied good and bad responses to social tensions. They are no unable to see that "real progress bears the same relation to it [a lack of progress, social struggle] that a happy girl laughing bears to an hysterical girl who cannot stop laughing" (pp. 29–30): to them, it all just looks like laughter. At the same time, Chesterton highlights that the Pollyannas who produce the sciences of eugenics routinely abandoned their own data graphs and legalistic arguments to make all manner of exceptions to their own personal benefit (e.g., unhappy wealthy people). This convoluted and self-contradictory science reflects the process by which "the Eugenist *has to treat everybody, including himself, as an exception to a rule that isn't there*" (p. 33).

Chesterton further believed that eugenicists, in their hunt for feeble-minded and emotionally negative individuals, may have become far worse that the witch-hunting inquisition. At least the witch-hunting inquisitors saw witches as powerful and influential; eugenicists, on the other hand, said "unfit" individuals were weak-willed and feeble-minded:

> I have more respect for the *old witch-finders* than for the Eugenists, who go about persecuting the fool of the family; because the witch-finders, according to their own conviction, ran a risk. Witches were not the feeble-minded, but the strong-minded—the evil mesmerists, the rulers of the elements. Many a raid on a witch, right or wrong, seemed to the villagers who did it a righteous popular rising against a vast spiritual tyranny, a papacy of sin. Yet we know that the thing degenerated into a rabid and despicable persecution of the feeble or the old. *It ended by being a war upon the weak. It ended by being what Eugenics begins by being.* (p. 65)

According to Chesterton, eugenics is a form of an attack on humanity, specifically on those who were considered socially lower or unacceptable:

> *The thing that really is trying to tyrannise through government is Science.* The thing that really does use the secular arm is Science. And the creed that really is levying tithes and capturing schools, the creed that really is enforced by fine and imprisonment, the creed that really is proclaimed not in sermons but in statutes, and spread not by pilgrims but by policemen—that creed is the great but disputed *system of thought which began with Evolution and has ended in Eugenics. Materialism is really our established Church; for the Government will really help it to persecute its heretics.* (pp. 77–78)

Eugenicists' views on the human condition, Chesterton argued, were not only tyrannical, but also intent on establishing a world order where faith in science was an absolute requirement. He claimed that their insistence on accepting science blindly was

> the real secret of this confusion, the secret of what the Eugenists really want. *They want to be allowed to find out what they want.* Not content with the endowment of research, they desire the establishment of research; that is the making of it a thing official and compulsory, like education or state insurance; but still it is only research and not discovery. In short, *they want a new kind of State Church*, which shall be an Established Church of Doubt—instead of Faith. (They have no Science of Eugenics at all, but they do really mean that *if we will give ourselves up to be vivisected they may very probably have one some day.* I point out, in more dignified diction, that this is a bit thick.) (p. 86)

In response to the often contradictory and groundless claims of eugenics, Chesterton refers to the "science" as "*our happy holiday in the land of nonsense*" (p. 87).

Chesterton's critique highlighted that eugenics was based on the need felt by wealthy British men to experience "*a much greater manliness in his pride*" and "*a much greater sincerity in his optimism*" (p. 117). In regard to eugenics' false optimism and its denials of others' humanity, Chesterton noted in 1920s that the eugenicists are like a "*Self-Helper who bore the adorable name of Smiles [who] told the English tramp [the poor] that he carried a coronet in his bundle [should just look at the bright side of life]*" (p. 120). He concluded that eugenics is inhumane and malevolent: "*There is one strong, startling, outstanding thing about Eugenics, and that is its meanness. Wealth, and the social science supported by wealth, had tried an inhuman experiment*" (p. 147).

"The Actual Unhappiness of the American Housewife" and the "Feminist Killjoy"

Like other critics, Chesterton noted that women bore the brunt of scientific Pollyannaism. According to Chesterton, eugenics required "*a Superwoman*," a female to be "called Eugenette" because women and were described as devoting themselves to the production of perfect pre-natal conditions (p. 181). They [were demanded to have] "*eliminated everything from their lives which did not tend towards complete happiness*" (p. 181). As noted above, De Beauvoir (1949) similarly questioned these scientifically-based requirements for women's happiness. Similarly, Betty Friedan (1963), in her groundbreaking book *The Feminine Mystique*, describes this requirement for women to be happy as a form of social oppression, stating that

> in 1960, *the problem that has no name burst like a boil through the image of the happy American housewife*. In the television commercials the pretty housewives still beamed over their foaming dishpans… *But the actual unhappiness of the American housewife* was suddenly being reported. (pp. 19–20)

Despite these notable critiques of scientific Pollyannaism and the image of the happy housewife, the enforcement of women's happiness remains an important force in Western culture. Distinguished feminist scholar, Sara Ahmed, in an article entitled *Killing Joy: Feminism and History of Happiness* summarizing her 2010 book *The Promise of Happiness*, highlighted that past and present discussions of happiness have persisted, especially in their a-contextualized, as racism- and sexism-blind forms. According to Ahmed (2010b) histories and studies of happiness reflect a "white male European inheritance" by focusing on their philosophical and intellectual treatises of positive emotions" (p. 572). Ahmed argued that "*treating happiness as an intellectual history amounts to becoming blind to how differences matter within that history as differences that trouble the very form of its coherence*" (p. 572). Instead, Ahmed argued that, in most organized societies, ideas of happiness are closely allied with "wishful politics" which "demands that others live according to a wish," a measurable and commoditized "social good" (p. 572).

Ahmed, echoing the writings of many critics, suggests that our focus must remain on unhappiness, as well as the realities of those who are "*banished from it [happiness] or who enter this history only as troublemakers, wretches, strangers, dissenters, killers of joy*" (p. 573). Ahmed proposed that feelings, including positive feelings, are not independent phenomena related to individual agency and choice, but socio-political constructions based on cultural demands. Ahmed's asks us to consider who defines what happiness is and for what social purpose. Women, she argued, especially women of color, have been conditioned to define their realities according to happiness of the dominant group, while simultaneously being punished for being the cause of personal and collective lack of happiness and well-being. Writers and poets, as Audre Lorde (1978) does in her poem entitled *A Litany for Survival*, can offer an acknowledgment of suffering in face of social oppression that deny one's full humanity, while drawing attention to the ways that suffering is silenced.

> For those of us who live at the shoreline
> standing upon the constant edges of decision
> crucial and alone...
> For those of us
> who were imprinted with fear
> like a faint line in the center of our foreheads
> learning to be afraid with our mother's milk
> for by this weapon
> this illusion of some safety to be found
> the heavy-footed hoped to silence us
> For all of us
> this instant and this triumph
> We were never meant to survive.

Ahmed (2010a, 2010b) noted that especially for women of color, "*The happiness duty is also a negative duty not to speak about racism in the present*" (p. 591). Indeed, proponents of scientific Pollyannaism have attacked anti-racist individuals for being too negative: according to positive psychology founder Seligman (2002) in his *Authentic Happiness*, it is the "contemporary American demagogues who play the race card, invoking reminders of slavery... at every opportunity, create the same vengeful mindset in their followers" (p. 76). In my article, *Don't Worry, Be Happy: Erasure of Racism, Sexism, and Poverty in Positive Psychology*, I further document efforts to minimize and deny social oppression, while blaming those who try to address social inequality for threatening individual and collective forms of happiness (Yakushko, 2018).

Ahmed (2010a, 2010b) further argued that enforced positivity and happiness requires false consciousness and defensive denials of reality in order to ensure person's acquiescence to a social status quo:

> *We can retrieve a model of false consciousness in critiquing claims to happiness.* You would not be saying "You are wrong; you are not happy; you just think you are because you have a false belief." Rather, you would be saying that there is something false about our consciousness of the world: *we learn not to be conscious; we learn not to see what happens right in front of us.* It is not that an individual person suffers from false consciousness but that *we inherit a certain false consciousness when we learn to see and not to see things in a certain way.* (p. 590)

To ensure social compliance, individuals are pressured to concede their own perceptions while replacing them with required "positive" responses, especially by denying the existence and impact of sexism, racism, and other forms of social violence. Ahmed suggests: "*Happiness can involve an immanent coercion, a demand for agreement.* Coercion is usually thought of as an external force that requires the obedience of subjects through the use of threats, intimidation, or pressure" (p. 580). In turn, Ahmed notes, when individuals name social inequalities and social violence, they are often accused of being the source of unhappiness themselves, for being "feminist killjoys" or "angry black women" (p. 593). Ahmed summarized this pattern:

> *You cause unhappiness by revealing the causes of unhappiness.* And you can become the cause of the unhappiness you reveal. *In becoming an unhappiness-cause, one can certainly be affected unhappily.* People often say that the struggle against racism is like banging your head against a brick wall. The wall keeps its place, so it is you who gets sore. Struggling against racism means being willing to labor over sore points. *Not only do we need to labor our points, as a laboring over sore points, but we also might even need to stay as sore as our points.* (p. 593)

Lastly, Ahmed, like others who critique scientific Pollyannaism, reminds the readers that opponents of and anti-negativity movements embrace a different relationship to human emotional reactions, a relationship that acknowledges their full emotional spectrum. This attitude views happiness, like other human emotions, as a state that can be examined in its multiplicity and contradictions, its context and values. When happiness or positivity are understood in this way, unhappiness or the opposite of happiness can also be welcomed, because all emotional reactions are permitted in reaction to all manner of human experiences (e.g., anger in reaction to abuse or oppression, sorrow in reaction to loss). Ahmed's reframing of happiness in relation to "hap"—to what happens, to possibility, including the possibility of an unhappy reaction–holds a vastly different and liberating potential. In her words,

> Happiness is offered here as a sense of possibility. To turn happiness into an expectation is to annul that sense of possibility. When happiness is not something we promise to another, is not something we imagine is due to us or which we have a duty toward, is not something that we anticipate will accumulate from the right points, then others things can happen. Hap

> can happen. I now think of political movements as hap movements rather than happiness movements. It is not about the unhappy ones becoming the happy ones. As I have suggested, *revolutionary forms of political consciousness involve heightening our awareness of what there is to be unhappy about.* Yet this does not mean that unhappiness becomes our political cause. In refusing to be constrained by happiness, we can open up other ways of being, of being perhaps. (pp. 593–594)

The Political Use of Human Emotions: The Case of Neo-Liberalism

Other contemporary scholars who critique the movements I call scientific Pollyannaism (e.g., positive psychology), similarly emphasize the political nature of human emotions as well as their usefulness as socio-political tools (Ahmed, 2004; Rose, 1990; Rose & Abi-Rached, 2013). Berlant (2011) proposed that conditions of neo-liberality, which have become dominant in the U.S. and the U.K. since 1980s, have contributed to what she termed "*cruel optimism.*" Neo-liberalism, related to fundamentalist or late-stage capitalism, has been defined as "the characteristic political-economic and social imaginary of our time, a form of governmentality that takes market relations as its model for social relations" (Yen, 2015, p. 421). According to Berlant (2011), contemporary society faces severe economic, environmental, and social deterioration, which denies majority individuals access to "good life." Meanwhile, neo-liberal society insists on instilling positive fantasies about an easy access to this "good life" with "clusters of promises" (p. 23). In her view, such misleading and false optimism in neo-liberal societies makes these fantasies profoundly cruel.

Similarly, Judith Butler (2004) noted that, in reaction to terrifying social events such as September 11th, individuals and even entire countries reject their vulnerability or capacity to mourn, embracing reactive aggression rather than shared suffering. According to Butler,

> *One can even experience that abhorrence, mourning, anxiety, and fear, and have all of these emotional dispositions lead to a reflection on how others have suffered arbitrary violence at the hands of the US, but also endeavor to produce another public culture and another public policy in which suffering unexpected violence and loss and reactive aggression are not accepted as the norm of political life.* (p. XIV)

Numerous other scholars specifically highlighted the link between the rise of fundamentalist capitalism and the emphases on the economic survival of the fittest via encouragements of personal optimism and perpetually hopeful attitudes. Lynne Layton (2010) drew attention to the "*irrational exuberance*" that often underlies justifications of neoliberal cultural claims (p. 303). Binkley (2014) offered an evaluation of positivity movements, calling attention to ways that the focus on happiness has intensified alongside an unprecedented rise in neo-liberal values. Binkley argued that these new positivity movements seek to create a perception that, if you feel badly, something must be wrong with your own feelings, rather than circumstances. This sense of wrongness or unhappiness in oneself must then be changed through business exchanges such as purchasing self-help propaganda, restructuring positivity cognitive, and other commoditized forms of therapeutic-type help. According to Binkley (2014), "*happiness is the problem for people who don't have a problem*" (p. 18). On the other hand, Binkley argues, individuals' implicit or unconscious refusal to be perpetually happy is its own form of resistance to these enforced positivity transactions. Using Foucault's analysis of self-confessed demonic possessions during the era of Inquisition as a form of resistance, Binkley wonders about ways that individuals unconsciously resist social demands for perpetual happiness by not being perpetually happy. However, while such resistance remains implicit, unconscious, or unnamed, these unhappy individuals become the subjects of new projects of governability, as they are punished for emotional transgressions and lured in by the elusive utopian states available only through purchasing more and more commoditized happiness products (Davies, 2015; De La Fabián & Stecher, 2018; Honneth, 2004; Yen, 2015). De La Fabián and Stecher (2018) noted that "*positive psychology accomplishes... the transcendence of the classical capitalist disjunction between work—associated with the present moment of production and sacrifice—and consumption—associated with the future moment of satisfaction and happiness*" (p. 602). Moreover, Friedli and Stearn (2015) have shown that entire governments will adopt "positive affect as coercive strategy," specifically towards individuals in need of governmental assistance because of their poverty or disabilities. In their view, Western governments who demand happy positive attitudes from people requiring their help engage in "*psycho-compulsion*" (p. 42) enacted as part of the "*psychological fundamentalism*" associated with psychological industries of well-being (p. 45).

Dire warnings about the absence of happiness or the refusal or inability to pursue it are central to contemporary scientific Pollyannaism movements. In the words of one of the most popular scholars of positive psychology, Lyubomirsky (2008), "If you are not happy today, then you won't be happy tomorrow" (p. 39). Such tautological arguments are common to many forms of scientific Pollyannaism. Thus, De La Fabián and Stecher (2018) noted in relation to positive psychology: "Only happy people can be even happier; only happy workers can enhance their happiness" (p. 602). Moreover, in conditions of capitalism and neo-liberalism, self-enhancement via pursuit of happiness is sold not only as a product, but as an expression of personal liberty and choice (Binkley, 2014; Rose, 1990; Yen, 2015). Thus, scientific Pollyannaism has become essential to capitalism, and capitalism remains foundational to scientific Pollyannaism. De La Fabián and Stecher (2018) summarize: "the overlap between certain forms of conducting the conduct of others, embedded in the neoliberal subjectivity of the entrepreneur of himself, certain games of truth (positive psychology), and the new kind of subjectification enabled by them: *already happy individuals who invest this initial human capital in becoming even happier*" (p. 617).

"Psytizens" and the "Happiness Industry"

Cabanas (2016) further argues that the "happiness industry" creates what he terms "psytizens," myopically focused on the pursuit of personal happiness, flow, and authentic optimism (p. 467). According to Cabanas,

> *Happiness has become a new moral regime* in neoliberal societies that defines what is right and wrong and stresses the insource of responsibility. More importantly, *happiness stands out as a new model of selfhood that aligns with the neoliberal ideology of individualism and consumerism at the same time that legitimizes and rekindles this same ideology in seemingly nonideological terms through the discourse of science.* (p. 467)

Cabanas' term psytizen indicates a position individuals are required to occupy, in which they are defined by their personal self-development, and in which they must rid themselves of concern for external circumstance and focus exclusively themselves:

> Happiness also stands out as a new and pervasive model of selfhood which defines individuals of neoliberal societies as what we might call psytizens, that is, as self-governed individuals whose *identity is only constrained by and linked to their psychological self-development*, a goal which is achieved through self-reflexive acts of choice and consumption. (p. 469)

Psytizenship, first and foremost, requires becoming a consumer of happiness and positive psychology products in order to achieve emotional rationality, flourishing, authenticity, and other similarly vague but supposedly desirable states. Offered numerous scales assuring them that, in one way or another, they lack this perfected emotional and behavioral state of authenticity or resilience or creativity or self-control or satisfaction or flourishing, the psytizen can find a route to self-improvement through the many available positive psychology products offered by the "happiness industry" (Cabanas, 2016; Davies, 2015). Thus, any difficulties adjusting to life's circumstances–feelings of depression and sorrow–are treated as solely personal problems, which are individually created and controlled. In Cabanas' (2016) words,

> since happiness is a matter of individual's responsibility, society tends to blame those who suffer for their failure to be happier and more optimistic, just as it blames smokers and the physically unfit for their failure to live healthier lives, or the unemployed for their failure to develop their working projects... *The imperative of happiness makes individuals bear the responsibility for the inherent structural economic and political contradictions and paradoxes of society, so criticisms addressed to this dominant discourse of happiness, as well as to its increasing commodification, are in fact criticisms directed against these contradictions and paradoxes, which are, instead of the "psyche," the principal loci of human suffering in neoliberal societies.* (p. 477)

In conclusion, critics scientific Pollyannaism emphasize the role of enforced happiness in maintaining the social status quo, especially when particular groups are marginalized and then punished for being or behaving "negatively." Ehrenreich (2009) wrote a book called *Bright-Sided* (also published under the title *Smile or Die*), which describes the enormous social cost of enforced positivity on individuals and society, tracing wars, the collapse of businesses, and abusive policies back to this insistence on happiness. She also provided detailed journalistic accounts of her interviews with Seligman, and describes the field positive psychology as an enormously lucrative and dishonest business. In response to this exposé, Ehrenreich, an award-winning author and journalist, was attacked in Seligman's (2011) *Flourish* for her so-called "rants" (p. 202). Seligman also accused her of "intellectual dishonesty" and "dangerous journalistic malpractice" (p. 203). Ehrenreich is one among many journalists and social critics, including many reviewed in this book, who point to the many problems inherent in scientific Pollyannaism. Another award-winning journalist, Chris Hedges, has documented the problematic nature of American positive psychology in relation to the social and political numbness common among Americans. According to his book *Empire of Illusion* (2009), "*Here, in the land of happy thoughts, there are no gross injustices, no abuses of authority, no economic and political systems to challenge, and no reason to complain. Here, we are all happy*" (p. 139).

References

Ahmed, S. (2004). *Cultural politics of emotion.* New York: Routledge.

Ahmed, S. (2010a). Killing joy: Feminism and the history of happiness. *Signs, 35*(3), 571–594. https://doi.org/10.1086/648513.

Ahmed, S. (2010b). *The promise of happiness.* Durham, NC: Duke University Press.

Berlant, L. G. (2011). *Cruel optimism.* Durham, NC: Duke University Press.

Binkley, S. (2014). *Happiness as enterprise: An essay on neoliberal life.* Albany, NY: State University of New York Press.

Butler, J. (2004). *Precarious life: The powers of mourning and violence.* London, UK: Verso.

Cabanas, E. (2016). Rekindling individualism, consuming emotions: Constructing "psytizens" in the age of happiness. *Culture & Psychology, 22*(3), 467–480.

Chesterton, G. K. (1922). *Eugenics and other evils: An argument against the Scientifically organized state.* London: Inkling Books.

Davies, W. (2015). *The happiness industry: How the government and big business sold us well-being.* London, UK: Verso Books.

De Beauvoir, S. (1949). *The second sex* (H. M. Parshley, Trans., 1974). New York: Vintage.

De La Fabián, R., & Stecher, A. (2018). Positive psychology and the enhancement of happiness: A reply to Binkley (2018). *Theory & Psychology, 28*(3), 411–417.

Ehrenreich, B. (2009). *Bright-sided: How the relentless promotion of positive thinking is undermining America*. New York, NY: Metropolitan Books.
Friedan, B. (1963/2010). *The feminine mystique*. New York: W. W. Norton.
Friedli, L., & Stearn, R. (2015). Positive affect as coercive strategy: Conditionality, activation and the role of psychology in UK government workfare programmes. *Medical Humanities, 41*(1), 40–47.
Graves, R. (1960). The case for Xanthippe. *The Kenyon Review, 22*(4), 597–605.
Hedges, C. (2009). *Empire of illusion: The end of literacy and the triumph of spectacle*. Toronto: Knopf Canada.
Honneth, A. (2004). Organized self-realization: Some paradoxes of individualization. *European Journal of Social Theory, 7*(4), 463–478.
Layton, L. (2010). Irrational exuberance: Neoliberal subjectivity and the perversion of truth. *Subjectivity, 3*(3), 303–322.
Lorde, A. (1978). *The black unicorn*. New York: Norton.
Lyubomirsky, S. (2008). *The how of happiness: A scientific approach to getting the life you want*. New York, NY: Penguin.
Rose, N. (1990). *Governing the soul: The shaping of the private self*. Florence, KY: Taylor & Francis/Routledge.
Rose, N., & Abi-Rached, J. M. (2013). *Neuro: The new brain sciences and the management of the mind*. Princeton, NJ: Princeton University Press.
Seligman, M. E. (2002). *Learned optimism: How to change your mind and your life*. New York, NY: Vintage.
Seligman, M. E. (2011). *Flourish: A visionary new understanding of happiness and well-being*. New York, NY: Simon & Schuster.
Yakushko, O. (2018). Don't worry, be happy: Erasing racism, sexism, and poverty in positive psychology. *Psychotherapy and Politics International, 16*(1), e1433.
Yen, J. (2015). Happiness as enterprise: An essay on neoliberal life. *Theory and Psychology, 25*(4), 541–542.

CHAPTER 9

Re-telling the Story of Orphaned Girl Named Pollyanna

The term "Pollyannaism" is based on a fairytale story about a young orphan named Pollyanna (Porter, 1913). Pollyanna is presented as a perpetually optimistic child, as someone who plays the "glad games," no matter how much she suffers (i.e., loss of her parents, profound neglect) or what suffering she observes (e.g., poverty, racism). Pollyanna, unlike other famous orphans in literature and film (e.g., Annie, Oliver), has the chance to live with distant and unkind relatives rather than be placed at an institution for orphans. In the book, Pollyanna supposedly learns her "glad games" from her father, who dies when she is still a young child, and these games are described as a type of connection she with her deceased parent. Pollyanna subsequently uses these glad games to cope with all manner of life's difficulties and disappointments. When, as a Christmas gift, Pollyanna receives a broken piece of a crutch rather than the doll she requested, Pollyanna plays her "glad game" to pretend the crutch was a gift she desired (i.e., it supposedly reminds her to be thankful that she did not need a crutch). She plays these games when she is punished without cause or when she severely hurts herself.

Pollyanna's story became an inspiration for many individuals and groups, especially those with an interest in explaining away difficult circumstances (Keith, 2001). Central to Pollyanna's story is the denial of dire violent circumstances faced by most orphans at the turn of twentieth century. Orphans were poor, frequently brutalized, and generally viewed as an undesirable social refuse. Scholars have shown that, at the turn of twentieth century, orphans were subjected to chilling conditions,

O. Yakushko, *Scientific Pollyannaism*,
https://doi.org/10.1007/978-3-030-15982-5_9

including extensive physical and sexual violence, neglect, and other forms of abuse (Shealy, 1995; Smith, 2011). Darwinists and eugenicists, who were socially and politically powerful during the time Pollyanna's story took place, considered orphans to be genetically defective (i.e., feeble-minded) and problematic for evolution (Darwin, 1889; Popenoe & Johnson, 1935).

Many eugenic psychologists ran the asylums into which most orphans were placed, and used their position to experiment on orphaned children (Goddard, 1912; Terman, 1916; Watson, 1914, 1919, 1928). Deborah Kallikak, who became the poster child for the dangers of feeble-mindedness and the evolutionary "sciences" of biological inferiority or superiority, was an orphan (Goddard, 1912; Selden, 1999; Smith, 1985; Tucker, 1996; Zenderland, 2001). Lewis Terman's (1916) arguments about the heritability of intelligence were based on the study of orphans, who he claimed had defective "germo-plasms." The abusive behaviorist experiments carried out by John B. Watson (1919, 1928, 1930), likewise made use of orphaned children as test subjects.

Twin studies, developed by eugenicists such as Terman (1916) to show the genetic and biological determinants of personality characteristics and intelligence, exclusively utilized twin children given up for adoption and separated from each other during the early stages of their lives. These twin studies remain central to eugenic-based sciences: the racist Pioneer Fund has supported such scientific work, including studies by T. Bouchard (1996), who ran the University of Minnesota's Twin and Adoption Study Project.

Orphans, especially at turn of twentieth century, were often children of color, since the genocide of American Indian/Native American/indigenous Northern American groups involved the mass extermination of adults among tribal groups. Crucial to North American policies was the removal of indigenous children into boarding schools, with the intention of re-educating them according to Western ideologies and to make them compliant (Holt, 2001; Zinn, 2010). The horrific violence of slavery and it legacy likewise resulted in great numbers of orphaned African American children (Zinn, 2010). These children were often placed in the worst orphanages and kept in inhumane conditions (Morton, 2000).

Children who are orphaned or who removed from parents by the state continue to remain at significant risk of violence. Contemporary scholars have shown that, even prior to being orphaned, many of these children are likely to have experienced abusive, neglectful, and dysfunctional home conditions (Cates, 1991; Shane, 1996; Tjaden & Thoennes, 1992).

The myth of the intact family, in which a child looses both parents who treated the child well but left the child without any subsequent care, is a myth. Children who are orphaned and institutionalized have been found to face numerous detrimental outcomes, such as delays in physical and cognitive development, as well as subsequent sexual and physical violence (Sherr, Roberts, & Gandhi, 2017). Being an orphan is a terrible and terrifying social condition for a child to face. Requiring that such a child be perpetually happy and optimistic only serves the adults or systems which seek to perpetuate violence toward such children (e.g., Goddard's eugenic asylums) or to ignore such violence (e.g., happy orphan fairytales).

Children who are traumatized, especially repeatedly, often process their trauma in predictable patterns. One of these ways, noted by Freud (1908, 1917) and many other psychoanalytic theorists (e.g., Ferenczi, Kline, Winnicott, Mahler), can be found in the practices of play which children use to replicate and manage their traumatic experiences. Winnicott (1967) highlighted the vital importance of symbolic play for children, who require a space to understand and manage their relational worlds. In play, children enact fantasies of what they wish adults in their lives could do, in order to help them process troubling situations and relationships. Play is a space into which children can retreat to escape, processing their experiences of both interpersonal and cultural experiences (Levy-Warren, 1994; Winnicott, 1965, 1967).

Sandor Ferenczi (1949), one of the most influential early psychoanalysts, noted that adults often their own project desires and needs unto children, which children then are required to play out. He called this process "the confusion of tongues" (p. 156). Ferenczi mostly wrote about cases of sexual abuse, but also noted that all manner of demands from the adults (e.g., for a child to be perpetually happy no matter what the circumstances) can result in the child identifying with these aggressive acts by adults in order to cope and survive. Children who experience trauma, especially the loss of a parent or situations of neglect and abuse, are likely to develop emotional defense strategies, which may help them manage these unbearable realities. According to Ferenczi,

> *this is the terrorism of suffering. Children have the compulsion to put to rights all disorder in the family, to burden, so to speak, their own tender shoulders with the load of all the others*; of course this is not only out of pure altruism, but is in order to be able to enjoy again the lost rest and the care and attention accompanying it. (p. 166)

Child researcher Margaret Mahler, Pine, and Bergman (1973) noted that children as young as infants seek to adapt their behavior to their environments, shaping themselves into what adults want them to be.

Numerous psychoanalytic scholars have shown that such adaptation can result in a false sense of self (e.g., a persona that defensively masks a person's real feelings and leads to feelings of derealization, disconnection, and emptiness) (Fairbairn, 1963; Kline, 1946; Winnicott, 1960). Karen Horney (1936, 1937, 1967) discussed the development of the "false self" in reaction to relational and societal requirements, including patriarchal ones, which demand that the individual always present an idealized façade. Other noted psychoanalysts, such as Kline (1946) and Fairbairn (1963), discussed how children who experienced difficulties in their relationships with caregivers often split the world into entirely good and entirely bad experiences, typically placing goodness outside of themselves (i.e., their caregivers, other adults, the world) while unconsciously maintaining that badness must be rooted in themselves. According to Winnicott (1965, 1967), a false sense of self always arises in relation to an abnormal environment, which rejects spontaneous authentic human reactions to life and others (e.g., anger or sorrow), resulting in a defensive personality donning on a defensive façade. In the case of Pollyanna, her defensive response to loss and the many challenges of her early life as an orphan was to develop an idealistically cheery persona. Her defensive façade involved her childhood "glad games," for which she is routinely praised by adults in her life. According to Levy-Warren's (1994) work on children playing in chaotic and troubling environments:

> In this repetitive play (which is the child's safe and orderly world), *the child has recreated the world of disorder as s(he) experiences it but is now master of the disorder*. The usual roles are reversed: it is the adult who finds the world incomprehensible, rather than the child. It is the adult who is anxious about what is really going on… The child has thus managed to turn passive into active. The play is an act of mastery. (p. 363)

Bowlby (1983), one of the most noted child researchers and founder of attachment theory, whose primary work focused on childhood loss, has shown that when children are unable to experience the full spectrum of their emotions, especially in reaction to demands by adults to not "tantrum" or "whine," they grow into psychologically stunted adults:

> In many families anger with an adult leads to punishment... Moreover a tearful appeal for comfort and help can lead to rejection and humiliation... It is perhaps too often forgotten by clinicians that many children, when they become distressed and weepy and are looking for comfort, are shooed off as intolerable little cry-babies. (p. 152)

Bowlby's work emphasized that childhood challenges, such as loss or social issues like poverty, become pathological when a child's caregivers are unable or unwilling to view the child as a whole person who experiences multiple emotional states and needs. Thus, children may be damaged, not only by their difficult circumstances, but by pathological adult caregiver treatment, especially when these caregivers rejects healthy emotional reactions like fear, sorrow, or anger.

Erich Fromm (1941, 1955) argued that a false sense of self can stem not only from immediate relationships with caregivers, but also relationships with society at large—with a society that demands compliance and self-negation. In his book, *Escape from Freedom*, Fromm (1941) described the social pressure for individuals to abandon their own feelings, especially feelings of distress, in order to fit societal demands, and thus become "*automatons*" (p. 208). Instead of "genuine" thinking and feelings, individuals adopt "pseudo-thinking" (p. 213). Fromm showed that in a society, as in all relational situations which demand absolute compliance, such pseudo-thinking and feeling become so crippling that individuals are no longer able to identify their own genuine experience. In one of his examples, a man who is a war veteran notices a momentary onset of grief and sorrow at a party, which he entirely dismisses because he conceives of himself as a very cheerful person who enjoys attending happy parties. This happy presentation, in fact, is what is desired by others, who are unwilling to recognize or accept his anger, sorrow, and trauma. Instead, this man has nightmares, in which his detached, undesired feelings become more manifest, pointing to the more genuine feelings that are held at bay. According to Fromm, "all his gaiety was a mask; it did not originate in himself, but covered what 'he' really felt: fear and anger" (p. 222). Fromm's example is of a person who, like many others, "*is accustomed to feel what he is supposed to feel*" (p. 223). In order to manage social threats and feelings of isolation, individuals, according to Fromm, will abandon their freedom to "think, feel and act as they [others] please" in order to fit in or to meet social expectations (p. 209). Pollyanna's circumstances show precisely this type of the environment, where her cheerful happy "glad game" compliance is what is desired and rewarded.

Other forms of oppression, especially when experienced during childhood, can also result in profound self-alienation and suffering. Children of color who must adapt to violently racist environments must also manage their false sense of self (White, 2002) or, in Fanon's (1959) terms, become "black" people donning "white masks." The disordered, damaging world of racism faced by children of color or children results in a "neurosis" of otherness (e.g., "neurosis of blackness") because their humanity is pitted against their perceived identity (Hook, 2012). Gloria Anzaldua (1987), a Chicana/Mexican-American feminist scholar, in her critical books on the intersectional nature of identity, noted that permission to express one's full spectrum of emotional or relational desires is often denied both by our cultures of origin as well as the dominant culture. Anzaldua called the repressed parts of self "the Shadow-Beast," which she described as that "*unacceptable aspect of the self our mother/culture/race*" rejects (p. 42). She further highlighted how in an effort to "*avoid rejection, some of us conform to the values of our culture and push the unacceptable parts into the shadows*" (p. 42).

Numerous historians and social scholars have pointed to the requirement, insisted on by the dominant culture, that children and people of color present themselves as perpetually happy or they will be treated as dangerous and punished accordingly (Merskin, 2011; Zinn, 2010). Resisting such representations is often profoundly difficult, because they are unconsciously held and maintained by the culture at large, as well as by oppressed individuals themselves (Hook, 2012). For example, in her discussion of the importance of anger as a vital response to racism, even between members of communities with shared legacies of oppression, Audre Lorde (1981/2007) proclaimed "*I cannot hide my anger to spare your guilt, nor hurt feelings, nor answering anger; for to do so insults and trivializes all our efforts… my response to racism is anger*" (p. 125). Anger, she asserted, is the mobilizing energy toward change: "anger between peers births change, not destruction, and the discomfort and sense of loss it often causes is not fatal, but *a sign of growth*" (p. 126). Orphan girls, or housewives, or enslaved people–all have been told to remain perpetually pleasant and happy, to focus on bright visions of the future, and to be content with their place in the predetermined order of the world (Ahmed, 2010a, 2010b; Merskin, 2011; Zinn, 2010).

Scientific Pollyannaism is also detrimental to democracy. Bollas (2018), in his new book entitled *Meaning and Melancholia*, noted that inability to accept individual internal states that are diverse and complex may contribute to a general incapacity to accept such diversity and complexity in human communities. This lack of inner capacity to accept divergent emotional states in oneself, Bollas suggested, may lead to the failure to form a genuine democratic process from diverse communities or societies. The demand for cheerful compliance and perpetual peace with others is opposed to democracy of ideas, diversity of social views, and creativity of human expressions.

Pollyanna, an orphan child who faces abusive difficult circumstances, survives by playing the "glad games": optimistic diversions from reality, which are desired by the adults in her life. These adults are unwilling to recognize or accept her genuine sorrow, or anger, or fear. Pollyanna's adaptation, while understandable, is also heart breaking. In contemporary society, where alienation from one self and others is common, Pollyanna's emotional efficiency and positivity are a seductive refuge and remedy for suffering. But the "glad games," are, in truth, empirically enforced forms of control over human lives, which are often marked by suffering, whether natural (i.e., our normal human losses) or socially generated (e.g., social oppression).

Scientific Pollyannaism requires us to orphan any emotional states or human conditions that it defines as being negative or unacceptable. We must orphan, disinherit, and reject our own anger or sorrow, just as we must treat other individuals' distress as undesirable orphans, including distress over their social circumstance. Prior to twentieth century versions of scientific Pollyannaism, the glad games drew on both religious views and the sciences of their day in order to rid the world of negative emotions and these people who display them (e.g., *Malleus Malleficarum*). Contemporary scientific Pollyannaism, from Darwinist eugenic "science of human betterment" to positive psychology, seeks to achieve the same extermination of negativity, and justifies their effort by insisting that their glad games are entirely based on empirical studies and scientific theories.

As noted throughout the book, the glad games deny both the fullness humanity and the realities of social oppression. The glad games, because of their social, religious, and scientific patronage, are also profitable games. Similar to Marx's (1843/1970) views on religion, contemporary scientific Pollyannaism serves as a numbing force, distracting individuals and communities who must remain unconscious about their sources of discontent. In Marx's words,

> The abolition of [scientific Pollyannaism] as the illusory happiness of the people is the demand for their real happiness. To call on them to give up their illusions about their condition is to call on them to give up a condition that requires illusions. The criticism of [scientific Pollyannaism] is, therefore, in embryo, the criticism of that vale of tears of which [scientific Pollyannaism] is the halo. (based on Introduction, paras. 4–5)

This book is an invitation to question both these glad games and the science behind them. It is an invitation to refuse to let parts of our own humanity and the entire sections of humanity at large become orphaned. It is a call to reclaim these orphaned pieces of ourselves and others– though I recognize that we have all been unconsciously conditioned to perceive many human emotions as alien, sick, wicked, wretched, and demonic. It is an invitation to reclaim unhappiness as our personal, political, and social right.

Thomas Ogden (2010, 2016), a psychoanalytic theorist, discussing therapeutic work with individuals who consistently display false self, stated that the possibility of change can occur when the whole person can be fully accepted, including in those feelings and behaviors that the person has had to reject or hide as inacceptable. Ogden uses the psychoanalytic language of objects, which constitute both real relationships and a sense of oneself as an autonomous valued self or object. According to Ogden (2010),

> *The most fundamental psychological principle underlying this conception of psychological growth is the idea that all psychological maturation involves the patient's genuine acceptance of himself [sic.] and, by extension, acceptance of others.* That acceptance is achieved by means of the work of *coming to terms with the full range of aspects of oneself, including one's disturbing, infantile, split-off identifications*… Psychological change of this sort creates the possibility of discovering a world of people and experiences that exists outside of oneself, a world in which *it is possible to feel curious, surprised, delighted, disappointed, homesick, and so on. The world of thought, feeling and human relatedness that is opened by such self-acceptance is a world in which one feels no compulsion to transform the realities of one's human relationships* into something other than what they are. (p. 114)

Zinn (2010) in his iconoclastic *People's History of the United States*, documented many such cases of resistance to whole-sale positivity, including the efforts of some Black leaders to persuade African Americans to willingly and gladly embrace their position under Jim Crow laws. In contrast, like many feminists, anti-colonial fighters, and all others who demanded justice, many African Americans have also mobilized the people by genuinely embracing anger and sorrow. Howard Zinn cited one such call to action: a public plea from John Hope, a young African American teacher working in the American South during the late 1800s. I read his call as a cry of resistance to Scientific Pollyannaism: "*Rise! … Be discontented. Be dissatisfied … Be as restless as the tempestuous billows on the boundless sea. Let your discontent break mountain-high against the wall of prejudice, and swamp it to the very foundation*" (quoted in Zinn, 2010, p. 193).

By acknowledging the discontent and dissatisfaction in ourselves and others, we may stop playing the Pollyanna glad games, where scientific theories and empirical figures set the rules and control human beings like pawns. By accepting our full spectrum of emotions, we may create personal and social spaces in which the whole, diverse human race can acknowledge the full spectrum of our individual and collective humanity. Our sorrow and our joy, our rage and our serenity, our fears and our certainties will be treated not as alienated and isolated orphaned states, but as vital capacities that keep us connected to our shared humanity and empower us to work toward a justly shared world.

References

Ahmed, S. (2010a). Killing joy: Feminism and the history of happiness. *Signs, 35*(3), 571–594. https://doi.org/10.1086/648513.

Ahmed, S. (2010b). *The promise of happiness*. Durham, NC: Duke University Press.

Anzaldua, G. (1987). *Borderlands: La Frontera*. San Francisco: Aunt Lute Publications.

Bollas, C. (2018). *Meaning and melancholia: Life in the age of bewilderment*. New York: Routledge.

Bouchard, T. J. (1996). Galton lecture: Behaviour genetic studies of intelligence, yesterday and today: The long journey from plausibility to proof. *Journal of Biosocial Science, 28*(4), 527–555.

Bowlby, J. (1983). *Attachment: Attachment and loss*. New York, NY: Basic Books Classics.

Cates, J. A. (1991). Residential treatment in the 1980s: Characteristics of children served. *Residential Treatment for Children & Youth, 9*(1), 75–84.
Darwin, C. (1889). *The expression of the emotions in man and animals*. London: Murray.
Fairbairn, W. R. D. (1963). Synopsis of an object-relations theory of personality. *International Journal of Psycho-Analysis, 44*, 224–250.
Fanon, F. (1959/2008). *Black skin, white masks*. San Francisco, CA: Grove Press.
Ferenczi, S. (1949). Confusion of the tongues between the adults and the child. *The International Journal of Psycho-Analysis, 30*, 225–230.
Freud, S. (1908/1953). Creative writers and day-dreaming.In *The standard edition of the complete psychological works of Sigmund Freud* (Translation from the German by J. Strachey, A. Freud, & A. Richards, Vol. 9). London, UK: Hogarth Press.
Freud, S. (1917). Mourning and melancholia. In *The standard edition of the complete psychological works of Sigmund Freud, volume XIV (1914–1916): On the history of the psycho-analytic movement, papers on metapsychology and other works* (A. Strachey & A. Tyson, Trans., pp. 237–258). London, UK: Hogarth Press.
Fromm, E. (1941). *Escape from freedom*. Oxford, UK: Farrar & Rinehart.
Fromm, E. (1955). *The sane society*. Oxford, UK: Rinehart & Co.
Goddard, H. H. (1912). *The Kallikak family: A study in the heredity of feeble-mindedness*. New York: Macmillan.
Holt, M. I. (2001). *Indian orphanages*. Lawrence: University Press of Kansas.
Hook, D. (2012). *A critical psychology of the postcolonial: The mind of apartheid*. New York: Routledge.
Horney, K. (1936). Culture and neurosis. *American Sociological Review, 1*(2), 221–230.
Horney, K. (1937). *The neurotic personality of our time*. New York: W. W. Norton.
Horney, K. (1967). *Feminine psychology*. New York, NY: Springer.
Keith, L. (2001). *Take up thy bed and walk: Death, disability and cure in classic fiction for girls*. New York, NY: Taylor & Francis.
Klein, M. (1946). Notes on some schizoid mechanisms. *International Journal of Psycho-Analysis, 27*, 99–110.
Levy-Warren, M. H. (1994). Child's play amidst chaos. *American Imago, 51*(3), 359–368.
Lorde, A. (1981/2007). *Sister outsider: Essays & speeches*. Berkeley, CA: Crossing Press.
Mahler, M. S., Pine, F., & Bergman, A. (1973). *The psychological birth of the human infant*. New York: Basic Books.
Marx, K. (1843/1970). *Introduction to a contribution to the critique of Hegel's philosophy of right*. Collected works (J. O'Malley, Ed., A. Jolin & J. O'Malley,

Trans., Vol. 3). New York, NY: Cambridge University Press. Retrieved on January 14, 2019 at https://www.marxists.org/archive/marx/works/1843/critique-hpr/intro.htm.
Merskin, D. L. (2011). *Media, minorities, and meaning: A critical introduction*. Philadelphia, PA: Peter Lang.
Morton, M. J. (2000). Surviving the great depression: Orphanages and orphans in Cleveland. *Journal of Urban History, 26*(4), 438–455.
Ogden, T. H. (2010). Why read fairbairn? *The International Journal of Psychoanalysis, 91*(1), 101–118.
Ogden, T. H. (2016). *Reclaiming unlived life: Experiences in psychoanalysis*. New York, NY: Routledge.
Popenoe, P., & Johnson, R. H. (1935). *Applied eugenics* (2nd ed.). New York: Macmillan.
Porter, E. (1913). *Pollyanna*. Boston, MA: Colonial Press.
Selden, S. (1999). *Inheriting shame: The story of eugenics and racism in America*. New York: Teachers College Press.
Shane, P. G. (1996). *What about America's homeless children? Hide and seek*. Thousand Oaks, CA: Sage.
Shealy, C. N. (1995). From boys town to oliver twist: Separating fact from fiction in welfare reform and out-of-home placement of children and youth. *American Psychologist, 50*(8), 565–570.
Sherr, L., Roberts, K. J., & Gandhi, N. (2017). Child violence experiences in institutionalised/orphanage care. *Psychology, Health & Medicine, 22*(Suppl. 1), 31–57.
Smith, J. D. (1985). *Minds made feeble: The myth and legacy of the Kallikaks*. Rockville, MD: Aspen.
Smith, W. B. (2011). *Youth leaving foster care: A developmental, relationship-based approach to practice*. New York, NY: Oxford University Press.
Terman, L. M. (1916). *The measurement of intelligence*. New York: Houghton Mifflin.
Tjaden, P. G., & Thoennes, N. (1992). Predictors of legal intervention in child maltreatment cases. *Child Abuse and Neglect, 16*(6), 807–821.
Tucker, W. H. (1996). *The science and politics of racial research*. Carbondale: University of Illinois Press.
Watson, J. B. (1914). *Behavior: An introduction to comparative psychology*. New York, NY: H. Holt.
Watson, J. B. (1919). *Psychology: From the standpoint of a behaviorist*. Philadelphia, PA: Lippincott.
Watson, J. B. (1928). *Psychological care of infant and child*. New York: W. W. Norton.
Watson, J. B. (1930). *Behaviorism* (Rev. ed.). New York, NY: W. W. Norton.

White, K. P. (2002). Surviving hating and being hated: Some personal thoughts about racism from a psychoanalytic perspective. *Contemporary Psychoanalysis, 38,* 401–422. https://doi.org/10.1080/00107530.2002.10747173.
Winnicott, D. W. (1960). The theory of the parent-infant relationship. *International Journal of Psycho-Analysis, 41,* 585–595.
Winnicott, D. W. (1965). *The maturational process and the facilitating environment.* London, UK: Penguin Books.
Winnicott, D. W. (1967). *Playing and reality.* Harmondsworth, UK: Penguin Books.
Zenderland, L. (2001). *Measuring minds: Henry Herbert Goddard and the origins of American intelligence testing.* New York: Cambridge University Press.
Zinn, H. (2010). *The twentieth century: A people's history.* New York: Harper & Row.

References

Achterberg, J. (2013). *Woman as healer*. Boulder, CO: Shambhala Publications.

Ahmed, S. (2004). *Cultural politics of emotion*. New York: Routledge.

Ahmed, S. (2010a). Killing joy: Feminism and the history of happiness. *Signs, 35*(3), 571–594. https://doi.org/10.1086/648513.

Ahmed, S. (2010b). *The promise of happiness*. Durham, NC: Duke University Press.

American Breeders Magazine: A Journal of Genetics and Eugenics. (1912). Washington, DC: American Breeders Association.

American Eugenics Society. (2015). *Members, officers, and directors activities database*. Retrieved on June 9, 2019 at https://ia801305.us.archive.org/25/items/AMERICANEUGENICSSOCIETYMEMBERS/AMERICAN%20EUGENICS%20SOCIETY%20MEMBERS.pdf.

The American Renaissance. (2019). *About us*. Retrieved on January 14, 2019 at https://www.amren.com/about/.

Angelou, M. (1983). *I know why the caged bird sings*. New York, NY: Bantam.

Ankarloo, B., & Clark, S. (1999). *Witchcraft and magic in Europe*. Philadelphia: University of Pennsylvania Press.

Anzaldua, G. (1987). *Borderlands: La Frontera*. San Francisco: Aunt Lute Publications.

Bajema, C. J. (1976). *Eugenics then and now*. Stroudsburg, PA: Dowden, Hutchinson & Ross.

Bakan, D. (2013). Politics and American psychology. In R. W. Rieber & K. Salzinger (Eds.), *Psychology: Theoretical–historical perspectives* (pp. 125–144). New York: Academic Press.

Baker, L. R. H. (1912). *Race improvement or eugenics*. New York: Dodd, Mead, & Co.

O. Yakushko, *Scientific Pollyannaism*,
https://doi.org/10.1007/978-3-030-15982-5

Baldwin, J. (1965, August). White man's guilt. *Ebony Magazine*, pp. 47–48.

Bannister, R. C. (1991). *Sociology and Scientism: The American Quest for Objectivity, 1880–1940*. Chapel Hill: The University of North Carolina Press.

Bannister, R. C. (2010). *Social Darwinism: Science and myth in Anglo-American social thought*. Philadelphia, PA: Temple University Press.

Barstow, A. L. (1988). On studying witchcraft as women's history: A historiography of the European witch persecutions. *Journal of Feminist Studies in Religion, 4*(2), 7–19.

Bartlett, K. R. (Ed.). (2011). *The civilization of the Italian Renaissance: A sourcebook*. Toronto, ON, Canada: University of Toronto Press.

Bashford, A., & Levine, P. (Eds.). (2010). *The Oxford handbook of the history of eugenics*. New York: Oxford University Press.

Beck, H. P., Levinson, S., & Irons, G. (2009). Finding little Albert: A journey to John B. Watson's infant laboratory. *American Psychologist, 64*(7), 605–614.

Becker, D., & Marecek, J. (2008). Positive psychology: History in the remaking? *Theory & Psychology, 18*(5), 591–604.

Behar, R. (2001). Sexual witchcraft, colonialism, and women's powers: Views from the Mexican Inquisition. In B. P. Levak (Ed.), *Gender and witchcraft: New perspectives on witchcraft, magic, and demonology* (pp. 218–246). New York, NY: Routledge.

Bell, A. G. (1908). *A few thoughts concerning eugenics*. New York, NY: Judd & Detweiler.

Béné, C., Wood, R. G., Newsham, A., & Davies, M. (2012). *Resilience: New utopia or new tyranny? Reflection about the potentials and limits of the concept of resilience in relation to vulnerability reduction programmes* (IDS Working Papers 405), 1–61. Brighton: Institute of Development Studies.

Ben-Yehuda, N. (1980). The European witch craze of the 14th to 17th centuries: A sociologist's perspective. *American Journal of Sociology, 86*(1), 1–31.

Bergman, J. (2014). *The Darwin Effect: It's influence on Nazism, Eugenics, Racism, Communism, Capitalism & Sexism*. Green Forest: New Leaf Publishing Group.

Berlant, L. G. (2011). *Cruel optimism*. Durham, NC: Duke University Press.

Binkley, S. (2011). Happiness, positive psychology and the program of neoliberal governmentality. *Subjectivity, 4*(4), 371–394.

Binkley, S. (2014). *Happiness as enterprise: An essay on neoliberal life*. Albany: State University of New York Press.

Biswas-Diener, R., Linley, P. A., Govindji, R., & Woolston, L. (2011). Positive psychology as a force for social change. In K. M. Sheldon, T. B. Kashdan, & M. F. Steger (Eds.), *Designing positive psychology: Taking stock and moving forward* (pp. 410–418). New York: Oxford University Press.

Black, E. (2003). *War against the weak: Eugenics and America's campaign to create a master race*. New York: Four Walls Eight Windows.

Blackburn, S. (2005). *The Oxford dictionary of philosophy*. Oxford, UK: Oxford University Press.

Bogen, H. (1992). *The luckiest orphans: A history of the Hebrew orphan asylum of New York*. Urbana-Champaign: University of Illinois Press.

Bollas, C. (2018). *Meaning and melancholia: Life in the age of bewilderment*. New York: Routledge.

Bouchard, T. J. (1996). Galton lecture: Behaviour genetic studies of intelligence, yesterday and today: The long journey from plausibility to proof. *Journal of Biosocial Science, 28*(4), 527–555.

Boucher, J., & Osgood, C. E. (1969). The Pollyanna hypothesis. *Journal of Memory and Language, 8*(1), 1–8.

Bowlby, J. (1983). *Attachment: Attachment and loss*. New York, NY: Basic Books Classics.

Brauner, S. (2001). *Fearless wives and frightened shrews: The construction of the witch in early modern Germany*. Amherst: University of Massachusetts Press.

Breuer, H. (2009). *Crafting the witch: Gendering magic in medieval and early modern England*. New York, NY: Routledge.

Brigham, C. C. (1923). *A study of American intelligence*. Princeton, NJ: Princeton University Press.

Brody, D., & Lamb, S. (2018). *The faith of Donald J. Trump: A spiritual biography*. New York, NY: HarperCollins.

Brooke, E. (1997). *Medicine women: A pictorial history of women healers*. New York, NY: Quest Books.

Brown, N. J., Sokal, A. D., & Friedman, H. L. (2013). The complex dynamics of wishful thinking: The critical positivity ratio. *The American Psychologist, 68*(9), 801–813.

Brown, N. J., Sokal, A. D., & Friedman, H. L. (2014). Positive psychology and romantic scientism. *The American Psychologist, 69*(6), 636–637.

Buckley, K. W. (1989). *Mechanical man: John Broadus Watson and the beginnings of behaviorism*. New York: Guilford Press.

Burns, W. E. (2003). *Witch hunts in Europe and America: An encyclopedia*. Westport, CT: Greenwood Publishing Group.

Buss, D. M. (1984). Evolutionary biology and personality psychology: Toward a conception of human nature and individual differences. *American Psychologist, 39*(10), 1135–1147.

Buss, D. M. (1995). Psychological sex differences: Origins through sexual selection. *American Psychologist, 50*(3), 164–168. https://doi.org/10.1037/0003-066X.50.3.164.

Buss, D. M. (2000). The evolution of happiness. *American Psychologist, 55*(1), 15–23.

Buss, D. M. (2009). The great struggles of life: Darwin and the emergence of evolutionary psychology. *American Psychologist, 64*(2), 140.

Buss, D. M. (2015). *Evolutionary psychology: The new science of the mind*. New York, NY: Psychology Press.

Buss, D. M. (2016). *The evolution of desire: Strategies of human mating*. New York, NY: Basic books.

Butler, J. (1995). Melancholy gender-refused identification. *Psychoanalytic Dialogues, 5*, 165–180.

Butler, J. (2004). *Precarious life: The powers of mourning and violence*. London, UK: Verso.

Butler, S. (1911). *Evolution, old and new: Or the theories of Buffon, Dr. Erasmus Darwin and Lamarck, as compared with that of Charles Darwin*. London, UK: Kessinger Publishing.

Cabanas, E. (2016). Rekindling individualism, consuming emotions: Constructing "psytizens" in the age of happiness. *Culture & Psychology, 22*(3), 467–480.

Carpenter, E. (1889). *Civilsation: Its cause and cure*. London, UK: George Allen and Unwind Ltd.

Cates, J. A. (1991). Residential treatment in the 1980s: Characteristics of children served. *Residential Treatment for Children & Youth, 9*(1), 75–84.

Cattell, R. B. (1987). *Beyondism: Religion from science*. New York: Praeger.

Cayman Taxonomy Meeting. (1999). Retrieved on January 14, 2019 at https://ppc.sas.upenn.edu/opportunities/conference-archives.

Center for Disease Control. (2018). *Drug overdose mortality by state*. Retrieved on January 14, 2019 at https://www.cdc.gov/nchs/pressroom/sosmap/drug_poisoning_mortality/drug_poisoning.htm.

Center for Disease Control. (2019). *Suicide mortality by state*. Retrieved on January 14, 2019 at https://www.cdc.gov/nchs/pressroom/sosmap/suicide-mortality/suicide.htm.

Chase, A. (1980). *The legacy of Malthus: The social costs of the new scientific racism*. Urbana-Champaign: University of Illinois Press.

Chesterton, G. K. (1922). *Eugenics and other evils: An argument against the Scientifically organized state*. London: Inkling Books.

Chirot, D. E., & Seligman, M. E. (Eds.). (2001). *Ethnopolitical warfare: Causes, consequences, and possible solutions*. Washington, DC: American Psychological Association.

Chodorow, N. (1978). *The reproduction of mothering*. Berkeley: University of California.

Clifford, S., & Lemery-Chalfant, K. (2015). Molecular genetics of resilience. In M. Pluess (Ed.), *Genetics of psychological well-being: The role of heritability and genetics in positive psychology* (p. 177). New York, NY: Oxford University Press.

Cogdell, C. (2010). *Eugenic design: Streamlining America in the 1930s*. Philadelphia: University of Pennsylvania Press.

Conrad, S. (2012). Enlightenment in global history: A historiographical critique. *The American Historical Review, 117*(4), 999–1027.

Cornum, R., Matthews, M. D., & Seligman, M. E. (2011). Comprehensive soldier fitness: Building resilience in a challenging institutional context. *American Psychologist, 66*(1), 4–11.

Coyne, J. C., Stefanek, M., & Palmer, S. C. (2007). Psychotherapy and survival in cancer: The conflict between hope and evidence. *Psychological Bulletin, 133*(3), 367–394. https://doi.org/10.1037/0033-2909.133.3.367.

Coyne, J. C., & Tennen, H. (2010). Positive psychology in cancer care: Bad science, exaggerated claims, and unproven medicine. *Annals of Behavioral Medicine, 39*(1), 16–26. https://doi.org/10.1007/s12160-009-9154-z.

Cronin, V. (2011). *The Florentine Renaissance.* New York, NY: Random House.

Csikszentmihalyi, M. (1997). *Finding flow: The psychology of engagement with everyday life.* New York: Basic Books.

Currell, S., & Cogdell, C. (Eds.). (2006). *Popular eugenics: National efficiency and American mass culture in the 1930s.* Athens: Ohio University Press.

Cushman, P. (1996). *Constructing the self, constructing America: A cultural history of psychotherapy.* Reading, MA: Addison-Wesley/Addison Wesley Longman.

The Daily Beast. (2011). *List of the most tolerant and the least tolerant states.* Retrieved on January 14, 2019 at https://www.thedailybeast.com/ranking-the-most-tolerant-and-least-tolerant-states.

Danieli, Y. (1984). Psychotherapists' participation in the conspiracy of silence about the Holocaust. *Psychoanalytic Psychology, 1*(1), 23–42.

Darwin, C. (1859). *On the origin of species: Or, the preservation of favoured races in the struggle for life.* London: Down, Bromley, Kent.

Darwin, C. (1888). *The descent of man and selection in relation to sex.* London: Murray.

Darwin, C. (1889). *The expression of the emotions in man and animals.* London: Murray.

Darwin, C. (1898). *The life and letters of Charles Darwin, including an autobiographical chapter* (F. Darwin, Ed., Rev. ed.). London, UK: John Murray.

Darwin, F. (1914). Francis Galton. *The Eugenics Review, 6*(1), 1–4.

Davenport, C. B. (1910). *Eugenics. The science of human improvement by better breeding.* New York: Henry Holt.

Davenport, C. B. (1911). *Heredity in relation to eugenics.* New York: H. Holt.

Davenport, C. B. (1913). *State laws limiting marriage selection examined in the light of eugenics.* Cold Springs, NY: Eugenics Record Office.

Davies, W. (2015). *The happiness industry: How the government and big business sold us well-being.* London, UK: Verso Books.

Dawkins, R. (1981). Selfish genes in race or politics. *Nature, 289,* 528.

De Beauvoir, S. (1949). *The second sex* (H. M. Parshley, trans., 1974). New York: Vintage.

De La Fabián, R., & Stecher, A. (2018). Positive psychology and the enhancement of happiness: A reply to Binkley (2018). *Theory & Psychology, 28*(3), 411–417.

Diener, E. (2009). Positive psychology: Past, present, and future. In S. J. Lopez & S. R. Snyder (Eds.), *Oxford handbook of positive psychology* (pp. 7–11). New York: Oxford University Press.

Diener, E. (Ed.). (2009b). *The science of well-being: The collected works of Ed Diener*. New York, NY: Springer Science & Business Media.

Deiner, E., Kesebir, P., & Lucas, R. (2008). Benefits of accounts of well-being—For societies and for psychological science. *Applied Psychology: An International Review, 57*(Suppl. 1), 37–53. https://doi.org/10.1111/j.1464-0597.2008.00353.x.

Diener, E., & Seligman, M. E. (2004). Beyond money toward an economy of well-being. *Psychological Science in the Public Interest, 5*(1), 1–31.

Dovidio, J. F., & Gaertner, S. L. (2004). Aversive racism. *Advances in Experimental Social Psychology, 36*, 4–56.

Duke, D. E. (1999). *My awakening: A path to racial understanding*. Convington, LA: Free Speech Press.

Dusek, V. (1999). Sociobiology sanitized: Evolutionary psychology and gene selectionism. *Science as Culture, 8*(2), 129–169.

Easton, M. (2006). *Does diversity make us unhappy?* American Renaissance. Retrieved on January 14, 2019 at https://www.amren.com/news/2006/06/does_diversity/.

Ehrenreich, B. (2007). John Templeton's universe. *The Nation*. Retrieved on January 14, 2019 at https://www.thenation.com/article/john-templetons-universe/.

Ehrenreich, B. (2009). *Bright-sided: How the relentless promotion of positive thinking is undermining America*. New York, NY: Metropolitan Books.

Ehrenreich, B., & English, D. (2010). *Witches, midwives, and nurses: A history of women healers*. New York, NY: Feminist Press.

Eugenical News. (1916–1922). Monthly publication of the Eugenics Record Office, Cold Springs, NY. Retrieved on February 22, 2018 at https://babel.hathitrust.org/cgi/pt?id=coo.31924063788834.

Evans, G. (2018). The unwelcome revival of 'race science'. *The Guardian*. Retrieved on November 27, 2018 at https://www.theguardian.com/news/2018/mar/02/the-unwelcome-revival-of-race-science.

Evans, R. B., Sexton, V. S. E., & Cadwallader, T. C. (1992). *The American Psychological Association: A historical perspective*. Washington, DC: APA.

Evans, W. S. (1931). *Organized eugenics*. New Haven, CT: American Eugenics Society.

Fairbairn, W. R. D. (1963). Synopsis of an object-relations theory of personality. *International Journal of Psycho-Analysis, 44*, 224–250.

Fanon, F. (1959/2008). *Black skin, white masks.* San Francisco, CA: Grove Press.

Fausto-Sterling, A. (2012). *Sex/gender: Biology in a social world.* New York: Routledge.

Ferenczi, S. (1949). Confusion of the tongues between the adults and the child—(The language of tenderness and of passion). *International Journal of Psycho-Analysis, 30*, 225–230.

Fischer, R., & Chalmers, A. (2008). Is optimism universal? A meta-analytical investigation of optimism levels across 22 nations. *Personality and Individual Differences, 45*(5), 378–382.

Fisher, R. A. (1924). The elimination of mental defect. *Eugenics Review, 16*, 114–116.

Fitzpatrick, M., Jones, P., Knellwolf, C., & McCalman, I. (Eds.). (2004). *Enlightenment world.* New York, NY: Psychology Press.

Flatley, J., & Flatley, J. (2009). *Affective mapping: Melancholia and the politics of modernism.* Cambridge, MA and London: Harvard University Press.

Fredrickson, B. (2009). *Positivity: Top-notch research reveals the 3 to 1 ratio that will change your life.* New York, NY: Three Rivers Press.

Fredrickson, B. L. (2013). Updated thinking on positivity ratios. *American Psychologist, 68*(9), 814–822. https://doi.org/10.1037/a0033584.

Fredrickson, B. L., & Losada, M. F. (2005). Positive affect and the complex dynamics of human flourishing. *American Psychologist, 60*, 678–686. https://doi.org/10.1037/0003-066X.60.7.678.

Freud, S. (1908/1953). Creative writers and day-dreaming. In *The standard edition of the complete psychological works of Sigmund Freud* (Translation from the German by J. Strachey, A. Freud, & A. Richards, Vol. 9). London, UK: Hogarth Press.

Freud, S. (1909). Analysis of a phobia in a five-year-old boy. In *The standard edition of the complete psychological works of Sigmund Freud, volume X (1909): Two case histories* ('Little Hans' and the 'Rat Man') (pp. 1–150). London, UK: Hogarth Press.

Freud, S. (1916/1977). *Introductory lectures on psychoanalysis.* New York: W. W. Norton.

Freud, S. (1917). Mourning and melancholia. In *The standard edition of the complete psychological works of Sigmund Freud, volume XIV (1914–1916): On the history of the psycho-analytic movement, papers on metapsychology and other works* (A. Strachey & A. Tyson, Trans., pp. 237–258). London, UK: Hogarth Press.

Freud, S. (1920). *A general introduction to psychoanalysis.* New York, NY: Horace Liveright.

Freud, S. (1930). *Civilization and its discontents* (Standard ed.). London: Hogarth Press.
Freud, S. (1953). *The standard edition of the complete psychological works of Sigmund Freud*. (Translation from the German by J. Strachey, A. Freud, & A. Richards). London, UK: Hogarth Press.
Fridlund, A. J., Beck, H. P., Goldie, W. D., & Irons, G. (2012). Little Albert: A neurologically impaired child. *History of Psychology, 15*(4), 302–327.
Friedan, B. (1963/2010). *The feminine mystique*. New York: W. W. Norton.
Friedli, L., & Stearn, R. (2015). Positive affect as coercive strategy: Conditionality, activation and the role of psychology in UK government workfare programmes. *Medical Humanities, 41*(1), 40–47.
Fromm, E. (1941). *Escape from freedom*. Oxford, UK: Farrar & Rinehart.
Fromm, E. (1955). *The sane society*. Oxford, UK: Rinehart & Co.
Frosh, S. (2004). Freud, psychoanalysis and anti-semitism. *The Psychoanalytic Review, 91*(3), 309–330. https://doi.org/10.1521/prev.91.3.309.38302.
Frosh, S. (2015). *Hate and the 'Jewish science': Anti-Semitism, Nazism and psychoanalysis*. London: Springer.
Froyum, C. M. (2010). The reproduction of inequalities through emotional capital: The case of socializing low-income black girls. *Qualitative Sociology, 33*(1), 37–54.
Gadjev, I. (2015). Nature and nurture: Lamarck's legacy. *Biological Journal of the Linnean Society, 114*(1), 242–247. https://doi.org/10.1111/bij.12439.
Galton, F. (1865). Hereditary talent and character. *Macmillan's Magazine, 12*(157), 318–327.
Galton, F. (1869). *Hereditary genius: An inquiry into its laws and consequences*. New York, NY: Macmillan.
Galton, F. (1883). *Inquiries into the human faculty & its development*. London, UK: J.M. Dent.
Galton, F. (1904). Eugenics: Its definition, scope, and aims. *American Journal of Sociology, 10*(1), 1–25.
Galton, F. (1907). *Probability: The foundation of eugenics*. London, UK: Clarendon Press.
Gana, N. (2011). *Signifying loss: Toward a poetics of narrative mourning*. Lewisburg: Bucknell University Press.
Garrett, H. E. (1961). The equalitarian dogma. *Perspectives in Biology and Medicine, 4*, 480–484.
Garrett, H. E., & Bonner, H. (1961). *General psychology*. New York: American Book Company.
Gay, P. (1996). *The enlightenment: An interpretation*. New York, NY: W. W. Norton.

Geronimus, A. T., Bound, J., & Colen, C. G. (2011). Excess black mortality in the United States and in selected black and white high-poverty areas, 1980–2000. *American Journal of Public Health, 101*(4), 720–729.

Gesche, I. E. M. A. (1927). The color preferences of one thousand one hundred and fifty-two Mexican children. *Journal of Comparative Psychology, 7*(4), 297–311.

Giroux, H. A. (2011). The disappearing intellectual in the age of economic Darwinism. *Policy Futures in Education, 9*(2), 163–171.

Goddard, H. H. (1911). The elimination of feeble-mindedness. *The Annals of the American Academy of Political and Social Science, 37*(2), 261–272.

Goddard, H. H. (1912). *The Kallikak family: A study in the heredity of feeble-mindedness.* New York: Macmillan.

Goddard, H. H. (1914). *Feeble-mindedness.* New York: Macmillan.

Goddard, H. H. (1917). Mental tests and the immigrant. *Journal of Delinquency, 2,* 243–277.

Goddard, H. H. (1919). *Psychology of the normal and subnormal.* New York: Dodd, Mead.

Goddard, H. H. (1948). *Our children in the atomic age.* Mellott, IN: Hopkins Syndicate.

Gottfredson, L. S. (1994a). Egalitarian fiction and collective fraud. *Society, 31*(3), 53–59.

Gottfredson, L. S. (1994b). The science and politics of race-norming. *American Psychologist, 49*(11), 955–963.

Gottfredson, L. S. (2005). Suppressing intelligence research: Hurting those we intend to help. In R. H. Wright & N. A. Cummings (Eds.), *Destructive trends in mental health: The well-intentioned path to harm* (pp. 155–186). New York, NY: Taylor & Francis.

Gottfredson, L. S. (2012). Resolute ignorance on race and Rushton. *Personality and Individual Differences, 55,* 218–223. https://doi.org/10.1016/j.paid.2012.10.021.

Gould, S. J. (1996). *The mismeasure of man.* New York, NY: W. W. Norton & Company.

Graves, R. (1960). The case for Xanthippe. *The Kenyon Review, 22*(4), 597–605.

Green, K., & Bigelow, J. (1998). Does science persecute women? The case of the 16th–17th century witch-hunts. *Philosophy, 73*(02), 195–217. https://doi.org/10.1017/s0031819198000187.

Green, C. D., & Cautin, R. L. (2017). 125 years of the American Psychological Association. *American Psychologist, 72*(8), 722–736.

Greenleaf, R. E. (1969). *The Mexican Inquisition of the sixteenth century.* Albuquerque: University of New Mexico Press.

Gregg, J. E. (1925). The comparison of races. *The Scientific Monthly, 20*(3), 248–254.

Griffin, R. A. (2012). I AM an angry Black woman: Black feminist autoethnography, voice, and resistance. *Women's Studies in Communication, 35*(2), 138–157.

Grossi, G., Kelly, S., Nash, A., & Parameswaran, G. (2014). Challenging dangerous ideas: A multi-disciplinary critique of evolutionary psychology. *Dialectical Anthropology, 38*(3), 281–285.

Guthrie, R. V. (2004). *Even the rat was white: A historical view of psychology*. Upper Saddle River, NJ: Pearson Education.

Guyer, M. F. (1916). *Being well-born: An introduction to eugenics*. New York, NY: Bobbs-Merrill Company.

Hague, W. G. (1913). *The eugenic mother and baby: A complete home guide*. London, UK: Hague.

Hall, G. S. (1881). *Aspects of German culture*. Boston: J.R. Osgood.

Hall, G. S. (1903). The white man's burden versus indigenous development of the lower races. *The Journal of Education, 58*(4, 1438), 83.

Hall, G. S. (1909). Evolution and psychology. In E. B. Poulton & G. S. Hall (Eds.), *Fifty years of Darwinism: Modern aspects of evolution* (pp. 251–267). Boston: H. Holt.

Hall, G. S. (1917). *Jesus, the Christ, in the light of psychology*. New York: Doubleday, Page.

Hall, G. S. (1917). Practical relations between psychology and the war. *Journal of Applied Psychology, 1*(1), 9–16. https://doi.org/10.1037/h0070238.

Halpern, C. (2002). *Suffering, politics, power: A genealogy in modern political theory*. Albany: SUNY Press.

Hannush, M. J. (1987). John B. Watson remembered: An interview with James B. Watson. *Journal of the History of the Behavioral Sciences, 23*(2), 137–152.

Harris, B. (2011). Letting go of Little Albert: Disciplinary memory, history, and the uses of myth. *Journal of the History of the Behavioral Sciences, 47*(1), 1–17.

Harris, S. (2006). What is your dangerous idea? In podcast series *Science Must Destroy Religion*. Retrieved on January 14, 2019 at https://samharris.org/science-must-destroy-religion.

Hartley, M. (with Commire, A.) (1991). *Breaking the silence*. New York: Signet Book.

Hartley, M., & Commire, A. (1990). *Breaking the silence*. New York, NY: GP Putnam's Sons.

Hedges, C. (2009). *Empire of illusion: The end of literacy and the triumph of spectacle*. Toronto: Knopf Canada.

Heinsohn, G., & Steiger, O. (1982). The elimination of medieval birth control and the witch trials of modern times. *International Journal of Women's Studies, 5*, 193–214.

Held, B. S. (2002). The tyranny of the positive attitude in America: Observation and speculation. *Journal of Clinical Psychology, 58*(9), 965–991.

Held, B. S. (2004). The negative side of positive psychology. *Journal of Humanistic Psychology, 44*(1), 9–46.

Herrnstein, R. J., & Murray, C. (1996). *The bell curve*. New York: Simon & Schuster.

Holbrook, M. L. (1897). *Homo-culture: Or, the improvement of offspring through wiser generation*. London, UK: ML Holbrook.

Hollingworth, L. S. (1924). Provisions for intellectually superior children. In M. V. O'Shea (Ed.), *The child: His nature and his needs* (pp. 277–299). New York, NY: The Children's Foundation.

Holt, M. I. (2001). *Indian orphanages*. Lawrence: University Press of Kansas.

Honeywill, R. (2008). *Lamarck's evolution: Two centuries of genius and jealousy*. New York: Allen & Unwin.

Honneth, A. (2004). Organized self-realization: Some paradoxes of individualization. *European Journal of Social Theory, 7*(4), 463–478.

hooks, B. (2006). *Outlaw culture: Resisting representations*. New York, NY: Routledge.

Hook, D. (2012). *A critical psychology of the postcolonial: The mind of apartheid*. New York: Routledge.

Horney, K. (1936). Culture and neurosis. *American Sociological Review, 1*(2), 221–230.

Horney, K. (1937). *The neurotic personality of our time*. New York: W. W. Norton.

Horney, K. (1967). *Feminine psychology*. New York, NY: Springer.

Horowitz, I. (2018). The happiness of the people. In I. Horowitz (Ed.), *Culture and civilization* (pp. 11–25). New York, NY: Routledge.

Horsley, R. A. (1979). Who were the witches? The social roles of the accused in the European witch trials. *The Journal of Interdisciplinary History, 9*(4), 689–715. https://doi.org/10.2307/203380.

Hosbawm, E. (1997). *On history*. London, UK: Abacus Books.

Hunt, M. (1999). *The new know-nothings: The political foes of the scientific study of human nature*. New Brunswick, NJ: Transaction.

Hunter, G. W. (1914). *A civic biology: Presented in problems*. New York: American Book Co.

Hunter, W. S., & Sommermier, E. (1922). The relation of degree of Indian blood to score on the Otis Intelligence Test. *Journal of Comparative Psychology, 2*(3), 257–277.

Hurlock, E. B. (1927). Color preferences of white and negro children. *Journal of Comparative Psychology, 7*(6), 389–404.

Huxley, J. S. (1936). Eugenics and society. *Eugenics Review, 28*(1), 11–31.

Ilies, R., Arvey, R. D., & Bouchard, T. J. (2006). Darwinism, behavioral genetics, and organizational behavior: A review and agenda for future research. *Journal of Organizational Behavior, 27*(2), 121–141.

Independent Review Report. (2015). *American Psychological Association*. Retrieved on October 5, 2016 at https://www.apa.org/independent-review/APA-FINAL-Report-7.2.15.pdf.

Itzkoff, S. W. (1994). *The decline of intelligence in America: A strategy for national renewal*. Westport, CT: Greenwood Publishing Group.

Iyer, V. R. K. (1990). *Human rights and human wrong*. Ann Arbor: University of Michigan Press.

Jacobs, T. (2013). *Study: Extreme conservatives make happier people*. American Renaissance. Retrieved on January 14, 2019 at https://www.amren.com/news/2013/07/study-extreme-conservatives-make-happier-people.

Jacoby, R. (1975). *Social amnesia: A critique of conformist psychology from Adler to Laing*. Boston, MA: Beacon Press.

Jennings, H. S., Watson, J. B., Meyer, A., & Thomas, W. I. (1917). *Suggestions of modern science concerning education*. New York: Macmillan.

Joseph, S., & Murphy, D. (2013). Person-centered approach, positive psychology, and relational helping: Building bridges. *Journal of Humanistic Psychology, 53*(1), 26–51.

Kamin, L. J. (2012). *The science and politics of IQ*. New York, NY: Routledge.

Kaminsky, I. (2013). Of strangeness that wakes us. *Poetry, 201*(4), 469–478.

Kanazawa, S., & Li, N. P. (2015). Happiness in modern society: Why intelligence and ethnic composition matter. *Journal of Research in Personality*. Retrieved on January 14, 2019 at https://www.amren.com/news/2017/12/happiness-modern-society-intelligence-ethnic-composition-matter/.

Karolides, N. J., Bald, M., & Sova, D. B. (1999). *100 banned books: Censorship histories of world literature*. New York, NY: Checkmark Books.

Kenealy, A. (1920). *Feminism and sex extinction*. London, UK: T. Fisher Unwin.

Keith, L. (2001). *Take up thy bed and walk: Death, disability and cure in classic fiction for girls*. New York, NY: Taylor & Francis.

Keith, T. (2017). *How positive thinking helped propel Trump to presidency*. NPR All Things Considered Report. Retrieved on January 14, 2019 at https://www.npr.org/2017/01/19/510628862/how-positive-thinking-helped-propel-trump-to-the-presidency.

Kellicott, W. E. (1915). *The social direction of human evolution: An outline of the science of eugenics*. New York: D. Appleton.

Klein, M. (1946). *Envy and gratitude and other works, 1946–1963*. New York, NY: Delacorte.

Klein, M. (1946). Notes on some schizoid mechanisms. *International Journal of Psycho-Analysis, 27*, 99–110.

Kline, W. (2001). *Building a better race: Gender, sexuality, and eugenics from the turn of the century to the baby boom*. Berkeley: University of California Press.

Kozlowski, S. W., Chen, G., & Salas, E. (2017). One hundred years of the Journal of Applied Psychology: Background, evolution, and scientific trends. *Journal of Applied Psychology, 102*(3), 237–253.

Kristjánsson, K. (2010). Positive psychology, happiness, and virtue: The troublesome conceptual issues. *Review of General Psychology, 14*(4), 296–310.

Kristjánsson, K. (2012). Positive psychology and positive education: Old wine in new bottles? *Educational Psychologist, 47*(2), 86–105. https://doi.org/10.1080/00461520.2011.610678.

Kropotkin, P. (1914/2012). *Mutual aid: A factor of evolution*. Mineola, NY: Dover.

Kruse, M. (2017). The power of Trump's positive thinking. *The Politico*. Retrieved on January 14, 2019 at https://www.politico.com/magazine/story/2017/10/13/donald-trump-positive-thinking-215704.

Kuhl, S. (2002). *The Nazi connection: Eugenics, American racism, and German national socialism*. New York: Oxford University Press.

Laenui, P. (2000). *Processes of decolonization*. Reclaiming indigenous voice and vision. Retrieved on November 13, 2016 at http://www.sjsu.edu/people/marcos.pizarro/courses/maestros/s0/Laenui.pdf.

Lamarck, J.-B. (1809). Zoological philosophy. In J. A. Hammerton (Ed.) (2008), *The world's greatest books* (Vol. 15). Science. Wm. H. Wise & Co. (Online).

Layton, L. (2010). Irrational exuberance: Neoliberal subjectivity and the perversion of truth. *Subjectivity, 3*(3), 303–322.

Levack, B. P. (1995). *The witch-hunt in early modern Europe*. Essex, UK: Pearson.

Levy-Warren, M. H. (1994). Child's play amidst chaos. *American Imago, 51*(3), 359–368.

Lewontin, R. C., Rose, S., & Kamin, L. J. (1984). *Not in our genes: Biology, ideology, and human nature*. New York, NY: Pantheon.

Lippman, W. (1922). The mental age of Americans. *New Republic, 32*(412–417), 213–215, 246–248, 275–277, 297–298, 328–330, 9–11.

Lipsitz, G. (2006). *The possessive investment in whiteness: How white people profit from identity politics*. Philadelphia, PA: Temple University Press.

Lombardo, P. A. (2008). *Three generations, no imbeciles: Eugenics, the Supreme Court, and Buck v. Bell*. Baltimore, MD: Johns Hopkins Press.

Lombardo, P. A. (Ed.). (2011). *A century of eugenics in America: From the Indiana experiment to the human genome era*. Bloomington: Indiana University Press.

Lombardo, P. A., & Dorr, G. M. (2006). Eugenics, medical education, and the Public Health Service: Another perspective on the Tuskegee syphilis experiment. *Bulletin of the History of Medicine, 80*(2), 291–316.

Lopez, S. J. (Ed.). (2011). *The encyclopedia of positive psychology*. New York, NY: Wiley.

Lopez, S. J. (2013). *Making hope happen: Create the future you want for yourself and others*. New York, NY: Simon & Schuster.

Lopez, S. J., & Edwards, L. M. (2008). The interface of counseling psychology and positive psychology: Assessing and promoting strengths. In S. D. Brown & R. W. Lent (Eds.), *Handbook of counseling psychology* (4th ed., pp. 86–99). Hoboken, NJ: Wiley.

Lopez, S. J., Floyd, R. K., Ulven, J. C., & Snyder, C. R. (2000). Hope therapy: Helping clients build a house of hope. In C. R. Snyder (Ed.), *Handbook of hope: Theory, measures, and applications* (pp. 123–150). New York, NY: Academic Press.

Lopez, S. J., & Gallagher, M. W. (2009). A case for positive psychology. In S. J. Lopez & S. R. Snyder (Eds.), *Oxford handbook of positive psychology* (pp. 3–6). New York: Oxford University Press.

Lopez, S. J., Magyar-Moe, J. L., Petersen, S. E., Ryder, J. A., Krieshok, T. S., O'Byrne, K. K., … Fry, N. A. (2006). Counseling psychology's focus on positive aspects of human functioning. *The Counseling Psychologist, 34*(2), 205–227.

Lopez, S. J., Pedrotti, J. T., & Snyder, C. R. (2018). *Positive psychology: The scientific and practical explorations of human strengths.* Thousand Oaks, CA: Sage.

Lorde, A. (1978). *The black unicorn.* New York: Norton.

Lorde, A. (1981/2007). *Sister outsider: Essays & speeches.* Berkeley, CA: Crossing Press.

Lourde, A. (1997). *The collected poems of Audre Lorde.* New York, NY: W. W. Norton.

Love, H. (2007). Compulsory happiness and queer existence. *New Formations, 63,* 52–65.

Lynn, R. (2001). *Eugenics: A reassessment.* New York: Praeger.

Lynn, R. (2001). *The science of human diversity: A history of the Pioneer fund.* Lanham, MD: University Press of America.

Lynn, R. (2007, July). *Race and psychopathic personality.* American Renaissance. Retrieved at https://www.amren.com/news/2008/08/race_and_psycho/.

Lyubomirsky, S. (2008). *The how of happiness: A scientific approach to getting the life you want.* New York, NY: Penguin.

MacInnis, C. C., Busseri, M. A., Choma, B. L., & Hodson, G. (2013). The happy cyclist: Examining the association between generalized authoritarianism and subjective well-being. *Personality and Individual Differences, 55*(7), 789–793.

Madison, G. (2013). *Passing of the great race.* New York, NY: Hardpress Limited.

Magyar-Moe, J. L., & Lopez, S. J. (2008). Human agency, strengths-based development and well being. *Biennial Review of Counseling Psychology, 1,* 157–175.

Magyar-Moe, J. L., Owens, R. L., & Scheel, M. J. (2015). Applications of positive psychology in counseling psychology: Current status and future directions. *The Counseling Psychologist, 43*(4), 494–507. https://doi.org/10.1177/0011000015581001.

Mahler, M. S., Pine, F., & Bergman, A. (1973). *The psychological birth of the human infant*. New York: Basic Books.

Martin, E. (2005). *Scientism: Encyclopedia of science, technology, and ethics*. Denver: University of Colorado.

Marx, K. (1843/1970). *Introduction to a contribution to the critique of Hegel's philosophy of right*. Collected Works (J. O'Malley, Ed., A. Jolin & J. O'Malley, Trans., Vol. 3.). New York, NY: Cambridge University Press. Retrieved on January 14, 2019 at https://www.marxists.org/archive/marx/works/1843/critique-hpr/intro.htm.

Matlin, M. W., & Stang, D. J. (1978). *The Pollyanna principle: Selectivity in language, memory, and thought*. New York, NY: Schenkman.

McDougall, W. (1914). Psychology in the service of eugenics. *The Eugenics Review, 5*(4), 295.

McDougall, W. (1921). *National welfare and national decay*. London: Methuen & Co. Ltd.

McGee, M. (2005). *Self-Help, Inc. Makeover culture in American life*. New York, NY: Oxford University Press.

McGurk, F. C. (1953). On white and Negro test performance and socio-economic factors. *The Journal of Abnormal and Social Psychology, 48*(3), 448–450.

McKinnon, S. (2006). *Neo-liberal genetics: The myths and moral tales of evolutionary psychology*. Chicago, IL: Prickly Paradigm Press.

McMahon, D. M. (2006). *Happiness: A history*. New York: Grove Press.

McMahon, D. M. (2010). What does the ideal of happiness mean? *Social Research, 77*(2), 469–490.

Mehler, B. (1997). Beyondism: Raymond B. Cattell and the new eugenics. *Genetica, 99*(2–3), 153–163.

Melendy, M. R. (1914). *The science of eugenics and sex life*. New York: W. R. Vansant.

Merchant, C. (1980). *The death of nature: Women, ecology, and the Scientific Revolution*. San Francisco, CA: Harper and Collins.

Merskin, D. L. (2011). *Media, minorities, and meaning: A critical introduction*. Philadelphia, PA: Peter Lang.

Messerly, J. G. (1996). *Piaget's conception of evolution: Beyond Darwin and Lamarck*. Lanham: Rowman & Littlefield.

Meyer, D. (1998). *The positive thinkers: Popular religious psychology from Mary Baker Eddy to Norman Vincent Peale and Ronald Reagan*. Middletown, PA: Wesleyan University Press.

Miller, A. (2008). A critique of positive psychology—Or 'the new science of happiness'. *Journal of Philosophy of Education, 42*(3/4), 591–608. https://doi.org/10.1111/j.1467-9752.2008.00646.x.

Morawski, J. G. (1982). Assessing psychology's moral heritage through our neglected utopias. *American Psychologist, 37*(10), 1082–1095.

Morton, M. J. (2000). Surviving the great depression: Orphanages and orphans in Cleveland. *Journal of Urban History, 26*(4), 438–455.

Nearing, S. (1912). *The super race: An American problem*. New York: B.W. Huebsch.

Nickerson, C. A. (2014). No empirical evidence for critical positivity ratios. *The American Psychologist, 69*(6), 626.

Ogden, T. H. (2010). Why read Fairbairn? *The International Journal of Psychoanalysis, 91*(1), 101–118.

Ogden, T. H. (2016). *Reclaiming unlived life: Experiences in psychoanalysis*. New York, NY: Routledge.

Oikkonen, V. (2013). *Gender, sexuality and reproduction in evolutionary narratives*. London, UK: Routledge.

Olson, R. (2008). *Science and scientism in nineteenth-century Europe*. Urbana-Champaign: University of Illinois Press.

Ong, A. D., & van Dulmen, M. H. (Eds.). (2006). *Oxford handbook of methods in positive psychology*. New York, NY: Oxford University Press.

Osteen, J. (2011). *Every day a Friday: How to be happier 7 days a week*. London, UK: Hachette.

Packard, A. S. (1901). *Lamarck, the founder of evolution: His life and work*. London, UK: Longmans, Green, and Company.

Palmer, S. C., Stefanek, M. E., Thombs, B. D., & Coyne, J. C. (2010). Psychological intervention and survival: Wishing does not make it so—Letter. *Clinical Cancer Research*. https://doi.org/10.1158/1078-0432.CCR-10-1703.

Parker, I. (2016). *Critical discursive psychology*. New York, NY: Springer.

Parrott, W. G. (Ed.). (2014). *The positive side of negative emotions*. New York, NY: Guilford Publications.

Pearson, K. (1905). *National life from the standpoint of science*. London: Adam and Black.

Pearson, K. (1911). *The scope and importance to the state of the science of national eugenics*. London, UK: Dulau and Company.

Pedrotti, J. T., Edwards, L. M., & Lopez, S. J. (2009). Positive psychology within a cultural context. In S. J. Lopez & S. R. Snyder (Eds.), *Oxford handbook of positive psychology* (pp. 49–57). New York: Oxford University Press.

Pérez-Álvarez, M. (2013). Positive psychology and its friends: Revealed. *Papeles del Psicólogo, 34*(3), 208–226.

Peterson, C., & Seligman, M. E. P. (2004). *Character strengths and virtues: A handbook and classification*. New York, NY: Oxford University Press.

Pew Research Center. (2018). *Attitudes toward spirituality and religion: Report*. Retrieved on January 14, 2019 at http://www.pewforum.org/2018/05/29/attitudes-toward-spirituality-and-religion.

PhysOrg. (2014). *Danish DNA could be key to happiness*. American Renaissance. Retrieved on January 14, 2019 at https://www.amren.com/news/2014/07/danish-dna-could-be-key-to-happiness.

Pinker, S. (2002). *The blank slate: The modern denial of human nature*. New York: Penguin.

Pinker, S. (2011). *The better angels of our nature: The decline of violence in history and its causes*. New York, NY: Penguin.

Pinker, S. (2018). *Enlightenment now: The case for reason, science, humanism, and progress*. New York: Penguin.

The Pioneer Fund. (2013). *Highlights of pioneer fund research and grants*. Retrieved on June 15, 2018 at https://web.archive.org/web/20130103005545/http://www.pioneerfund.org:80.

The Pioneer Fund. Retrieved on October 5, 2018 at https://www.splcenter.org/fighting-hate/extremist-files/group/pioneer-fund.

Pluess, M. (Ed.). (2015). *Genetics of psychological well-being: The role of heritability and genetics in positive psychology*. New York, NY: Oxford University Press.

Popenoe, P., & Johnson, R. H. (1935). *Applied eugenics* (2nd ed.). New York: Macmillan.

Porter, E. (1913). *Pollyanna*. Boston, MA: Colonial Press.

Prilleltensky, I. (2013). Wellness without fairness: The missing link in psychology. *South African Journal of Psychology, 43*(2), 147–155.

Pulla, V. (2016). *The Lhotsampa people of Bhutan: Resilience and survival*. New York, NY: Palgrave.

Robbins, B. D., & Friedman, H. (2008). Introduction to our special issue on positive psychology. *The Humanistic Psychologist, 36(*2), 93–95.

Robinson, V. (1908). *Comrade Kropotkin*. New York, NY: The Altrurians.

Rose, N. (1990). *Governing the soul: The shaping of the private self*. Florence, KY: Taylor & Francis/Routledge.

Rose, H., & Rose, S. (2010). *Alas poor Darwin: Arguments against evolutionary psychology*. New York: Random House.

Rose, N., & Abi-Rached, J. M. (2013). *Neuro: The new brain sciences and the management of the mind*. Princeton, NJ: Princeton University Press.

Ruickbie, L. (2004). *Witchcraft out of the shadows: A complete history*. London, UK: Robert Hale.

Rundle, D. (1995). A new golden age? More, Skelton and the accession verses of 1509. *Renaissance Studies, 9*(1), 58–76.

Russell, J. B. (1972). *Witchcraft in the middle ages*. Ithaca, NY: Cornell University Press.

Ruti, M. (2015). *The age of scientific sexism: How evolutionary psychology promotes gender profiling and fans the battle of the sexes*. Toronto, ON, Canada: Bloomsbury Publishing.

Rushton, J. P. (1990). Sir Francis Galton, epigenetic rules, genetic similarity theory, and human life-history analysis. *Journal of Personality, 58*(1), 117–140.

Rushton, J. P. (1995). *Race, evolution, and behavior*. New Brunswick, NJ: Transaction.

Rushton, J. P. (1999). Genetic similarity theory and the nature of ethnocentrism. In K. Thienpont & R. Cliquet (Eds.), *In-group/out-group behavior in modern societies: An evolutionary perspective*. Amsterdam, The Netherlands: Vlaamse Gemeeschap/CBGS.

Rushton, J. P. (2001). A scientometric appreciation of H.J. Eysenck's contributions to psychology. *Personality and Individual Differences, 31*(1), 17–39.

Rushton, J. P. (2002). The Pioneer Fund and the scientific study of human differences. *Albany Law Review, 66*, 207–262.

Rushton, J. P. (2012). No narrowing in mean Black-White IQ differences—Predicted by heritable g. *American Psychologist, 67*, 500–501.

Rushton, J. P., & Ankney, C. D. (2009). Whole brain size and general mental ability: A review. *International Journal of Neuroscience, 119*(5), 692–732.

Rushton, J. P., & Jensen, A. R. (2005). Wanted: More race realism, less moralistic fallacy. *Psychology, Public Policy, and Law, 11*(2), 328–336. https://doi.org/10.1037/1076-8971.11.2.328.

Said, E. W. (2003). *Freud and the non-European*. London: Verso.

Saini, A. (2018). Racism is creeping back into mainstream science—We have to stop it. *The Guardian*. Retrieved on December 1, 2018 at https://www.theguardian.com/commentisfree/2018/jan/22/eugenics-racism-mainstream-science.

Saleeby, C. W. (1911). *Woman and womanhood: A search for principles*. New York, NY: Kennerley.

Sanger, M. (1919, February). Birth control and racial betterment. *Eugenical News*.

Sanger, M. (1921). The eugenic value of birth control propaganda. *Birth Control Review, 5*(10), 1–10.

Scarre, G., & Callow, J. (2001). *Witchcraft and magic in sixteenth- and seventeenth-century Europe* (2nd ed.). Hampshire, UK: Palgrave.

Scharlieb, M. M. A. D. B. (1912). *Womanhood and race-regeneration*. New York, NY: Moffat, Yard.

Schultz, A. H. (1923). Comparison of White and Negro fetuses. In C. B. Davenport, H. F. Osborn, C. Wissler, & H. H. Laughlin (Eds.), *Scientific papers of the second international congress of eugenics* (Vol. 2). Baltimore, MD: Williams & Wilkins.

Schultz, E. (2016). Bhutanese refugee crisis: A brief history. *The Seattle Times.* Retrieved at https://www.seattletimes.com/seattle-news/bhutanese-refugee-crisis-a-brief-history/.

Science Daily. (2015). *How your brain reacts to emotional information is influenced by your genes.* American Renaissance. Retrieved on January 14, 2019 at https://www.amren.com/news/2015/07/how-your-brain-reacts-to-emotional-information-is-influenced-by-your-genes/.

The Science of Happiness. (2019). *Research-based tips for a meaningful life. A co-production with the Greater Good Science Center at UC Berkeley.* The Public Radio International. Retrieved on January 14, 2019 at https://www.pri.org/programs/science-happiness.

Selden, S. (1999). *Inheriting shame: The story of eugenics and racism in America.* New York: Teachers College Press.

Seligman, M. E. P. (1975). *Helplessness: On depression, development, and death.* New York, NY: WH Freeman/Times Books/Henry Holt & Co.

Seligman, M. E. P. (2002). *Learned optimism: How to change your mind and your life.* New York, NY: Vintage.

Seligman, M. E. P. (2006). *Authentic happiness: Using the new positive psychology to realize your potential for lasting fulfillment.* New York, NY: Simon & Schuster.

Seligman, M. E. P. (2007). *The optimistic child: A proven program to safeguard children against depression and build lifelong resilience.* New York, NY: Houghton Mifflin Harcourt.

Seligman, M. E. P. (2011). *Flourish: A visionary new understanding of happiness and well-being.* New York, NY: Simon & Schuster.

Seligman, M. E. P., & Csikszentmihalyi, M. (2000). Positive psychology: An introduction. *American Psychologist, 55*(1), 5–14.

Seligman, M. E. P., & Csikszentmihalyi, M. (2014). *Positive psychology: An introduction.* New York, NY: Springer.

Seligman, M. E. P., & Fowler, R. D. (2011). Comprehensive soldier fitness and the future of psychology. *American Psychologist, 66*(1), 82–86.

Seligman, M. E. P., Railton, P., Baumeister, R. F., & Sripada, C. (2017). *Homo prospectus.* New York, NY: Oxford University Press.

Seligman, M. E., Steen, T. A., Park, N., & Peterson, C. (2005). Positive psychology progress: Empirical validation of interventions. *American Psychologist, 60*(5), 410–421.

Shane, P. G. (1996). *What about America's homeless children? Hide and seek.* Thousand Oaks, CA: Sage.

Shealy, C. N. (1995). From Boys Town to Oliver Twist: Separating fact from fiction in welfare reform and out-of-home placement of children and youth. *American Psychologist, 50*(8), 565–570.

Sheldon, K. M., Frederickson, B., Rathunde, K., Csikszentmihalyi, M., & Haidt, J. (2000). *Positive psychology manifesto.* Retrieved on October 5, 2016 at http://www.positivepsychology.org/akumalmanifesto.html.

Sheldon, K. M., Kashdan, T. B., & Steger, M. F. (Eds.). (2010). *Designing positive psychology: Taking stock and moving forward.* New York: Oxford University Press.

Sherr, L., Roberts, K. J., & Gandhi, N. (2017). Child violence experiences in institutionalised/orphanage care. *Psychology, Health & Medicine, 22*(Suppl. 1), 31–57.

Shields, S. A., & Bhatia, S. (2009). Darwin on race, gender, and culture. *American Psychologist, 64*(2), 111–119. https://doi.org/10.1037/a0013502.

Silverblatt, I. (1983). The evolution of witchcraft and the meaning of healing in colonial Andean society. *Culture, Medicine and Psychiatry, 7*(4), 413–427.

Simonton, D. K. (2011). Positive psychology in historical and philosophical perspective: Predicting its future from the past. In K. M. Sheldon, T. B. Kashdan, & M. F. Steger (Eds.) (2010), *Designing positive psychology: Taking stock and moving forward* (pp. 447–454). New York: Oxford University Press.

Skaggs, E. B. (1930). Studies in attention and emotion. *Journal of Comparative Psychology, 10*(4), 375–419. https://doi.org/10.1037/h0071298.

Sloan, T. (1996). *Damaged life. The crisis of the modern psyche.* New York: Routledge.

Smedley, A., & Smedley, B. D. (2005). Race as biology is fiction, racism as a social problem is real: Anthropological and historical perspectives on the social construction of race. *American Psychologist, 60*(1), 16.

Smith, E. P., & Merkel-Holguin, L. (2017). *A history of child welfare.* New York, NY: Routledge.

Smith, J. D. (1985). *Minds made feeble: The myth and legacy of the Kallikaks.* Rockville, MD: Aspen.

Smith, W. B. (2011). *Youth leaving foster care: A developmental, relationship-based approach to practice.* New York, NY: Oxford University Press.

Snyder, C. R., & Lopez, S. J. (2005). The future of positive psychology: A declaration of independence. In C. R. Snyder & S. J. Lopez (Eds.), *Handbook of positive psychology.* New York, NY: Oxford University Press.

Snyder, C. R., & Lopez, S. J. (2007). *Positive psychology: The scientific and practical explorations of human strengths.* Thousand Oaks, CA: Sage.

Social Biology. (1973). A new name society for the study of social biology (Formerly the American Eugenics Society). *Social Biology, 20*(1), 1.

Soldz, S. (2016). The comprehensive soldier fitness program: Discontinued and misrepresented positive psychology. In S. Soldz & O. Yakushko (Co-chairs),

Ethics of social justice/Social justice of ethics: Implications for psychology and psychologists. Symposium presented at the meeting of the American Psychological Association, Denver, CO.

Sorell, T. (2013). *Scientism: Philosophy and the infatuation with science*. London, UK: Routledge.

The Source Watch. (2019). *John Templeton, Jr.* Retrieved on January 14, 2019 at https://www.sourcewatch.org/index.php/John_Templeton,_Jr.

South Dakota Suicide Prevention. (2018). *Suicide Factsheet*. Retrieved on January 14, 2019 at http://doh.sd.gov/documents/statistics/SuicideFactsheet.pdf.

Southern Poverty Law Center. (2017). *From eugenics to voter ID laws: Thomas Farr's connection to the Pioneer Fund*. Retrieved on June 15, 2018 at https://www.splcenter.org/hatewatch/2017/12/04.

Southern Poverty Law Center. (2019). *Fighting hate/extremist files: The American Renaissance*. https://www.splcenter.org/fighting-hate/extremist-files/group/american-renaissance.

Steele, S. (1990). White guilt. *American Scholar, 59*, 497–506.

Stefanek, M. E., Palmer, S. C., Thombs, B. D., & Coyne, J. C. (2009). Finding what is not there. *Cancer, 115*(24), 5612–5616.

Steinbeck, J. (1939). *The grapes of wrath* (re-printed 2006). New York, NY: Penguin.

Steiner, E. A. (1909). *The immigrant tide: Its ebb and flow*. New York: F.H. Revell.

Stenmark, M. (2018). *Scientism: Science, ethics and religion*. New York, NY: Routledge.

Stern, A. M. (2015). *Eugenic nation: Faults and frontiers of better breeding in modern America*. Berkeley: University of California Press.

Sullivan, H. S. (1953). *Interpersonal theory of personality*. New York, NY: Norton.

Sumalla, E. C., Ochoa, C., & Blanco, I. (2009). Posttraumatic growth in cancer: Reality or illusion? *Clinical Psychology Review, 29*(1), 24–33.

Sunne, D. (1917). A comparative study of white and negro children. *Journal of Applied Psychology, 1*(1), 71–83.

Sutter, J. D. (2014). *List: States where rape is most common*. CNN Report. Retrieved on January 14, 2019 at https://www.cnn.com/2014/02/03/opinion/sutter-alaska-rape-list/index.html.

Taylor, J. (2011). *Genetics, personality, and race*. American Renaissance. Retrieved on January 14, 2019 at https://www.amren.com/news/2011/07/genetics_person/.

Templeton Foundation. (2019). *Funding areas*. Retrieved on January 14, 2019 at https://www.templeton.org/funding-areas.

Teo, T. (2008). From speculation to epistemological violence in psychology: A critical-hermeneutic reconstruction. *Theory & Psychology, 18*(1), 47–67.

Teo, T. (2010). What is epistemological violence in the empirical social sciences? *Social and Personality Psychology Compass, 4*(5), 295–303.

Terman, L. M. (1916). *The measurement of intelligence*. New York: Houghton Mifflin.

Thorndike, E. L. (1909). Darwin's contribution to psychology. *University of California Chronicle, 12*(1), 65–80.

Thornhill, R., & Palmer, C. T. (2000). *A natural history of rape*. Cambridge: MIT Press.

Thurston, R. W. (2007). *The witch hunts: A history of the witch persecutions in Europe and North America*. Upper Saddle River, NJ: Pearson Education.

Tjaden, P. G., & Thoennes, N. (1992). Predictors of legal intervention in child maltreatment cases. *Child Abuse & Neglect, 16*(6), 807–821.

Tuana, N. (1993). *The less noble sex: Scientific, religious, and philosophical conceptions of woman's nature*. Bloomington: Indiana University Press.

Tucker, W. H. (1996). *The science and politics of racial research*. Carbondale: University of Illinois Press.

UNESCO. (1969). *Four statements on the race question*. Paris, France: The United Nations Publications. Retrieved on April 1, 2019 at http://refugeestudies.org/UNHCR/UNHCR.%20Four%20Statements%20on%20the%20Race%20Question.pdf.

UNESCO Institute for Statistics. (2017). *UIS fact sheet: Women in science*. Retrieved on October 5, 2018 at http://uis.unesco.org/en/topic/women-science.

Versluysen, M. C. (1980). Old wives tales? Women healers in English history. In C. Davies (Ed.), *Rewriting nursing history* (pp. 75–99). London, UK: Croom Helm.

Walker, E. (1990). *Interview with James Watson*. Video recording retrieved from American Psychological Association Archives, Akron, OH.

Walsh, R. T., Teo, T., & Baydala, A. (2014). *A critical history and philosophy of psychology: Diversity of context, thought, and practice*. New York, NY: Cambridge University Press.

Washburn, M. F. (1923). A questionary study of certain national differences in emotional traits. *Journal of Comparative Psychology, 3*(6), 413–430.

Watkins, M., & Schulman, H. (2008). *Towards psychologies of liberation*. New York, NY: Palgrave Macmillan.

Watson, J. B. (1914). *Behavior: An introduction to comparative psychology*. New York, NY: H. Holt.

Watson, J. B. (1919). *Psychology: From the standpoint of a behaviorist*. Philadelphia, PA: Lippincott.

Watson, J. B. (1924). *Behaviorism*. New York, NY: Norton.

Watson, J. B. (1928). *Psychological care of infant and child.* New York: W. W. Norton.

Watson, J. B. (1930). *Behaviorism* (Rev. ed.). New York, NY: W. W. Norton.

Watson, J. B. (1935). *Behaviorism* (Rev. ed.). New York, NY: W. W. Norton.

Watson, J. B., & Lashley, K. S. (1920). A consensus of medical opinion upon questions relating to sex education and venereal disease campaigns. *Mental Hygiene, 4,* 769–847.

Watson, J. B., & Rayner, R. (1920). Conditioned emotional reactions. *Journal of Experimental Psychology, 3*(1), 1–14. https://doi.org/10.1037/h0069608.

Weikart, R. (2004). *From Darwin to Hitler: Evolutionary ethics, eugenics, and racism in Germany.* New York: Palgrave Macmillan.

Weiss, A., Adams, M. J., Widdig, A., & Gerald, M. S. (2011). Rhesus Macaques (Macaca Mulatta) as living fossils of hominoid personality and subjective well-being. *Journal of Comparative Psychology, 125*(1), 72–83.

White, K. P. (2002). Surviving hating and being hated: Some personal thoughts about racism from a psychoanalytic perspective. *Contemporary Psychoanalysis, 38,* 401–422. https://doi.org/10.1080/00107530.2002.10747173.

Whitney, E. (1995). The witch "she"/the historian "he": Gender and the historiography of the European witch-hunts. *Journal of Women's History, 7*(3), 77–101. https://doi.org/10.1353/jowh.2010.0511.

Whitney, G. (1997). Raymond B. Cattell and the Fourth Inquisition. *The Mankind Quarterly, 38*(1&2), 99–124.

Whitney, G. (1999). Introduction. In D. E. Duke (Ed.), *My awakening: A path to racial understanding* (pp. 2–11). Convington, LA: Free Speech Press.

Wiggam, A. E. (1923). *The new decalogue of science.* Indianapolis, IN: Bobbs-Merrill.

Williams, R. N., & Robinson, D. N. (Eds.). (2014). *Scientism: The new orthodoxy.* London, UK: Bloomsbury Publishing.

Williams, T. (2015). *What makes Templeton tick and just how scary is this place.* The Inside Philanthropy. Retrieved on January 14, 2019 at https://www.insidephilanthropy.com/home/2015/1/6/what-makes-templeton-tick-and-just-how-scary-is-this-place-a.html.

Wilson, E. O. (1975). *Sociobiology: The new synthesis.* Cambridge, MA: Harvard University Press.

Winnicott, D. W. (1960). The theory of the parent-infant relationship. *International Journal of Psycho-Analysis, 41,* 585–595.

Winnicott, D. W. (1965). *The maturational process and the facilitating environment.* London, UK: Penguin Books.

Winnicott, D. W. (1967). *Playing and reality.* Harmondsworth, UK: Penguin Books.

Witz, A. (2013). *Professions and patriarchy.* New York, NY: Routledge.

Wong, P. T. (2011). Reclaiming positive psychology: A meaning-centered approach to sustainable growth and radical empiricism. *Journal of Humanistic Psychology, 51*(4), 408–412.

Wright, R. (1994). *The moral animal: The new science of evolutionary psychology.* New York: Pantheon Books.

Wright, R. (1995). *The moral animal: Why we are, the way we are: The new science of evolutionary psychology.* New York: Vintage.

Wynn, R. (2000). Saints and sinners: Women and the practice of medicine throughout the ages. *Journal of the American Medical Association, 283*(5), 668–669.

Xenophon. (app. 400 BCE). *Symposium* (A. J. Bowen, Ed., 1998). Warminster, UK: Aris & Phillips.

Yakushko, O. (2018a). Don't worry, be happy: Erasing racism, sexism, and poverty in positive psychology. *Psychotherapy and Politics International, 16*(1), e1433.

Yakushko, O. (2018b). *Modern-day xenophobia: Critical historical and theoretical perspectives on the roots of anti-immigrant prejudice.* New York, NY: Springer.

Yakushko, O. (2018c). Witches, charlatans, and old wives: Critical perspectives on history of women's indigenous knowledge. *Women & Therapy, 41*(1–2), 18–29.

Yakushko, O. (2019). Eugenics and its evolution in history of western psychology: A critical archival review. *Psychotherapy and Politics International* (Online).

Yakushko, O., & Blodgett, E. (2018). Negative reflections about positive psychology: On constraining the field to a focus on happiness and personal achievement. *Journal of Humanistic Psychology.* https://doi.org/10.1177/0022167818794551.

Yen, J. (2010). Authorizing happiness: Rhetorical demarcation of science and society in historical narratives of positive psychology. *Journal of Theoretical and Philosophical Psychology, 30*(2), 67–78.

Yen, J. (2014). Positive psychology. In *Encyclopedia of critical psychology* (pp. 1431–1437). New York, NY: Springer.

Yen, J. (2015). Happiness as enterprise: An essay on neoliberal life. *Theory and Psychology, 25*(4), 541–542.

Yerkes, R. M. (1907). *The dancing mouse: A study in animal behavior.* New York, NY: Macmillan.

Yerkes, R. M. (1918). Psychology in relation to the war. *Psychological Review, 25*(2), 85–115.

Yerkes, R. M. (Ed.). (1920). *The new world of science: Its development during the war.* New York, NY: Century Company.

Yerkes, R. M. (Ed.). (1921). *Psychological examining in the United States Army.* Memoirs of the National Academic of Sciences. Washington, DC: Government Printing Office.

Yerkes, R. M. (1923). Eugenic bearing of measurements of intelligence. *The Eugenics Review, 14*(4), 225–229.
Young, P. C. (1929). Intelligence and suggestibility in whites and negroes. *Journal of Comparative Psychology, 9*(5), 339–359. https://doi.org/10.1037/h0075409.
Zenderland, L. (2001). *Measuring minds: Henry Herbert Goddard and the origins of American intelligence testing*. New York: Cambridge University Press.
Zinn, H. (2010). *The twentieth century: A people's history*. New York: Harper & Row.

Index

O. Yakushko, *Scientific Pollyannaism*,
https://doi.org/10.1007/978-3-030-15982-5

CPSIA information can be obtained
at www.ICGtesting.com
Printed in the USA
LVHW011723221219
641395LV00015B/1034/P

9 783030 159818